PRAISE FOR *WOE IS I*

"This work is a dream come true. . . . Darn, this is fun . . . a delightful romp through the intricacies of our language."

—*Library Journal*

"Woe Is I covers all those tricky grammar issues that can make or break your writing."　　　　　　　　　　—Write101.com

"Wow! Who would have thought that you could have such a delicious time with a grammar book? *Woe Is I* is great fun."

—Susan Isaacs

"When we all come to our senses and start recognizing truly important deeds, Patricia O'Conner will get a tickertape parade and a big, shiny medal. . . . This former *New York Times Book Review* editor has done more to keep the streets safe from bad grammar than just about anyone else, and we all owe her."　　　—*The Seattle Times*

"Funny, irreverent, and authoritative without being stuffy . . . *Woe Is I* is a charming, practical little book that deserves a spot on your shelf right next to Strunk & White."　　—*The Charlotte Observer*

"Hallelujah! This book works."　　　　　　—*The Des Moines Register*

"The best thing to happen to grammar since Strunk and White."

—Molly Ivins

"An invigorating and entertaining dissection of our ever-evolving language. . . . O'Conner . . . gleefully eviscerates poor sentence construction and dangling participles, soothes verb tension and debunks the frequently intimidating semicolon with finesse. Tempered with a heavy dose of wit . . . O'Conner's lively treatise is as vital as a dictionary for those who wish to be taken seriously in speech, in print or on Facebook."

—*Publishers Weekly* (starred review)

"If I found a man with the appeal of *Woe Is I*, I would be married before you could say 'Winston tastes good like a cigarette should'— that clinker that used to give English teachers fits."

—Cleveland *Plain Dealer*

"A fun read as well as a thorough reference guide."

—*Writer's Digest*

"Ms. O'Conner has the gift." —*The Dallas Morning News*

"It's a gem." —*The Arizona Republic*

"It is the best primer on English usage to come along since Strunk and White's *The Elements of Style*."

—*The Atlanta Journal-Constitution*

"Covers the conventional wisdom . . . at a merry skip rather than a resolute march." —*The Boston Globe*

WOE IS I

THE GRAMMARPHOBE'S GUIDE
TO BETTER ENGLISH IN PLAIN ENGLISH

PATRICIA T. O'CONNER

RIVERHEAD BOOKS
New York

RIVERHEAD BOOKS
An imprint of Penguin Random House LLC
penguinrandomhouse.com

Library of Congress Cataloging-in-Publication Data

Names: O'Conner, Patricia T., author.
Title: Woe is I : the grammarphobe's guide to better English in plain English /
Patricia T. O'Conner.
Description: Fourth Edition. | New York : Riverhead Books, an imprint of Penguin Random
House LLC, 2019 | "First Riverhead hardcover edition: September 2009"—T.p. verso. |
Includes bibliographical references and index.
Identifiers: LCCN 2018014756 | ISBN 9780525533054 (trade paperback) |
ISBN 9780525533061 (ebook)
Subjects: LCSH: English language—Grammar—Handbooks, manuals, etc. |
English language—Usage—Handbooks, manuals, etc.
Classification: LCC PE1112 .O28 2019 | DDC 428.2—dc23
LC record available at https://lccn.loc.gov/201801475
p.   cm.

G. P. Putnam's Sons hardcover edition: September 1996
First Riverhead hardcover edition: July 2003
Riverhead hardcover (Third edition): September 2009
First Riverhead trade paperback edition: July 2010
Riverhead trade paperback (Fourth edition): February 2019

Printed in the United States of America
9   10   8

For Stewart

CONTENTS

Some books can't sit still. They get fidgety and restless, mumbling to themselves and elbowing their authors in the ribs. "It's that time again," they say. "I need some attention here."

Books about English grammar and usage are especially prone to this kind of behavior. They're never content with the status quo. That's because English is not a stay-put language. It's always changing—expanding here, shrinking there, trying on new things, casting off old ones. People no longer say things like "Forsooth, methinks that grog hath given me the flux!" No, time doesn't stand still and neither does language.

So books about English need to change along with the language and those who use it. Welcome to the fourth edition of *Woe Is I*.

What's new? Most of the changes are about individual words and how they're used. New spellings, pronunciations, and meanings develop over time, and while many of these don't stick around, some become standard English. This is why your mom's dictionary, no matter how fat and impressive-looking, is not an adequate guide to standard English today. And this is why I periodically take a fresh look at what "better English" is and isn't.

The book has been updated from cover to cover, but don't expect a lot of earthshaking changes in grammar, the foundation of our language. We don't ditch the fundamentals of grammar and start over every day, or even every generation. The things that make English seem so changeable have more to do with vocabulary and how it's used than with the underlying grammar.

However, there are occasional shifts in what's considered grammatically correct, and those are reflected here too. One example is the use of *they*, *them*, and *their* for an unknown somebody-or-other, as in "Somebody forgot *their* umbrella"— once shunned but now acceptable. Another has to do with *which* versus *that*. Then there's the use of "taller *than me*" in simple comparisons, instead of the ramrod-stiff "taller *than I*." (See Chapters 1, 3, and 11.)

Despite the renovations, the philosophy of *Woe Is I* remains unchanged. English is a glorious invention, one that gives us endless possibilities for expressing ourselves. It's practical, too. Grammar is there to help, to clear up ambiguities and prevent misunderstandings. Any "rule" of grammar that seems unnatural, or doesn't make sense, or creates problems instead of solving them, probably isn't a legitimate rule at all. (Check out Chapter 11.)

And, as the book's whimsical title hints, it's possible to be too "correct"—that is, so hung up about correctness that we go too far. While "Woe is I" may appear technically correct (and even that's a matter of opinion), the lament "Woe is me" has been good English for generations. Only a pompous twit—or an author trying to make a point—would use "I" instead of "me" here. As you can see, English is nothing if not reasonable.

ACKNOWLEDGMENTS

Countless friends and colleagues helped make this book by contributing ideas, pointing out omissions, and sneering at my mistakes. I'm glad that I was able to provide you all with a socially acceptable outlet for your more aggressive impulses. Your patience and good humor were second only to mine, and I can't thank you enough.

I'm particularly grateful to those who read the manuscript: Laurie Asséo; David Feldman; Margalit Fox; Elizabeth Frenchman; Anita Gates; Neal, Margo, and Garth Johnston; Dimi Karras; Peter Keepnews; David Kelly; Eden Ross Lipson; Deborah Nye; Allan M. Siegal; Rachel Elkind Tourre; Gloria Gardiner Urban; Elizabeth Weis; and my mother, Beverly J. Newman.

For their support, encouragement, and advice, I thank Michael Anderson; Michael Barson; Alida Becker; Brenda Berkman; Charles Doherty; Tom Ferrell; Jan Freeman; Ken Gordon;

Pamela and Larry Kellerman; Harvey Kleinman; Charles Mc-Grath; Merrill Perlman; Tim Sacco; Michael Sniffen; Katlyn Stranger; Yves Tourre; Marilynn K. Yee; Arline Youngman; my sister, Kathy Richard; my aunt, Sydney Blanchard; and my encyclopedic father-in-law, Allen G. Kellerman.

Sam Freedman was generous with his time and advice, and passed along much valuable insight (especially about danglers) from his experiences as a reporter, an author, and a teacher. William Safire was kind enough to acquaint me with the invaluable Jeff McQuain, who expertly scoured the manuscript for errors. (Any boo-boos that remain are mine alone.) I'd be lost without my tireless agent, Dan Green, who has been with me every step of the way since 1994. And the book couldn't have been written without the help of a terrific editor, Jane Isay, whose idea it was in the first place.

I'm indebted as well to Dan Jacob and to all the readers whose kibitzing from the sidelines has helped make the book better, edition after edition: Stephen Ahearne-Kroll, Catalina Baker, David A. Ball, Brian Blank, Ron Blicq, Jason W. Brunk, Liz Copeland, Don Corken, Jr., Robert H. Dietrick, Steve Fischer, Eric Fluger, Victor Carl Friesen, Mary Laura Gibbs, Kathleen Gifford, Sherman Greene, David Hawkins, Cheryl Lynn Helm, Hunt B. Jones, Anita Kern, Ann J. Kirschner, Zilia L. Laje, Ruth M. McVeigh, Francis Mead, Jackson Miller, Ed Pearson, Jessica Raimi, Louie G. Robinson, Geoffrey Rommel, James Smith Rudolph, Gary G. Sackett, Jennifer Schwartz, Daniel Siepert, Bill Sowder, Elissa Steeves, Scott Summerville, Robert Swinney, and Kurt Yeung.

Anna Jardine, the pickiest copy editor on the face of the earth, has worked with me on every edition of the book since it was first published in 1996, and she's a wonder. Thanks for helping No. 4 along, Anna. Special thanks also go to Jake Morrissey, a gifted writer and editor, as well as to Kevin Murphy and the rest of the staff at Riverhead Books.

Finally, heartfelt thanks to my husband and frequent coauthor, Stewart Kellerman, for his conjugal as well as conjugational expertise. The book would not have been possible without his hard work and solid good sense. He's my best friend, and the best editor I know.

We all come from the factory wired for language. By the time we know what it is, we've got it. As toddlers, we don't think about language; we just talk. Only later are we aware of grammar, an ever-evolving set of rules for using words in ways that we can all agree on. Without rules, without a system for organizing words into sentences, we'd be spouting gibberish. But the laws of grammar come and go. English today isn't what it was a hundred years ago, and it's not what it will be a hundred years from now. As times change, we save what's useful and discard what isn't. If our language didn't keep up, our wires would get crossed and we'd fail to understand one another.

If language were flawless, perhaps this wouldn't happen. But the perfect language hasn't been invented. No, I take that back—it has been done. There are so-called rational languages (like the "universal" tongue Esperanto and the computer-generated

ELIZA) that are made up, designed to be logical, reasonable, sensible, easy to speak and spell. And guess what? They're flat and lifeless. What's missing are the quirks, the subtleties, the bumpy irregularities that make natural languages so exasperating and shifty—and so wonderful.

That's wonderful in the literal sense: full of wonders and surprises, poetry and unexpected charm. If English weren't so stretchy and unpredictable, we wouldn't have Lewis Carroll, Dr. Seuss, or the Marx Brothers. And just try telling a knock-knock joke in Latin!

But we pay a price for poetry. English is not easy, as languages go. It began over 1,500 years ago, when Germanic tribes (mainly Angles and Saxons) invaded Britain, a Celtic-speaking land already colonized by Latin-speaking Romans. Into this Anglo-Saxon broth went big dollops of French, Italian, Spanish, German, Danish, Portuguese, Dutch, Greek, and more Latin. Within a few hundred years, English was an extraordinarily rich stew. Today, it's believed to have the largest lexicon (that is, the most words) of any major European language—and it's still growing and evolving. Is there any wonder the rules get a little messy?

And let's face it, English *does* get messy. Bright, educated, technologically savvy people who can program a supercomputer with their toes may say or write things like:

"Come to lunch with the boss and I."

"I wish you would have called."

"Already housebroken, the Queen brought home a new corgi."

Every one of those sentences is faulty and could make a

smart person look clueless (if you don't see why, check out Chapters 1, 4, and 9).

On the other hand, some kinds of flubs become so widespread that they start to sound right. And in some cases, they become right. This is because as English evolves, so do the "rules," which are simply the linguistic conventions of the times. (When did you last hear someone say, "Whence cometh thou hither"?) So what used to be regarded as errors may now be acceptable or even preferred. What are we supposed to make of all this?

Woe Is I is a survival guide for intelligent people who probably have never diagrammed a sentence and never will. Most of us don't know a gerund from a gerbil and don't care, but we'd like to speak and write as though we did. Grammar is mysterious to each of us in a different way. Some very wise people mess up pronouns, and I've known brilliant souls who can't spell. Many people can't tell the difference between *it's* and *its*. Others go out of their way to avoid using quotation marks. Whatever your particular blind spot, *Woe Is I* can help you without hitting you over the head with a lot of technical jargon. No heavy lifting, no assembly required. There are sections on the worst pitfalls of everyday language, along with commonsense tips on how to avoid stumbling into them. Wherever possible, I've tried to stay away from grammatical terms, which most of us relish about as much as a vampire does garlic. You don't need them to use English well. If you come across a term that gives you trouble, there's a glossary in the back.

One last word before you plunge in. A dictionary is an essential tool, and everybody should have at least one. Yet the fact that a word can be found in the dictionary doesn't make it acceptable English. The job of a dictionary is to describe how words are used at a particular time. Formal or standard meanings are given, but so are colloquial, slang, dialect, non-standard, regional, and other current meanings. A dictionary may tell you, for example, what's meant by oddities like "restauranteur" or impostors like "irregardless"—but you wouldn't want to embarrass yourself by using them. Buy a reputable dictionary or consult one online (there are recommendations in the bibliography), and read the fine print.

The best of us sometimes get exasperated with the complexities of using English well. Believe me, it's worth the effort. Life might be easier if we could confine ourselves to classical Latin. But the quirks, the surprises, the ever-changing nature of English—these are the differences between a living language and a dead one.

CHAPTER 1

WOE IS I

THERAPY FOR PRONOUN ANXIETY

When a tiny word gives you a big headache, it's probably a pronoun.

Pronouns are usually small (*I, me, he, she, it*), but they're among the biggest troublemakers in the language. If you've ever been picked on by the pronoun police, don't despair. You're in good company. Hundreds of years after the first Ophelia cried "Woe is me," only a pedant would argue that Shakespeare should have written "Woe is I" or "Woe is unto me." (Never mind that the rules of English grammar weren't even formalized in Shakespeare's day.) The point is that no one is exempt from having their pronouns second-guessed.

Put simply, a pronoun is an understudy for a noun (a word for a person, place, or thing). *He* may stand in for "Ralph," *she* for "Alice," *they* for "the Kramdens," and *it* for "the stuffed piranha." Why do we need them? Take the following sentence:

*Ralph smuggled **his** stuffed piranha into the Kramdens' apartment, sneaked **it** out of **his** jacket, and was slipping **it** into **his** wife's curio cabinet, when suddenly Alice walked into **their** living room, clutched **her** heart, and screamed, "**You** get **that** out of **my** house!"*

If no one had invented pronouns, here's how that sentence would look: *Ralph smuggled Ralph's stuffed piranha into the Kramdens' apartment, sneaked the stuffed piranha out of Ralph's jacket, and was slipping the stuffed piranha into Ralph's wife's curio cabinet, when suddenly Alice walked into the Kramdens' living room, clutched Alice's heart, and screamed, "Ralph, get the stuffed piranha out of Alice's house!"*

See how much time pronouns save?

Simple substitutions (like *his* for *Ralph's*) are easy enough. Things get complicated when a pronoun, like any good understudy, takes on different guises, depending on the roles it plays in the sentence. Some pronouns are so well disguised that you may not be able to tell one from another. Enter *that* and *which*; *it's* and *its*; *who's* and *whose*; *you're* and *your*; *who* and *whom*; *everybody* and *nobody*; and *their*, *they're*, and *theirs*.

Now let's round up the usual suspects, as well as a few other shady characters.

THE WHICH TRIALS: WHICH OR THAT?

Bite on one of these: *Buster's bulldog, [**which** or **that**] had one white ear, won best in show.*

Pretty easy, right? The pause in the middle, set apart by commas, probably told you to choose *which*.

Now for a harder choice: *The dog [**which** or **that**] won best in show was Buster's bulldog.*

If you're confused, you've been spooked by *which*es. In that sentence, according to modern grammarians, you can use either *that* or *which*. (Americans are more likely to use *that* than the British, but both are correct.)

The old *that*-versus-*which* problem haunts everybody sooner or later. Here are two hints to help you figure out whether a clause (a group of words with its own subject and verb) should start with *that* or *which*.

- If the clause is not essential (your sentence is okay without it), use *which* and commas.
- If the clause is essential (your sentence is pointless without it), use either *that* or *which* and no commas.

Why does it matter whether the information in the clause is essential or not? Because we naturally pause to introduce stuff that's merely an interruption and not necessary to the meaning of a sentence. We separate it from the rest with commas and a *which*. But we don't pause for essential information—it runs right into the sentence with no interrupting commas, and it can start with either *which* or *that* (the choice is yours).

Let's take another look at the correct versions of those sentences: *Buster's bulldog, **which** had one white ear, won best in show. The dog **which** [or **that**] won best in show was Buster's bulldog.*

The point of each sentence is that Buster's dog won. What happens when we remove the *which* or *that* clause?

In the first sentence, the clause (**which** *had one white ear*) is disposable—without it, we still have the gist of the sentence: *Buster's bulldog won best in show.*

But in the second sentence, the clause (***which*** [or ***that***] *won best in show*) is essential. Without it, the sentence is pointless: *The dog was Buster's bulldog.* The point you were trying to make—Buster's dog won!—is missing.

Now let's take sentences that look more alike. All the versions are correct, though their meanings aren't the same.

> *The dogs,* ***which*** *had baths, smell better now.* (This means that all the dogs smell better because all of them had baths.)
> *The dogs* ***which*** [or ***that***] *had baths smell better now.* (This means that only the bathed dogs smell better.)

These next sentences also look alike, but the information—essential or not—comes at the end. Again, all the versions are correct, though their meanings aren't the same.

> *We threw out the bath towels,* ***which*** *were ruined.* (We dumped all the towels—they were all ruined.)
> *We threw out the bath towels* ***which*** [or ***that***] *were ruined.* (We dumped only the ruined towels.)

When information is essential and not set apart by commas, many people prefer *that* to *which*. They may think *that* is less of an interruption, or they may think *which* is incorrect (it's not). If you normally use *that* in these cases, by all means keep using it. Just don't sneer at those who use *which*.

WHICH CRAFT

Sometimes we start a statement with *which* to make a comment on the previous sentence. Which is perfectly all right, if the ideas are connected.

Orson saw himself as larger than life. **Which** *was true, after he gained all that weight.*

But *which* is often used in casual conversation to introduce an afterthought that comes out of nowhere.

He was a great Othello. **Which** *reminds me, where's that twenty dollars you borrowed?*

Conversation is one thing and written English is another. When you write a sentence starting with *which*, make sure there's a connection. Which is a rule that bears repeating!

AN ITSY-BITSY PROBLEM: IT'S OR ITS?

The smaller the word, the handier it is. And *it* is about as useful as they come. *It* can stand in for anything—a stuffed piranha, existentialism, the Monroe Doctrine, or buttered toast. It's a very versatile pronoun! But did you notice what just happened? We added an *s* and got *it's*—or should that be *its*? Hmmm. When do you use *it's*, and when do you use *its*?

This is a teeny-weeny problem that trips up even the smartest people. They go wrong when they assume that a word with an apostrophe must be a possessive, like **Bertie's** *aunt*. But an apostrophe can also stand for something that's been omitted (as in contractions, which are run-together words like *can't* and *shouldn't*). In this case, *it's* is short for *it is*. Plain *its* is the possessive form. So here's the one and only rule you need:

- If you can substitute *it is*, use *it's.*

> **NOTE:** *It's* can also be short for *it has*. There's more on *its* versus *it's* in the chapter on possessives, pages 41–42.

WHO'S (OR WHOSE) ON FIRST?

This problem is a first cousin of the one above (which you should look at, if you haven't already). As with *it's* and *its*, remember that *who's* is shorthand for *who is*, and unadorned *whose* is the possessive form.

- If you can substitute *who is*, use *who's.*

> **NOTE:** *Who's* can also be short for *who has*. There's more on *whose* versus *who's* in the chapter on possessives, pages 42–43.

YOU'RE ON YOUR OWN

"Your our kind of people," reads the hotel marquee. Eek! Let's hope impressionable children aren't looking. The sign should read: "You're our kind of people." *You're* is short for *you are*; *your* is the possessive form.

- If you can substitute *you are*, use *you're*.

WHO'S THAT?

Choose one: *The girl* **that** *married dear old Dad* or *The girl* **who** *married dear old Dad.*

If both sound right, it's because both are right. Despite what many people think, a person can be either a *that* or a *who*. A thing, on the other hand, is always a *that*.

But what about Benji and Morris? Dogs and cats aren't people, but they aren't quite things, either. Is an animal a *that* or a *who*?

If the animal is anonymous, it's a *that*: *There's the dog* **that** *won the Frisbee competition.*

An animal with a name, however, can be a *who* or a *that*: *Morris is a cat* **who** *knows what he likes.*

There's more about the old *that*-versus-*who* myth on page 245.

WHOM SWEET WHOM

Poor *whom*! Over the years, wordsmiths from Noah Webster to Jacques Barzun have suggested that maybe we should ditch it altogether and let *who* do the job of both. Not a bad idea.

It's pretty hard to imagine an outraged populace protesting, "*Whom* do you think you're messing with! Get your hands off our pronouns!" There's no doubt that in everyday speech and casual writing, *whom* has lost the battle.

So has the bell tolled for *whom?*

Not quite. Here we are, well into a new millennium, and against all odds, creaky old *whom* is still with us. With a few minor adjustments, we can do without it when we speak or write casually (I'll show you how on page 10). But anyone who wants to write formal English will have to get a grip on *whom.*

If you want to be absolutely correct, the most important thing to know is that *who* does something (it's a subject, like *he*), and *whom* has something done to it (it's an object, like *him*). You might even try mentally substituting *he* or *him* where *who* or *whom* should go: if *him* fits, you want *whom* (both end in *m*); if *he* fits, you want *who* (both end in a vowel). *Who* does something *to* (*at*, *by*, *for*, *from*, *in*, *toward*, *upon*, *with*, etc.) *whom.* The italicized words in parentheses, by the way, are prepositions—they "position" or situate words in relation to one another. A preposition often comes just before *whom*, but not always. A better way to decide between *who* and *whom* is to ask yourself *who* is doing what to *whom.*

This may take a little detective work. Miss Marple herself might have been stumped by the convolutions of some *who* or *whom* clauses (a clause, you'll recall, is a group of words with its own subject and verb). For instance, other words may get in between the subject and the verb. Or the object may end up in front of both the subject and the verb. Here are two pointers to help clear up the mystery, followed by examples of how they're used.

- Simplify, simplify, simplify: strip the clause down to its basic subject, verb, and object.
- Move the words around mentally to make it easier to identify the subject and the object.

*Nathan invited only guys [**who** or **whom**] he thought played for high stakes.* If you strip the mystery clause of its false clues—the words separating the subject and verb—you end up with **who** . . . *played for high stakes. Who* did something (played for high stakes), so it's the subject.

*Nathan wouldn't tell Miss Adelaide [**who** or **whom**] he invited to his crap game.* First strip the sentence down to the mystery clause, *[**who** or **whom**] he invited.* If it's still unclear, rearrange the words in your mind: *he invited **whom**.* You can now see that *whom* is the object—*he* did something to (invited) *whom*—even though *whom* comes ahead of both the verb and the subject.

> **NOTE:** A preposition isn't always followed by *whom*. It can be followed by a clause that starts with *who*. Consider this sentence: *After the crap game, Nathan was confused about [**who** or **whom**] owed him money.* Don't be misled by the preposition *about*; it's one of the false clues mentioned above. Instead, simplify, simplify, simplify, and look for the clause—in this case it's **who** *owed him money.* Since *who* did something (owed him money), it's the subject.

A CURE FOR THE WHOM-SICK

Now for the good news. In almost all cases, you can use *who* instead of *whom* in conversation or in informal writing—personal letters, casual memos, emails, and texts.

Sure, it's not a hundred percent correct, and I don't recommend using it on formal occasions, but *who* is certainly less stuffy, especially at the beginning of a sentence or a clause: **Who***'s the letter from? Did I tell you* **who** *I saw at the movies?* **Who** *are you waiting to see? No matter* **who** *you invite, someone will be left out.*

A note of caution: *Who* can sound grating if used for *whom* right after a preposition. You can get around this by putting *who* in front. *From* **whom***?* becomes **Who** *from?* So when a colleague tells you he's going on a Caribbean cruise and you ask, "Who with?" he's more likely to question your discretion than your grammar. See also page 244.

OBJECT LESSONS

THE ME GENERATION

These days, anyone who says "It is I" sounds like a stuffed shirt. It wasn't always so. In bygone days, you might have had your knuckles rapped for saying "It's me" instead of "It is I." Your crime? A pronoun following the verb *to be*, the English teacher insisted, should act like a subject (*I, he, she, they*) and not an object (*me, him, her, them*). But language is a living thing, always evolving, and *It is I* is just about extinct. In all but the most formal writing, even some of the fussiest grammarians accept *It's me*. Most of us find the old usage awkward, though I must admit that I still use "This is she" when someone asks for me on the phone. Old habits die harder than old rules.

Next time you identify the perp in a police lineup, feel free to point dramatically and say, "That's him, Officer!" For more, see page 244.

JUST BETWEEN ME AND I

Why is it that no one ever makes a mistake like this? *You'll be hearing **from I**.*

It's instinctive to use the correct form (*from **me***) when only a solitary pronoun follows a preposition. (Prepositions—*after, as, at, before, between, by, for, from, in, like, on, toward, upon, with,* and a slew of others—position other words in the sentence.) But when the pronoun isn't alone, instinct goes down the drain, and grammar with it. So we run into misdemeanors like *The odds were **against you and I***, although no one would dream of saying "against I."

I wouldn't be at all surprised to learn that the seeds of the *I*-versus-*me* problem are planted in early childhood. We're admonished to say, "I want a cookie," not "Me want a cookie." We begin to feel subconsciously that *I* is somehow more genteel than *me*, even in cases where *me* is the right choice—for instance, after a preposition. Trying too hard to be right, we end up being wrong. Hypercorrectness rears its ugly head.

My guess is that most people who make this mistake do so out of habit, without thinking, and not because they don't know the difference between *I* and *me*. If you find yourself automatically putting *you and I* after a preposition, try this: In your mind, eliminate the other guy, leaving the tricky pronoun (*I* or *me*) all by itself. Between you and me, it works.

> **NOTE:** I can hear a chorus of voices shouting, Wait a minute! Doesn't Shakespeare use *I* after a preposition in *The Merchant of Venice*? Antonio tells Bassanio, "All debts are clear'd between you and I, if I might but see you at my death." That's true. But then, we're not Shakespeare.

MORE THAN MEETS THE I

Some of the smartest people I know hesitate at the word *than* when it comes before a pronoun. What goes next, *I* or *me*? *he* or *him*? *she* or *her*? *they* or *them*?

The answer: All of the above! Use whatever seems natural to you.

Take *I* and *me* as examples, since they're the pronouns we use most (egotists that we are).

*Trixie is fatter **than me**.*
*Trixie is fatter **than I**.*

In a simple comparison like that, modern grammarians tell us, both sentences are correct and they mean the same thing. Many people find *than I* stuffier and more old-fashioned, but it's not more correct.

If you're used to making comparisons with *than I*, and if it seems natural to you, stick with it. But if you're more comfortable with *than me*, don't let anybody tell you it's wrong (see pages 241–242).

Beware, however, of more complicated comparisons. Some, like those with *more than* or *less than*, can be unclear if they end with just a pronoun.

For example, a sentence like *Trixie loves spaghetti* **more than me** could leave doubt about what's being compared with what. Here it's a good idea to fill out the sentence and make your meaning clearer. Choose one of these instead:

Trixie loves spaghetti **more than I do**.
Trixie loves spaghetti **more than she loves me**.

NOTE: Watch your spelling. The word used in comparisons is *than*, not *then*. See page 127.

OF ME I SING

One of the most splendid words in the English language is *me*. (And I say this in all humility.) Yet *me* gets no respect. All the glory goes to *I*. This is a great injustice, and it leads to all kinds of misconceptions about English.

Because many people feel there's something immodest— or perhaps not quite correct—about using *me*, they avoid it. Instead of *than* **me**, they think they have to use *than I* (see above and pages 241–242). Instead of *with Marcel and* **me**, they use *with Marcel and* **I** (see pages 11–12). Or they hedge their bets and use *myself* instead (see pages 14–15).

This *me* avoidance must stop! *Me* is an honorable and upright word and always has been. So give *me* its due and use it where it belongs.

Here's something else about *me* while we're on the subject (or rather the object). In English, *me* (along with the other object pronouns) is the default choice, linguists say. This means that when there's no clear indication one way or another, choose *me* (or *us*, *him*, *her*, *them*). In these kinds of sentences, objects rule!

What? **Me** *sing?*

Silly **me**.

Lucky **us**!

The real **her** *is coming out.*

Nobody else, just **him**.

Oh no, not **them** *again!*

And yes, sentence fragments are a valuable part of English. They're perfectly fine in speech and in ordinary writing. (You'll want to use full sentences in formal writing, though.)

SELF DENIAL

In the contest between *I* and *me*, the winner is often *myself.* That's because people who can't decide between *I* and *me* often choose *myself* instead. They say things like *Jack and* **myself** *were married yesterday.* (Better: *Jack and* **I***.*) Or: *The project made money for Reynaldo and* **myself***.* (Better: *for Reynaldo and* **me***.*) You've probably done it yourself.

Well, it's not grammatically wrong, but I don't recommend this *self*-promotion. Ideally, *myself* and the rest of the *self*-ish crew (*yourself, himself, herself,* etc.) shouldn't take the place of the ordinary pronouns *I* and *me, he* and *him, she* and *her,* and so on. They're better used for two principal purposes:

- To emphasize. *I made the cake* **myself**. *Love* **itself** *is a riddle. The detective* **himself** *was the murderer.* (The emphasis could be left out, and the sentence would still make sense.)
- To refer back to the subject. *She hates* **herself**. *And you call* **yourself** *a plumber! They consider* **themselves** *lucky to be alive. The problem practically solved* **itself**.

THEY AND COMPANY: THEY'RE, THEIR, THEIRS (AND THERE AND THERE'S)

These words remind me of the stateroom scene in the Marx Brothers movie *A Night at the Opera.* There seem to be half a dozen too many, all stepping on one another's feet.

Taken one at a time, though, they're pretty harmless.

- *They're* is shorthand for *they are*: **They're** *tightwads, and they always have been.*
- *Their* and *theirs* are the possessive forms for *they*: **Their** *money is* **theirs** *alone.*
- *There* (meaning "in or at that place," as opposed to "here") isn't even a pronoun, unlike the rest of the crowd

in the stateroom. Neither is *there's*, which is shorthand
for *there is*. But *there* and *there's* frequently get mixed up
with the sound-alikes *they're*, *their*, and *theirs*.

Sometimes a limerick says it best.

THE DINNER GUESTS

They seem to have taken on airs.
They're ever so rude with *their* stares.
They get *there* quite late,
There's a hand in your plate,
And *they're* eating what's not even *theirs*.

WHEN THEY IS NOBODY SPECIAL

What's wrong with this sentence? *Everybody likes the beach,
even if they don't swim.*

Answer: Nothing's wrong with it. The use of *they* to refer
to *everybody* is perfectly good English, in the opinion of modern grammarians. The following sentences, too, are just fine:

*Nobody goes to the dentist because **they** like it.*
*If anyone calls, tell **them** I've gone to lunch.*
*Somebody always parks **their** car in my spot.*
*Everyone who missed the concert was kicking **themselves**.*

So if you already use English like this, you can relax. If you
think it's wrong, here are the facts.

It's true that indefinite pronouns like *everybody* and *nobody* and *anyone* are used with singular verbs: *everybody **likes**, nobody **goes**, anyone **calls**,* and so on.

But they're not singular in meaning. Pronouns like these feel plural, because they stand for notions like "all people" or "no people" or "any people"—no one in particular. So there's no conflict in referring to them with the plural *they* or its sidekicks *them, their,* and *themselves.*

In modern English, forms of *they* can properly be used in these ways.

- To refer back to a plural (two or more in number): *All **people** think **their** children are above average.*
- To refer back to an unknown person or persons (no particular number): ***Everybody** thinks **their** children are above average.*

The same is true of ordinary nouns when they're indefinite and stand for an unknown person or persons.

> *No victim of a crime should blame **themselves** for what happened.*
> *The typical depositor puts too much trust in **their** local Bank & Trust.*

Yes, those subjects (*victim, depositor*) are grammatically singular too, and we use them with singular verbs. But here they don't mean just one individual. They stand for a whole pool of people, so using forms of *they* is normal and appropriate.

This is a case where an outdated rule has been discarded (see the chapter on grammar myths, pages 251–252). No, nothing has changed in actual usage. People have used *they* in this way for almost seven hundred years, even in the best writing. The only news here is that grammarians now recognize this as proper English. So there's no need to fumble around with awkward substitutes like *he or she, him or her,* and so on (*No victim of a crime should blame **himself or herself** for what happened*).

If you were taught differently and this sticks in your craw, nobody is forcing you to change your habits. Indefinite uses are easy enough to avoid if you want to. Just make the subject clearly plural instead of indefinite (***Victims** of a crime shouldn't blame **themselves** for what happened*).

In fact, a sentence is sometimes neater without an indefinite pronoun. Instead of *This book is for **everyone** who likes **their** thrillers on the dark side,* you can be more definite: *This book is for **readers** who like **their** thrillers on the dark side.*

But substituting *he or she* alternatives is clumsy and unnecessary. And *he* alone is inappropriate. *He* is no longer considered a universal "neuter" pronoun, and it will color your meaning.

However, if the subject is clearly masculine or feminine, by all means use forms of *he* or *she* instead of *they.*

*Somebody left **her** bra in the locker room.*
*No victim of a fraternity hazing should keep it to **himself**.*

NOTE: A special use of *they* and its other forms has been recognized by some dictionaries and usage guides. This *they* is the pronoun preferred by someone who doesn't identify as either male or female and doesn't want to be referred to as *he* or *she*. *Kim got an A-plus on **their** gender-studies paper. The professor told **them** that **they** scored higher than any other student*. This usage is still controversial, but it's something to be aware of. If you choose to use it in your own writing, avoid confusion. Make it clear that the pronoun refers to only one person.

WHAT'S WHAT?

Which sentence is correct?

*Lou sees **what appears** to be ghosts.*
*Lou sees **what appear** to be ghosts.*

Leaving aside the issue of Lou's sanity, should we choose *what appears* or *what appear*? And what difference does it make? Well, what we're really asking is whether the pronoun *what*, when used as a subject, takes a singular verb (*appears*) or a plural one (*appear*). The answer is that *what* can be either singular or plural; it can mean "the thing that" or "things that." In this case, Lou is seeing "things that" appear to be ghosts. So this is the correct sentence: *Lou sees **what appear** to be ghosts.*

NOTE: When *what* is the subject of two verbs in the same sentence, make the verbs match in number—both singular or both plural, not one of each. **What scares** *Lou the most* **is** *Bud's sudden disappearance.* (Both verbs are singular.) *But* **what seem** *to be supernatural events* **are** *really sleight of hand.* (Both verbs are plural.)

By the way, it takes a certain effort to get your *what*s straight. Few people do it automatically, so take your time and watch out for trapdoors. For more on *what* with verbs, see page 59.

CHAPTER 2

PLURALS BEFORE SWINE

BLUNDERS WITH NUMBERS

With grammar, it's always something. If it's not one thing, it's two—or four, or eight—and that's where plurals come in.

WHAT NOAH KNEW

The ark was filled symmetrically:
A boy for every girl.
Its claim to singularity
Resided in the plural.

Without plural words, we'd have to talk about one thing at a time! You couldn't eat a bag of *peanuts* at the ball game, you'd have to eat *peanut* after *peanut* after *peanut*. But English is very accommodating. A *bagful* here and a *bagful* there and—voilà—you've got *bagfuls*. See? There's nothing we can't have more of, even *infinities*, because anything that can be singular can also be plural.

In English, it's fairly easy to go forth and multiply. To make a singular noun (a word for a thing, person, place, or idea) into a plural one, we usually add *s* or *es* or *ies*, depending on its ending. In general, plurals are a piece (or pieces) of cake.

Of course, there are dozens of irregular plurals, but most of them are second nature to us by the time we're five or six. *Children* (not "childs") shouldn't play with *knives* (not "knifes"), and ganders are male *geese* (not "gooses"). A little later in life we pick up some of the more exotic plurals— *criteria*, *phenomena*, *hypotheses*, and the like—that are the offspring of other languages.

For most of us, plurals get sticky mainly when they involve proper names, nouns with several parts, or words that can be either singular or plural. How do we refer to more than one *Sanchez* or *spoonful* or *brother-in-law*? Is a word like *couple* or *politics* singular or plural—or can it be both?

To get right to the points, let's start with names.

KEEPING UP WITH THE JONESES: HOW NAMES MULTIPLY

Names are not all that mysterious. Then why do people mangle them almost beyond recognition when making them plural? *In my daughter's preschool class, there are two **Larries** [ouch!], three **Jennifer's** [oof!], and two **Sanchez'** [yipes!].* It's *Larrys, Jennifers,* and *Sanchezes.*

Getting them right isn't difficult. Whether you're dealing with a first name or a last, form the plural by adding *s*, or (if the name ends in *s*, *sh*, *ch*, *x*, or *z*) by adding *es*. A final *y* doesn't change to *ies* at the end of a name. And please, no apostrophes!

> *Charles and his friend Charles are just a couple of* **Charleses**.
>
> *When Eliza dated three guys named Henry, she couldn't keep her* **Henrys** *straight. What's more, two of them were* **Higginses**.
>
> *There are eight* **Joneses**, *two of them* **Marys**, *in Reggie's little black book.*
>
> *The* **Ricardos** *and the* **Mertzes** *had dinner with the* **Simpsons** *and the* **Flanderses** *at the home of the* **Cleavers**.

COMPOUND FRACTURES: WORDS THAT COME APART

Some nouns aren't simple; they're more like small construction projects. When a *spoon* is *full*, it's a *spoonful*—but are two of them *spoonsful* or *spoonfuls*? If your better half has two brothers, are they your *brothers-in-law* or your *brother-in-laws*? In other words, how do you make a plural of a noun with several parts? The answer, as it turns out, comes in parts:

- If a compound word is solid and has no hyphen (-), put the normal plural ending at the *end* of the word:

Churchmen love *soapboxes*.

Kipling appeals to *schoolchildren* *and* *fishwives*.

Doormen *are good at getting* *taxicabs*.

You don't find Biedermeier *bookcases* *in* *alleyways*.

Babies dump *spoonfuls* *of jam on* *footstools*.

- If the word is split into parts, with or without hyphens, put the plural ending on the root or most important part (underlined in the examples):

  <u>*Mothers*</u>*-in-law like to attend* <u>*courts*</u>*-martial*.

  Are they <u>*ladies*</u>*-in-waiting or just* <u>*hangers*</u>*-on?*

  Those <u>*counselors*</u>*-at-law ate all the* <u>*crêpes*</u>
      suzette.

  Do *rear* <u>*admirals*</u> *serve on* <u>*men*</u>*-of-war?*

- Watch out for *general* when it's part of a compound word. In a military title, *general* is usually the important part, so it gets the *s*. In a civilian title, *general* isn't the root, so it doesn't get the *s*:

  Two <u>*attorneys*</u> *general went dancing with two*
      major <u>*generals*</u>.

  Those <u>*consuls*</u> *general are retired* *brigadier*
      <u>*generals*</u>.

NOTE: Somebody passing by used to be called a *passer-by*, and several of them were *passers-by*. By and by, the hyphen fell out, giving us *passerby* and *passersby*. The plural *s* stayed in the middle. These things happen.

THE ICS FILES

Figuring out the mathematics of a noun can be tricky. Take the word *mathematics*. Is it singular or plural? And what about all those other words ending in *ics*—*economics*, *ethics*, *optics*, *politics*, and so on? Fortunately, it doesn't take a PhD in mathematics to solve this puzzle.

If you're using an *ics* word in a general way (as a branch of study, say), it's singular. If you're using an *ics* word in a particular way (as someone's set of beliefs, for example), it's plural.

> *"**Politics** stinks," said Mulder.*
> *"Mulder's **politics** stink," said Scully.*
> ***Statistics** isn't a popular course at the academy.*
> *Alien-abduction **statistics** are scarce.*

TWO-FACED WORDS: SOMETIMES SINGULAR, SOMETIMES PLURAL

A noun can be double trouble if it stands for a collection of things. Sometimes it's singular and sometimes it's plural. How do you know which is which? Amazingly, common sense (yes, it has a place in English usage!) should tell you. Ask yourself this question: Am I thinking of the baseball team, or the players? Let's take a swing at these problem words a few at a time.

COUNSELING FOR COUPLES

What is a *couple*, anyway? Is it a pair (singular), or two of a kind (plural)? Is it two peas (plural) in a pod, or a pod (singular) with two peas?

Couple is probably the most common of the two-faced words. It can be either singular or plural, depending on whether it's supposed to mean two individuals or a package deal. Ask yourself whether you have the two peas in mind, or the pod. Here's a hint: Look at the word (*a* or *the*) in front. *A couple*, especially when followed by *of*, is usually plural. *The couple* is usually singular. Each of these examples illustrates both uses (the verbs are underlined, one plural and one singular):

> A **couple** of tenants <u>own</u> geckos. The **couple** in 5G <u>owns</u> a
> family of mongooses.
> Only a **couple** of appointments <u>are</u> available. That **couple**
> <u>is</u> always late.

There's more about *couple* on pages 57 and 130.

GROUP THERAPY

Many words that mean a group of things—*total*, *majority*, and *number*, for example—can be singular or plural. Sometimes they mean the group acting as a whole, sometimes the members of the group.

As with the other two-faced words, ask yourself whether

you are thinking of the whole or the parts. A little hint: *The* before the word (*the total, the majority*) is usually a tip-off that it's singular, while *a* (*a total, a number*), especially when *of* comes after, usually indicates a plural. Each of these examples illustrates both (the verbs are underlined, one singular and one plural):

> *The* **majority** *is in charge. Still, a* **majority** *of voters are unhappy.*
> *The* **total** *was in the millions. A* **total** *of six were missing.*
> *The* **number** *of hats Bette owns is astounding. A* **number** *of them are pretty ridiculous.*

There's more about *total, majority,* and *number* in the chapter on verbs, page 57.

ALL OR NOTHING

All is a versatile word. It's all things to all people; in fact, it's all-encompassing. So all-inclusive is this little word that it can be either singular or plural. Another two-faced word!

Luckily, it's all too simple to decide whether *all* is singular or plural. Here's a foolproof way (the verbs in the examples are underlined):

- If *all* means "all of it" or "everything" or "the only thing," it's singular. *"All I eat is lettuce,"* said Charlotte. *"But* **all** *I lose is brain cells.* **All** *is not well with my waist."*

- If *all* indicates "all of them," it's plural. "***All** the men I date are confused,*" said Charlotte. "***All** prefer slender women with big appetites.*"

NOTE: The same logic holds for *any*. If it means "any of it," it's singular; if it means "any of them," it's plural. There's more about *any* and *all* in the chapter on verbs, page 57.

NONE SENSE

None is the most difficult of the two-faced words, those that can be either singular or plural. One reason it's so confusing is that generations of us were taught (incorrectly) as schoolchildren that *none* is always singular because it means "not one." Legions of people think of rather stiff sentences—***None** of the ladyfingers was eaten.* ***None** of the watercress sandwiches was touched*—as grammatically correct.

But *none* has always been closer in meaning to "not any," and most authorities agree it usually means "not any of them" and is plural: ***None** of the cheese puffs were eaten.* ***None** of the buffalo wings were touched.* *None* is singular only when it means "none of it" (that is to say, "no amount"): *However, **none** of the beer was wasted.*

Here's an easy way to decide whether *none* is singular or plural (the verbs are underlined):

- If it suggests "none of them," it's plural. ***None** of the guests are smiling.* ***None** are staying past nine o'clock.*

- If it means "none of it," it's singular. ***None*** *of the food* <u>*was*</u> *eaten.* ***None*** <u>*was*</u> *edible.*

> NOTE: When you really do mean "not one," it's better to say "not one," and use a singular verb: **Not one** of the bottles <u>was</u> broken and **not one** beer <u>was</u> spilled. There's more about *none* in the chapter on verbs, page 57, and on page 243.

Y'S AND WHEREFORES: WORDS THAT END IN Y

Some plurals are just a bowl of cherries. Words ending in *y* either add *s* or change the *y* to *ies*. Here's the scoop.

- If a word ends in *y* preceded by a consonant (a hard sound, like *b*, *d*, *l*, *r*, *t*, etc.), drop the *y* and add *ies*: *Well-bred **ladies** don't throw **panties** off the decks of **ferries**.*
- If a word ends in *y* preceded by a vowel (a soft, open-mouthed sound, like *a*, *e*, *o*, *u*), add *s*: ***Boys** born in **alleys** can grow up to be **attorneys**.*

For making plurals out of names that end in *y*, see pages 22–23. For making plural forms of single letters, like *y*, see pages 31–32.

IFS, ANDS, OR BUTS

In English, there are exceptions to every rule. When *man* or *woman* is part of a compound, often both parts become plural. For example, *manservant* becomes *menservants*; *woman doctor* becomes *women doctors*. A live *mouse* has baby *mice*. But a computer *mouse* multiplies as either *mice* or *mouses*. (Some wags prefer *meece*, *rats*, or *rodentia*.) And get this: *hotfoot* becomes *hotfoots*, and *still life* becomes *still lifes*. Go figure.

On occasion you may need to form a plural of a word like *yes*, *no*, or *maybe*. Well, since you're referring to them as nouns, just follow the normal rules for making nouns into plurals (except that here you don't change a final *y* to *ies*).

I feel a poem coming on.

WORDS TO THE WHYS

Ups *and* **downs** *and* **ins** *and* **outs**,
Forevers *and* **nevers** *and* **whys**.
Befores *and* **afters, dos** *and* **don'ts**,
Farewells *and* **hellos** *and* **good-byes**.

Life is a string of **perhapses**,
A medley of **whens** *and* **so whats**.
We rise on our **yeses** *and* **maybes**,
Then fall on our **nos** *and our* **buts**.

ONE POTATO, TWO POTATO:
WORDS THAT END IN O

O for a simple solution to this one! Unfortunately, there's no hard-and-fast rule that tells you how to form the plural of every word that ends in *o*.

- Most form their plurals by adding *s*: ***Romeos*** who wear ***tattoos*** and invite ***bimbos*** to their ***studios*** to see their ***portfolios*** are likely to be ***gigolos***.
- A small number of words that end in *o* form their plurals by adding *es*. Some of the most common are in this example: The ***heroes*** saved the ***cargoes*** of ***tomatoes*** and ***potatoes*** from the ***mosquitoes*** and ***tornadoes*** by hiding them in ***grottoes***.

If you're unsure about the plural of an *o* word, look it up in the dictionary. And if two plurals are given, the one that's listed first is often the more common.

PLURALS ON THE Q.T.:
ABBREVIATIONS, LETTERS, AND NUMBERS

Over the years, authorities have disagreed on how we should form the plurals of abbreviations (*GI, rpm, RBI*), letters (*x, y, z*), and numbers (*9, 10*). Should we add *s*, or *'s*? Where one style maven saw *UFO's*, another saw *UFOs*. One was nostalgic for the *1990's*, the other for the *1990s*.

The problem with adding *'s* is that we get plurals and possessives confused. Is *UFO's*, for example, a plural (*I see two* **UFO's**) or a possessive (*That* **UFO's** *lights are violet*)?

Here's what I recommend, and what most publishers do these days. To form the plurals of abbreviations and numbers, add *s* alone, but to form the plural of a single letter, add *'s*. **CPAs**, *who know the three* **R's** *and can add columns of* **9s** *in their heads, have been advising* **MDs** *since the* **1980s** *to dot their* **i's**, *cross their* **t's**, *and never accept* **IOUs**. *Things could be worse: there could be two* **IRSs**.

Why use the apostrophe with a single letter? Because without it, the plural is often impossible to read. Like this: *The choreographer's name is full of* **as**, **is**, *and* **us**. (Translation: *His name is full of* **a's**, **i's**, *and* **u's**.) See also pages 207 and 270.

BETWEEN AND FROM: THE NUMBERS GAME

OK, it's not something that's been keeping you awake nights. But it comes up all the time. The question: When a noun follows *between* or *from*, is it singular or plural? *The elevator stalled* **between** *the ninth and tenth [* **floor** *or* **floors** *], stranding the boss* **from** *the first to the third [* **week** *or* **weeks** *] in August.* See what I mean? A small problem, perhaps, but a common one.

The answer: *Between* is followed by a plural noun, and *from* is followed by a singular one: *The elevator stalled* **between** *the ninth and tenth* **floors**, *stranding the boss* **from** *the first to the third* **week** *in August.*

Another pair of examples:

Veronica said she lost her charm bracelet somewhere **between** *Thirty-third and Thirty-seventh* **streets**. *Archie searched every inch of pavement* **from** *Thirty-third to Thirty-seventh* **Street** *before realizing that she had been in a cab at the time.*

GRADUATE STUDIES

If one graduate is an *alumna*, what do you call two? In traditional usage, the correct terms depend on whether the graduates are men or women. Here's the scoreboard.

- *alumna*: one woman
- *alumnus*: one man
- *alumnae*: two or more women (see also page 171)
- *alumni*: two or more men, or a mix of men and women

Those terms are technically correct, but in my opinion they're antiquated and fussy. Besides, the division of the sexes is usually irrelevant. So in everyday usage, the unisex *alum* (singular) and *alums* (plural) are fine. They're standard English, just less formal.

THE SOUL OF KINDNESS:
ALL KINDS, SORTS, AND TYPES

You've probably heard sentences like this one: *I hate **these kind** of mistakes!* If it sounds wrong to you, you're right. It's ***these kinds*** of mistakes (or ***this kind*** of mistake).

The singulars—*kind* of, *sort* of, *type* of, and *style* of—when preceded by *this* or *that*, are followed by singular nouns: *George wears **this kind of hat**.*

The plurals—*kinds* of, *sorts* of, *types* of, and *styles* of—when preceded by *these* or *those*, are usually followed by plural nouns: *Louise hates **those kinds of hats**.*

Here are some more examples to help you sort things out:

*"I enjoy **this sort of cigar**," said George.*

*"**These sorts of cigars** disgust me," said Louise.*

*"**That type of car** is my ideal," said George.*

*"Only gangsters drive **those types of cars**," said Louise.*

Don't use *a* or *an* after the expressions *kind of, sort of, type of,* or *variety of*: *The beagle is **some kind of a** hound.* (Arf!)

NOTE: Some singular nouns can stand for just one thing (*Is the **meat** done?*) or a whole class of things (*The butcher sells many varieties of **meat***). Other singular nouns always stand for a set of things (*The **china** matches the **furniture***). When a singular noun stands for a group of things, it's all right (though not necessary) to use it with *those kinds,*

these sorts, and so on. ***Those kinds of china*** *break easily.*
This can be a subtle distinction, and when in doubt just
stick to the all-singular or all-plural rule (*this kind of china*).

SOME THINGS NEVER CHANGE

You're already familiar with nouns from the animal kingdom
that can stand for one critter or many: *fish, deer, moose, elk,
sheep, swine.* Well, some words ending in *s* are also the same in
singular and plural: *series, species,* and *headquarters,* which can
mean a base or bases.

> *Gizmo's* ***headquarters*** *was designed by Rube Goldberg.*
> *The two rival companies'* ***headquarters*** *were on opposite
> sides of town.*

LOOKS CAN BE DECEIVING

Loads of nouns look plural because they end in *s,* but they're
actually singular: *checkers* (also *billiards, dominoes,* and other
names of games); *measles* (also *mumps, rickets, shingles,* and
many other diseases); *molasses; news;* and *whereabouts. Basil
says* ***billiards*** *takes his mind off his* ***shingles***, *which is driving
him crazy.*

If that's not confusing enough, some singular nouns that
end in *s* are regarded as pairs—*scissors, trousers, tongs, pliers,
tweezers,* and *breeches,* for instance. Although these pair words

are singular, they're treated as plural. *The scissors were found, as were the tweezers, in the drawer where the pliers are kept.*

Then there's the word *pair* itself—singular or plural? This requires a pair of answers.

If you're talking about two separate things (*a pair of pumpkins*, for example), treat *pair* as plural: *A pair of pumpkins are in the window.*

If you're talking about one thing that just happens to have two parts (like *a pair of shoes*), treat *pair* as singular: *One pair of shoes is black.* But add another *pair* and you have multiple *pair* or *pairs*; either plural is fine. *Two pair [or pairs] are brown.*

Here's another wrinkle. Plural words are often treated as singulars in quantities and measurements like these:

- Money: *Bernice says four dollars is too much for a cup of coffee.*
- Time: *For a trip to Tuscany, three days isn't enough.*
- Distances: *The pizzeria says five miles is as far as it delivers.*
- Weights: *At Emma's height, 110 pounds is too skinny.*
- Temperatures: *In Phoenix, 90 degrees is springlike.*

And by the way, use *less than*, not *fewer than*, with amounts like these. For more about *fewer* and *less*, see pages 115–116.

NOTE: Some words that started out as plurals have since become singular, like *insignia* (which once meant badges or emblems), *stamina* (strengths or qualities), and *agenda* (items on a list). The words *data* and *media* have now joined the group. For the scoop on these two, see page 240. And if you want a little thrill—all right, I said a *little* thrill—look up *kudos* (singular or plural?) on page 132.

PLURALS WITH FOREIGN ACCENTS

A Californian I know, Dr. Schwartz, is a cactus fancier. Is his garden filled with *cactuses* . . . or *cacti*?

As dictionaries will tell you, either form is right. Although *cacti* may sound more scientific, that doesn't make it more correct.

With nouns of foreign origin, is it better to choose an Anglicized plural (like *curriculums*) or a foreign one (*curricula*)? There's no single answer. A century ago, the foreign ending would have been preferred, but over the years we've given English plural endings to more and more foreign-derived words. And in common (rather than technical or scientific) usage, that trend is continuing. So don't assume that an exotic plural is more educated. Only *ignorami* would say they live in *condominia*.

The right choice can be a close call. The race between *referendums* and *referenda*, for example, is a tie. When in doubt, consult a usage guide or your dictionary. If both are listed without reservation, both are OK, so the choice is yours. In case you'd like to use the one that's more common, here are some current preferences.

Anglicized: *chateaus, focuses, formulas, gymnasiums, indexes, memorandums, octopuses, stadiums, symposiums, ultimatums, virtuosos.*

Foreign: *addenda, algae, analyses, axes* (for *axis*), *bacteria, bases* (for *basis*), *crises, criteria, hypotheses, kibbutzim, larvae, oases, parentheses, phenomena, stimuli, strata, theses, vertebrae.*

Toss-ups: *beaus* or *beaux*; *cactuses* or *cacti*; *curriculums* or *curricula*; *funguses* or *fungi*; *millenniums* or *millennia*; *radiuses* or *radii*; *referendums* or *referenda*; *syllabuses* or *syllabi*; *tableaus* or *tableaux.*

And these plurals are often spelled differently for different meanings: *antennas* (on electronics) or *antennae* (on insects); *appendixes* (in anatomy) or *appendices* (in books).

Plurals can be singularly interesting. Take the octopus—a remarkable creature, grammatically as well as biologically. *Octopus* is from the Greek and means "eight-footed." The original plural was *octopodes*, Anglicized over the years to *octopuses*. Along the way, someone substituted the Latin ending *pi* for the Greek *podes* and came up with the polyglot *octopi.*

Though it's etymologically illegitimate, *octopi* is now so common that dictionaries list it as a second choice after *octopuses*. I'll stick to *octopuses*, thank you very much. *Octopi* is for suckers.

MULTIPLE MOLLUSKS
In the oceans, wriggling by,
Are *octopuses*, not *octopi.*

CHAPTER 3

YOURS TRULY

THE POSSESSIVES AND THE POSSESSED

For an acquisitive society, we're awfully careless about possessives. Have you ever driven through a vacation community and noticed the offhanded signs identifying the properties? *The Miller's, The Davis', The Jone's, Bobs Place*. Businesses are no better, imagining possessives where there aren't any. A now defunct theater near Times Square in New York called itself *The Ero's*. We've all seen places like *Harrys Muffler Shop* or *Glorias' House of Beauty* or *His' and Hers' Formal Wear*.

The word *its* is an Excedrin headache, a possessive that does not take the apostrophe (') we've come to expect. There are scores of other possessive puzzles: Are you a friend *of Jake*, or a friend *of Jake's*? Are you going to your *aunt and uncle's* house, or to your *aunt's and uncle's* house? Do you mind *me smoking*, or do you mind *my smoking*?

As long as there are haves and have-nots, there will be

questions about possessives. This chapter should answer the most troublesome ones.

POSSESSION IS NOT DEMONIC:
THE SIMPLE FACTS

The tool kit couldn't be simpler. All you need to make almost any word possessive is an apostrophe and the letter *s*. You add both of them together (*'s*) or just the apostrophe alone, depending on the circumstances:

- If the word is singular, always add *'s*, regardless of its ending. (This is true even if the ending is *s*, *z*, or *x*— whether sounded or silent.) *The waiter spilled red wine on* **Eula's** *dress, which came from* **Paris's** *finest shop. The* **dress's** *skirt, which resembled a tutu from one of* **Degas's** *paintings, was ruined.* **Flem's** *attitude was philosophical (he had been reading* **Camus's** *essays). "It wasn't* **Jacques's** *fault," he said, defending the waiter. "Besides, it's not this* **Bordeaux's** *best vintage."* Some names from antiquity may be exceptions; see page 46.
- If the word is plural and doesn't already end in *s*, add *'s*: *The* **children's** *menu was a rip-off, and the* **men's** *room was painted fuchsia.*
- If the word is plural and ends in *s*, add just the apostrophe: *The* **Snopeses'** *car was stolen by the valet parking attendant. The* **cops'** *attitude was surly. The* **victims'** *evening was now demolished.*

Incidentally, when you need a comma or a period after a possessive word that ends with an apostrophe, the comma or period goes after the apostrophe and not inside it: *The idea was the **girls'**, or maybe the **boys'**, but the responsibility was their **parents'**.*

> NOTE: Be sure you've formed the plural correctly before you add the apostrophe to the end. There's more about plural names in the chapter on plurals, pages 22–23. In a nutshell, if a name ends in *s* (like *Snopes*), the plural adds *es* (the **Snopeses**) and the plural possessive adds *es'* (*the **Snopeses'** car*). For a name that doesn't end in an *s* sound (*Babbitt*), the plural adds *s* (the **Babbitts**) and the plural possessive adds *s'* (*the **Babbitts'** car*).

ITS (OR IT'S?):
PUBLIC ENEMY NUMBER 1

What a difference an apostrophe makes. Every possessive has one, right? Well, not necessarily so. *It* (like *he* and *she*) is a pronoun—a stand-in for a noun—and pronouns don't have apostrophes when they're possessives: ***His** coat is too loud because of **its** color, but **hers** is too mousy.*

Now, as for *it's* (the one with the punctuation), the apostrophe stands for something that has been removed. *It's* is short for *it is*, and the apostrophe replaces the missing *i* in *is*. *The parakeet is screeching because **it's** time to feed him.*

Here's how to keep *its* and *it's* straight:

- If the word you want could be replaced by *it is*, use *it's*.
  If not, use *its*. (There's more on *its* and *it's* in the chapter
  on pronouns, pages 5–6.)

NOTE: Sometimes *it's* is short for *it has*, as in **It's** been
hours since he ate.

IT WIT

An itsy-bitsy problem
Used to give me fits.
Why use an apostrophe
With *it's* but not with *its*?

The answer to this little quiz:
The longer *it's* stands for "it is,"
While the *its* that's less impressive
Is the one that's a possessive.

WHO'S WHOSE?

The battle between *whose* and *who's* comes up less frequently
than the one between *its* and *it's* (see above), but the problems
are identical. If you can solve one, you've got the other one
whipped.

Don't be misled by the apostrophe. Not every possessive has
one. *Who* (like *it* and *he*) is a pronoun—a stand-in for a
noun—and pronouns don't have apostrophes when they're
possessives: "**Whose** *frog is this?" said Miss Grundy.*

Now, as for *who's*, the apostrophe stands for something that has been removed. *Who's* is short for *who is*, and the apostrophe replaces the missing *i* in *is*. *"And **who's** responsible for putting it in my desk?"*

Here's how to keep *whose* and *who's* straight:

- If you can substitute *who is*, use *who's*. If not, use *whose*.

NOTE: Sometimes *who's* is short for *who has*, as in **Who's had lunch?**

THERE'S A THEIR THERE!

What do you think of this sentence? *Nobody in their right mind pays retail.* (Hint: This question has nothing to do with shopping.)

If that sentence sounds wrong to you, then your English needs an update. In the opinion of modern grammarians, the use of *their* to refer to *nobody* is perfectly good English. People use *their* this way every day, even in the best English, and have for centuries. There's no need to change it to "*his* right mind," or "*her* right mind," or the clumsy "*his or her* right mind."

It's true that *their*, the possessive form of *they*, is plural. But it's often used in a way that's neither singular nor plural but indefinite. This happens when we use it with an indefinite subject, like *nobody*, *everyone*, *anybody*, etc. Those words are grammatically singular (we say *nobody **pays***, not *nobody **pay***), but they aren't singular in meaning. They stand for "no people," "all people," "any people," and so on. So the use of *their* for an unknown somebody-or-other is now considered standard English.

If you're skeptical, check out the chapters on pronouns (pages 16–18) and on grammar myths (pages 251–252). Meanwhile, if you mix up *their* and its sound-alikes, see pages 15–16.

GROUP OWNERSHIP: WHEN POSSESSIVES COME IN PAIRS

When something has two owners, who really owns it? When two people share an experience, whose experience is it? Who, in other words, gets the apostrophe when Sam and Janet spend an evening out—is it **Sam and Janet's** *evening,* or **Sam's and Janet's** *evening?*

- If two people (*Sam and Janet*) possess something (an *evening*) in common, consider them a single unit and put a single *'s* at the end: **Sam and Janet's** *evening was ruined when their date ended at the police station.*
- If two people possess something (or some things) individually, rather than jointly, each name gets an *'s*: **Sam's and Janet's** *furniture—his Danish modern, her French rococo—would never work in the same apartment.* Or: **Sam's and Janet's** *couches came from the same store.*

- If the names of the two owners are replaced by pronouns (stand-ins for nouns, like *your, my, our*, etc.), don't use them side by side, as in *"**Your and my** furniture can't live together,"* said Janet. The sentence sounds much better with the noun in between: *"**Your** furniture **and mine** can't live together."*

NOBODY'S FOOL

Body language is no problem in the possessive. Words like *anybody, everybody, somebody,* and *nobody* become possessive when you add *'s: anybody's, everybody's, somebody's, nobody's.*

When *else* is added, the *'s* goes after *else*: *"Stella is mine, and **nobody else's**,"* said Stanley. This seems pretty obvious to us now, but there was a time when it was considered correct to leave the apostrophe with the pronoun: *Is that your suit of armor, Sir Lancelot, or **somebody's else**?*

OH, FOR GOODNESS' SAKE!

Some word formations are just too much for us to get our tongues around. That's the only good reason I can think of for this next exception to the usual rules on possessives.

We may do something for *pity's* sake, for *heaven's* sake, for the *nation's* sake, for our *children's* sake. But with some "sake" phrases—*for **goodness'** sake, for **conscience'** sake, for* *convenience' sake, for **righteousness' *sake—*we don't add (or pronounce) the final *s* that normally follows the apostrophe. Call it tradition. I suppose our English-speaking forebears decided there was enough hissing in those words already, without adding another sibilant syllable (say those last two words five times in rapid succession).

The traditional custom has also been to drop the final *s* when writing the possessives of ancient classical or biblical names that already end in *s*: *Whose biceps were bigger, **Hercules' *or **Achilles'*? However, this old tradition is no longer universally followed. Today the final *s* is optional: **Aeschylus'** *plays* or **Aeschylus's** *plays*, **Moses'** *laws* or **Moses's** *laws*, **Jesus'** *teachings* or **Jesus's** *teachings*.

How do you decide? Let your pronunciation choose for you. If you add an extra syllable when pronouncing one of these possessive names (MO-zus-uz), then add the final *s* (*Moses's*). If you don't pronounce that *s* (and many people don't, especially if the name ends in an EEZ sound, like *Euripides*), then don't write it.

ARE YOU TOO POSSESSIVE?

One way to make a noun possessive is to add *'s*; another way is to put *of* in front of it.

What about using both? Are two possessives better than one? Should we say *a friend **of Jake's***? Or *a friend **of Jake***?

I'll end the suspense. Both are correct. There's nothing

wrong with using the *'s* in addition to *of*: *Brett is an old girl-friend **of Jake's** [or **of Jake**].* The choice is yours.

But when a pronoun is involved, make it a possessive pronoun (a friend **of his**, not a friend **of him**). *She's a friend **of his** and a client **of mine**.*

DOING TIME

Time is money, we say, and both are valuable, which may be why they're sometimes expressed in a way that looks possessive. It's long been the custom in English that we may, if we wish, describe periods of time and amounts of money by using apostrophes: *After an **hour's** wait in court, Butch was given two **years'** probation for stealing fifty **dollars'** worth of change from the collection plate.*

Why the apostrophes? After all, that *hour* doesn't possess anything, and neither do the *years* or the *dollars*.

The reason is that an apostrophe doesn't always imply ownership. It implies something like *of* or *amounting to*. When we write *an **hour's** wait*, we mean *a wait of one hour*. Similarly, *two **years'** probation* means *probation of two years*, and *fifty **dollars'** worth* means *worth amounting to fifty dollars*.

This is why we see apostrophes in such common expressions as *two **days'** time, five **years'** experience, one **week's** notice*, and so on. This is also why historians normally write the *Seven Years' War* and the *Hundred Years' War* with apostrophes. No real ownership is implied. Just imagine words like *of* or *amounting to* or *lasting* in place of the apostrophe: *time amounting to two days, experience amounting to five years, notice of one week, war lasting seven years.*

If you want, you can express yourself without using apostrophes: *After waiting an hour in court, Butch was given probation of two years for stealing fifty dollars in change from the collection plate.*

> NOTE: The same principle is at work in phrases like *a* **summer's** *day* (a day of summer), *a good* **night's** *sleep* (a sleep lasting all night), *for* **old times'** *sake* (for the sake of old times), *in* **harm's** *way* (in the way of harm), and *at our* **wits'** *end* (at the end of our wits).

SINGLES' BAR?

Some people are possessive about apostrophes and some aren't. That's why the University of Iowa has a Writers' Workshop while *The Kenyon Review* has a Writers Workshop.

Both are correct, and the difference is very slight. As I said on the previous page, there are times when an apostrophe doesn't suggest actual ownership. Instead, the apostrophe implies something else, something like *of*. So ***writers' workshop*** implies a workshop of writers. The apostrophe-free version, ***writers workshop***, is merely a descriptive adjective: it tells you what kind of workshop this is, one for writers (I told you the difference was slight).

The choice here is often up to you, which is why we read

both *citizens' group* and *citizens group*, *teachers' college* and *teachers college*, *veterans' affairs* and *veterans affairs*.

But when there's obviously no *of* implied, you can safely forget the apostrophe: *You'll never get into the **honors** program by hanging out in **singles** bars.*

DO YOU MIND ME . . . UH . . . MY SMOKING?

For many of us, this one is the Gordian knot of possessive puzzles. Actually, it's not hard to untie, once you know the secret. First, let's see how you do on your own. Which of these is correct?

*1. He resents **my going**.*
*2. He resents **me going**.*

If you picked number 2, you're less than perfect, but don't beat up on yourself. You're a member of a large and distinguished club. To see why so many of us slip up, let's look at two similar examples:

*1. He resents **my departure**.*
*2. He resents **me departure**.*

I'll bet you didn't have any trouble with that one. Obviously, number 1 is correct. *Departure* is a noun (a thing), and when it is modified or described by a pronoun (a word that stands in for a noun), the pronoun should be a possessive: *my*, *your*, *his*, *her*, and so on.

Now look again at the first set of examples:

1. *He resents **my going**.*
2. *He resents **me going**.*

If you still feel like picking number 2, it's because *ing* words are chameleons. They come from verbs—*go*, in the case of *going*—and usually act like verbs. But every once in a while they step out of character and take on the role of nouns. For all intents and purposes they may as well be nouns; in this example, *going* may as well be the noun *departure*.

The $64,000 question: How do we figure out whether an *ing* word is acting like a verb or like a noun? Here's a hint: If you can substitute a noun for the *ing* word—*departure* in place of *going*, for example, or *habit* for *smoking*—then treat it like a noun. That means making the word in front a possessive (*my*, not *me*): *He can't stand **my** smoking.*

LOOSE ENDS

The preceding explanation unties the Gordian knot, and you can stop there if you want. But here are a couple of loose ends you may want to tie up.

Sometimes it's too clumsy to use a possessive with an *ing* word—for instance, when you'd have to make a whole string of words possessive, not just one. Here's an example: *Basil objects to* **men and women kissing** *in public.* Using the possessive (*men's and women's kissing*) would create a monster. It's good to follow a rule, except when it leads you off a cliff. Since there's no way to mistake the meaning, leave it alone. But if there's just a pronoun in front, stick to the rule and make it a possessive: *Basil objects to* **our kissing** *in public.* (Not: *Basil objects to* **us kissing** *in public.*)

Another complication is the kind of sentence that can go either way:

> *Basil dislikes that* **woman's wearing** *shorts.*
> *Basil dislikes that* **woman wearing** *shorts.*

Both are correct, but they mean different things. In the first example, Basil dislikes shorts on the woman. In the second, he dislikes the woman herself. The lesson? Lighten up, Basil!

CHAPTER 4

THEY BEG
TO DISAGREE

PUTTING VERBS IN THEIR PLACE

The verb is the business end of a sentence, the sentence's reason for being. That's where the action is. Without a verb or even the hint of one, there's nothing going on, just a lot of nouns standing around with their hands in their pockets. A verb is easy to spot. Just look for the moving target, the center of activity, the part that tells you what's going on. No wonder the verb is often the most interesting word in a sentence.

It's also the most complicated. Because a verb expresses action, it has a dimension that other words lack—time. It has to tell you whether something happens in the present, the past, the future, or some combination of times: *sneeze, sneezed, will sneeze, would have sneezed,* and so on. The verb has another dimension, too. It varies according to the subject (who or what is performing the action): *I sneeze, you sneeze, he sneezes, they sneeze*, and so on.

There are plenty of reasons a verb can go astray. The most common is that it doesn't match the subject: one is singular and the other plural (*Harry and I **was sneezing***, for example). The next most common reason is that the verb's timing—its tense—is off (*Yesterday she **sneezes***).

Then there are those pesky little verbs that are as annoying as ants at a picnic, and just about as hard to tell apart: *sit* and *set*, *rise* and *raise*, *lie* and *lay*.

This makes verbs sound daunting, but they're actually not that bad. Taken one at a time (which is how you encounter them, after all), problems with verbs can be made to disappear.

MAKING VERBS AGREEABLE

Some rules of grammar may shift every eon or so, but you can bet the bank that this one will never change: Subject and verb must agree. If the subject is singular, then so is the verb (*Ollie **stumbles***). If the subject is plural, the verb has to be plural too (*Stan and Ollie **stumble***).

If your verb (the action word) doesn't match its subject (who or what is doing the action), you probably have the wrong subject in mind. That's not unusual, since the real subject isn't always easy to see. If you find it a breeze to write a simple sentence but start hyperventilating when a few bells and whistles are added, you're not alone. Here's what I mean:

*Every part of Ollie **needs** a massage.*

No problem. The subject (*part*) is singular, so the verb (*needs*) is singular. Now let's add a few of Ollie's aching parts:

*Every part of Ollie—his legs, his neck, his shoulders, his feet—[**needs** or **need**] a massage.*

Since the closest word is *feet*, a plural, you might be tempted to pick *need*. But in fact, the verb stays the same, *needs*, despite the extraneous details. That's because the subject (*part*) hasn't changed. The key to making subject and verb agree is to correctly identify the subject, and for that you have to simplify the sentence in your mind. Here are some pointers.

- Extra information inserted between subject and verb doesn't alter the verb.
  *Spring's glory **was** lost on Ollie.*
  *Spring's glory, with its birds and its flowers and its trees, **was** lost on Ollie.*
  The subject, *glory*, is still singular.
- Phrases such as *accompanied by, added to, along with, as well as, coupled with, in addition to,* and *together with,* inserted between subject and verb, don't alter the verb.
  *Spring **was** a tonic for Stan.*
  *Spring, along with a few occasional flirtations, **was** a tonic for Stan.*
  The subject is still *spring*, and is singular.

- Descriptions (adjectives) added to the subject don't alter the verb.

  > *A substance **was** stuck to Stan's shoe.*
  >
  > *A green, slimy, and foul-smelling substance **was** stuck to Stan's shoe.*

  The subject is *substance*, and it stays singular no matter how many disgusting adjectives you pile on.

SPLIT DECISIONS

Often the subject of a sentence—whoever or whatever is doing the action—is a two-headed creature with *or* or *nor* in the middle: ***Milk or cream*** *is fine, thank you.*

When both halves of the subject—the parts on either side of *or* or *nor*—are singular, so is the verb: *Neither alcohol nor tobacco **is** allowed.* When both halves are plural, so is the verb: *Ties or cravats **are** required.*

But how about when one half is singular and the other plural? Do you choose a singular or a plural verb? *Neither the eggs nor the milk [**was** or **were**] fresh.*

The answer is simple. If the part nearer the verb is singular, the verb is singular: *Neither the eggs nor **the milk was** fresh.* If the part nearer the verb is plural, the verb is plural: *Neither the milk nor **the eggs were** fresh.* (Treat *or* the same way, whether or not you use it with *either*: **Is the milk** *or the eggs returnable?* **Are** *either **the eggs** or the milk returnable?*)

The same rule applies when subjects are paired with *not only* and *but also*: *Not only the chairs but also **the table was** sold.* Or: *Not only the table but also **the chairs were** sold.*

NOTE: There's more about *either* and *or*, *neither* and *nor*, on pages 139–141. As you'll see, the multitalented *either* and *neither* can juggle more than two things at once.

THE SUBJECT
WITH MULTIPLE PERSONALITIES

Say you've identified the subject of a sentence, and it's a word that could be interpreted as either singular or plural, like *couple*, *total*, *majority*, *number*, *any*, *all*, or *none*. Is the verb singular or plural?

Here's how to decide.

Words that stand for a group of things—*couple*, *total*, *majority*, and *number*—sometimes mean the group as a whole (singular), and sometimes mean the individual members of the group (plural). The presence of *the* before the word (*the couple, the total, the majority*) is often a clue that it's singular, so use a singular verb: **The couple lives** in apartment *9A*. When *a* comes before the word, and especially when *of* comes after (*a couple of, a number of*), the word is probably plural, so use a plural verb: **A couple of** deadbeats **live** in apartment *9A*.

The words *all*, *any*, and *none* can also be either singular or plural. If you're using them to suggest *all of it, any of it*, or *none of it*, use a singular verb: **All** the money [all of it] **is** spent. If you're suggesting *all of them, any of them*, or *none of them*, use a plural verb: **All** the customers [all of them] **are** gone.

There's more about these two-edged words in the chapter on plurals, pages 25–29.

PERCENTAGE POINTERS

Choose the right verb: *Only a small percentage of new students in our dorm [***plan*** or ***plans****] to attend New Student Days.* (Hint: The subject is *percentage*.)

The correct verb is *plan*. Well, you had a fifty percent chance of getting it right.

Percentage is another subject with a multiple personality. Technically the noun is singular (*percentages* is the plural), but it's used with both singular and plural verbs. How do you choose? Start by looking at the article (*a* or *the*) preceding *percentage*.

- *the percentage*, no matter what follows, gets a singular verb. **The percentage** *of students who get care packages from their parents* **is** *just amazing!*
- *a percentage*, followed by *of* plus a singular noun, gets a singular verb. **A** *good* **percentage** *of the mail delivered to students* **includes** *food.*
- *a percentage*, followed by *of* plus a plural noun, gets a plural verb. **A** *large* **percentage** *of the goodies* **are** *consumed on the spot.*

For more about *percentage*, see page 266.

WHAT AND WHATNOT

What is another multiple personality—a word that can be treated as either singular or plural. Take a look at these examples:

What is *going on here?* **What are** *your intentions, Mister?*

As you can see, *what* can be either singular or plural when it's the subject of a verb. If *what* stands for one thing, use a singular verb (*is*, in this case). If it stands for several things, use a plural verb (*are*, for example).

But how do you choose? Consider this sentence: *Natalie is wearing* **what** *[look* or *looks] like false eyelashes.* Just ask yourself whether *what* refers to "a thing that" or "things that." In this case, she is wearing *things that look* like false eyelashes. Use the plural verb: *Natalie is wearing* **what look** *like false eyelashes.*

NOTE: When *what* affects two verbs in the same sentence, the verbs should be alike—both singular or both plural, not one of each: **What gives** away Natalie's age **is** her bad knees. In other words, the thing about Natalie that gives away her age is the fact that she has bad knees. On the other hand, if you want to emphasize that several things about Natalie show her age, you should choose plurals for both verbs: **What give** away Natalie's age **are** the knees and the bad face-lift. As you may suspect, there can be disagreement about whether *what* should be singular or plural. What's important to remember is that if *what* affects two verbs, they should match—both singular or both plural.

There's more about *what* in the chapter on pronouns; see pages 19–20.

THERE, THERE, NOW!

When a statement starts with *there*, the verb can be either singular or plural. We can say *there is* (*there's*, if you prefer), or we can say *there are*:

"**There is** [or **there's**] *a fly in my soup!" said Mr. LaFong.
"And **there are** lumps in the gravy!"*

The choice can be tricky, because *there* is only a phantom subject. In the first example, the real subject is *fly*; in the second, it's *lumps*. If the subject is hard for you to see, just delete *there* in your mind and turn the statement around: *"A fly **is** in my soup! And lumps **are** in the gravy!"*

So far so good. The rule to remember is that the verb after *there* should agree with the following subject: *there is* (or *there's*) when the real subject is singular, *there are* when it's plural. This is easy to see when the subject is one noun, like *fly* or *lumps*.

But what if the subject has more than one noun, like *chicken, vegetables, and gravy*? Technically, a compound subject like that is plural (*Chicken, vegetables, and gravy **are** in the soup*).

However, when the compound subject follows *there*, you have a choice:

- You can follow the formal rule and use a plural verb.
  There are *chicken, vegetables, and gravy in the soup.*
- You can make the verb agree with the closest noun. **There's** [or **There is**] *chicken, vegetables, and gravy in the soup.*

Today, either choice is acceptable in standard English. For more about starting a sentence with *there*, see pages 241 and 250.

WHEN EACH IS A REACH

Finish this sentence: **Each** *of the horses* **has its** *[or* **have their***] own personality.* (Hint: It pays to be single-minded here.)

In any sentence beginning with *each*, the subject is singular and has a singular verb. This is true even if *each* is followed by *of* and a plural noun. So the answer is **Each** *of the horses* **has its** *own personality.*

But what about this sentence: *The horses* **each has its** *[or* **have their***] own personality?* Aha! Here we have a horse (or horses) of a different color. The subject this time is *horses*, not *each*. And *horses*, a plural subject, takes a plural verb: *The horses* **each have their** *own personality.*

The word *each* can play a lot of different roles in a sentence, but there's a simple way of keeping the accompanying verbs in line. If you follow these tips, you can't go wrong:

- *Each*, at the beginning of a sentence, is accompanied by a singular verb. **Each** *of the horses* **is** *frisky.* **Each** *horse* **is** *frisky.* **Each** *of them* **is** *frisky.* **Each** **is** *frisky.*
- *Each*, when it follows a plural subject, is accompanied by a plural verb. *The horses* **each are** *frisky.* *They* **each are** *frisky.*

WISHFUL THINKING: I WISH I WAS . . .
OR . . . I WISH I WERE?

"Difficult do you call it, Sir?" the lexicographer Samuel Johnson once said after hearing a violinist perform. "I wish it were impossible."

Were? Why not *I wish it **was** impossible*? Well, in English we have a special way of speaking wishfully. We say, *I wish I **were** in love again*, not *I wish I **was** in love again*. There's a peculiar, wishful kind of grammar for talking about things that are desirable, as opposed to things as they really are. When we're in a wishful mood (a grammarian would call it the subjunctive mood), *was* becomes *were*:

> *I wish I **were** in Paris.* (I'm not in Paris.)
> *They wish he **weren't** so obnoxious.* (He is so obnoxious.)
> *She wishes pizza **were** a health food.* (It isn't a health food, unfortunately.)
> *He wishes Julia **were** home more often.* (Julia isn't home more often.)

IFFY SITUATIONS: IF I WAS . . .
OR . . . IF I WERE?

What a difference an *if* makes. An ordinary, straightforward statement like *I **was** taller* becomes quite another proposition when we insert one little word: *If I **were** taller*.

Why is this? It's because there's a special, "what if" sort of grammar that kicks in when we talk about something that's untrue. When we're in this iffy mood—the subjunctive mood, if you want to be technical—*was* becomes *were.* That's why the father in *Fiddler on the Roof* sings, "If I *were* a rich man," not "If I *was* a rich man." When a sentence or a clause (a group of words with its own subject and verb) starts with *if,* and what's being talked about is contrary to fact, here's what happens:

*If I **were** king, no one would pay retail.* (I'm not king.)
*If she **were** older, she'd know better.* (She's not older.)
*We could go shopping if it **were** Saturday.* (Today is not Saturday.)

NOTE: Not all *if* statements fall into this category, only those that are undeniably contrary to fact. In cases where the statement may actually be true, *was* remains *was:*

*If I **was** rude, I apologize.* (I may have been rude.)
*If she **was** there, I guess I missed her.* (She may have been there.)
*If it **was** Thursday, I must have gone to bed early.* (It may have been Thursday.)

AS IF YOU DIDN'T KNOW

The same rules that apply to *if* statements apply to those starting with *as if* or *as though*:

> *He acts as if he* **were** *infallible.* (He's not infallible.)
> *She behaves as though money* **were** *the problem.*
>   (Money is not the problem.)

For more about *as if* and *as though*, see page 103.

KNOCK WOULD

When we use wishful language to talk about the past, we sometimes make it more complicated than it needs to be. We stick in the phrase *would have* where a simple *had* should go. In this case, simpler is better.

> Incorrect: *I wish you* ***would have*** *called.*
> Correct: *I wish you* ***had*** *called.*

A similar problem arises when we use iffy language to talk about the past. We use *would have* twice when once is enough. Again, simpler is better.

> Incorrect: *If you* ***would have*** *called, I* ***would have*** *gotten the message.*
> Correct: *If you* ***had*** *called, I* ***would have*** *gotten the message.*

SUGGESTIVE LANGUAGE

Sometimes, English slips through a time warp and into another dimension. In cases where we'd normally use the verb *was* or *were*, we use *be* instead. You may have wondered why we say *I **was** quiet*, but *They requested that I **be** quiet*. What's going on here? The answer is that in English we have a special way of suggesting or demanding something (another example of the subjunctive mood). This is what you need to remember:

Use *be* instead of *was* or *were* after someone *asks*, *demands*, *insists*, *orders*, *requests*, *requires*, or *suggests* that something be done:

> *I demand that I **be** excused.*
> *The judge ordered that the suspect **be** tried.*
> *Olivia insisted they **be** admitted free.*
> *The law requires that you **be** fingerprinted.*

If *be* sounds unnatural to your ear, just imagine an unspoken *should* in front of it:

> *I demand that I (should) **be** excused.*
> *The judge ordered that the suspect (should) **be** tried.*
> *Olivia insisted they (should) **be** admitted free.*
> *The law requires that you (should) **be** fingerprinted.*

By the way, the form of the verb used here—*be* instead of *was* or *were*—is similar to the one used for a command: ***Be good! Be quiet! Be there or be square!***

NOTE: *Was*, *were*, and *be* give us the most trouble when we're suggesting or demanding something. But other verbs must also be in the command form when they're forced to give "command" performances: *Mom demanded that Ricky **change** his clothes. We suggest that she **get** a job. He urged that Barbra **negotiate**. Grandma insisted he **have** fruitcake.* Again, if this feels unnatural, imagine an unspoken *should* in front of the verb: *Grandma insisted he (should) **have** fruitcake.*

MAYDAY! MAYDAY!

May is a source of our word *maybe*, and that's a good clue to how it's used. We attach it to another verb (***may take*** or ***may forget*** or ***may have learned***, for example) to show that something is or was possible.

We can use *might* in the same way, attaching it to a main verb to indicate possibility (***might take***, ***might have forgotten***, ***might learn***). Then how do we know which to choose as our auxiliary, or "helping," verb—*may* or *might*?

Tradition says that what *may* happen is more possible than what *might* happen. But never mind. Today most people see little or no difference in the degree of possibility, and that old distinction is largely ignored. In modern English, *may* and *might* are interchangeable—almost. Grammarians still recommend *might* in certain cases.

Here's what to remember.

- If the sentence has only one main verb (with or without *have*), you can accompany it with either *may* or *might*. Here we're talking about things that are still possible.

    *Hermione **may** [or **might**] take the train.*
    *Hermione **may** [or **might**] have taken the train.*
    *She **may** [or **might**] forget her wand.*
    *She **may** [or **might**] have forgotten her wand.*
    *She **may** [or **might**] learn new tricks at the conference.*
    *She **may** [or **might**] have learned new tricks at the conference.*

- If the sentence has an additional verb in the present tense (underlined here), you can use either *may* or *might* with the other verb. Here again, we're talking about things that are still possible.

    *Hermione **<u>thinks</u>** she **may** [or **might**] take the train.*
    *She **<u>is</u>** afraid she **may** [or **might**] have forgotten her wand.*
    *She **<u>says</u>** she **may** [or **might**] learn new tricks at the conference.*

- If the sentence has an additional verb in the past tense (underlined here), I recommend using *might* with the other verb, though *may* is often seen in informal English. Here we're talking about things that were possible in the past.

    *Hermione **<u>thought</u>** she **might** take the train.*

*She **was** afraid she **might** leave [or **might** have left] her
wand behind.*

*She **said** she **might** learn new tricks at the conference.*

Why use *might* in speaking of possibilities from the past? Since *might* is technically the past tense of *may*, it mixes better with past-tense verbs.

> **NOTE:** Because there's an "iffy," hypothetical element in *may* and *might*, they're often used in *if* statements. Don't let that throw you. Just follow the advice above about using either *may* or *might* when there are other present-tense verbs and *might* when there are other past-tense ones: *If Hermione **goes** to the Arithmancy lecture tonight, she **may** [or **might**] run into Professor Vector. If Hermione **went** to the Arithmancy lecture tonight, she **might** run into Professor Vector. If Hermione **had gone** to the Arithmancy lecture tonight, she **might** have run into Professor Vector.*

May is used in another sense: to indicate permission. See the section on *can* versus *may*, pages 107–108. And for more about *might*, which is a mighty complicated word, see the box below.

WHAT MIGHT HAVE BEEN

In some kinds of sentences, as you've just seen, there's not much difference between *might* and *may*. Here comes one now: *Moose **might** [or **may**] have flunked the course.* Both versions express a possibility: Moose could have flunked.

But sometimes *might* branches out on its own. It no longer acts like a version of *may*, so it loses its sense of possibility and becomes negative. This *might*—often it's a *might have*—is about things that are contrary to fact.

Here's the kind of sentence I mean: *Given enough time, Moose **might have** graduated.* This means that in retrospect, he didn't have enough time, so he didn't graduate.

When we're being contrary, we often use *might* and *might have* to speak of nonevents—things that "*might* be" but aren't, or that "*might have* been" but weren't. Here are some more examples of this contrary-to-fact *might*:

*"You **might** have helped me move that heavy armoire," snapped Moose's mom.* (He didn't help.)
*"You **might** tell me next time you have to miss a test," said Moose's professor.* (He didn't tell the prof.)
*Had Moose gone to class, he **might** have learned something.* (He didn't learn.)
*If Moose hadn't played hooky, he **might** not have flunked.* (He did flunk.)

Only certain kinds of situations lend themselves to a contrary-to-fact *might*. This is the *might* that refers to possibilities that never came to pass, or that reproaches someone who fails to fulfill an expectation. (Sometimes, the failure is our own, so we reproach ourselves: "*I **might** have known!*")

JUST ONE OF THOSE THINGS

Here's one of the things that [*drives* or *drive*] us crazy. Should the verb be singular or plural? *Drives*? Or *drive*? In other words, what kind of verb goes with a phrase like *one of the*, *one of those*, or *one of these*? Here's the time-honored solution.

- If a *that* or a *who* comes before the verb, it's plural. *He's one of the authors who **say** it best.*
- If not, it's singular. *One of the authors **says** it best.*

In the first example, *one* is not the subject of the verb *say*. The actual subject is *who*, which is plural because it refers to *authors*. In the second example, the subject really is *one*. If you don't trust me, just turn the sentences around in your mind and you'll end up with the correct verbs: *Of the authors who **say** it best, he is one. Of the authors, one **says** it best.*

NEVER-NEVER LAND

Poor verbs! We tend to spread them a little thin sometimes. Any sentence with *never have and never will* is probably doomed. There's almost no way to finish it correctly, because so few verbs go with both *have* and *will*.

Here's the kind of sentence I mean: *They **never have and never will** forget Paris.* What we intend to say is, *They **never have forgotten** and **never will forget** Paris.* But what we've actually said is, *They **never have forget** and **never will forget** Paris*. That odd, crackling noise you hear is the sound of a sentence short-circuiting. This problem comes up when we use *have* and *will* with the same verb. Another major culprit is *always have and always will*.

Only a couple of dozen verbs (*cut*, *hit*, *hurt*, *put*, and *read* among them) will work with *never have and never will*, because they're the same in all tenses. *I **never have and never will put** ketchup on a hot dog.*

But most verbs don't work that way. Only when a verb would appear the same way twice in the full sentence (*I **never could forget and never would forget** Paris*) can you omit one: *I **never could and never would forget** Paris.*

> **NOTE:** If you don't want to seem repetitive by using different forms of the same verb, rearrange the sentence: *They **never have** forgotten Paris and **never will**.* The part you omit—*forget Paris*—is cut from the end, where it won't be missed.

IZE IN OUR HEADS: ARE THESE VERBS LEGIT?

For centuries, we've been creating instant verbs in English simply by adding *ize* to nouns (*demon → demonize*) or to adjectives (*brutal → brutalize*). The ancient Greeks were the ones who gave us the idea. The *ize* ending (often *ise* in British spellings) has given us loads of useful words (*agonize, burglarize, fantasize, mesmerize, pasteurize, pulverize*). It's just as legitimate to add *ize* to the end of a word as it is to add *un* or *pre* to the beginning.

Yet there can be too much of a good thing, and that's what has happened with *ize*. Verbs should be lively little devils, and just adding *ize* to a word doesn't give it life. Fortunately, many recent horrors (*credibilize, effectivize, permanentize, respectabilize*) have failed to catch on. But some lifeless specimens have slipped into the language, among them *absolutize, securitize,* and *uniformize*, and they'll probably be around for a while.

I have two pieces of advice about verbs ending in *ize*:

- Don't coin any new ones.
- Don't use any recent ones you don't like. If we ignore them, maybe they'll go away.

ANTS AT THE PICNIC: PESKY LOOK-ALIKES

Who hasn't confused *lie* and *lay*? *Sit, set,* and *sat*? *Rise* and *raise*? It's nothing to be ashamed of. You could commit them all to memory, of course. Or you could *lay* your cares aside, *sit* tight, *rise* to the occasion, and look up the answer.

Here's the *lay* of the land (or, as they say in Britain, the *lie* of the land).

LIE (to recline): *She **lies** quietly. Last night, she **lay** quietly. For years, she **has lain** quietly.*
LIE (to fib): *He **lies**. Yesterday he **lied**. Frequently he **has lied**.*

LAY (to place): *She **lays** it there. Yesterday she **laid** it there. Many times she **has laid** it there.* (When *lay* means "to place," it's always followed by an object, the thing being placed.)

SIT (to be seated): *I **sit**. I **sat** last week. I **have sat** many times.*

SET (to place): *He **sets** it there. He **set** it there yesterday. He **has set** it there frequently.* (*Set* meaning "to place" is always followed by an object, the thing being placed.)

RISE (to go up or get up): *You **rise**. You **rose** at seven. You **have risen** even earlier.*

RAISE (to bring something up): *I **raise** it. I **raised** it last year. I **have raised** it several times.* (The verb *raise* is always followed by an object, the thing being brought up.)

FITTED TO BE TIED

Several verbs ending in *t* or *d* have all but dropped the *ed* ending in the past tense. Once we would have said, *Mr. Pecksniff **quitted** the firm, **betted** on the horses, and **wetted** his whistle, then **wedded** his sweetheart in a suit that **fitted** him perfectly.* The British still sometimes use those endings, but Americans are now more likely to use the shorter *quit, bet, wet, wed*, and *fit. Mr. Pecksniff **quit** the firm, **bet** on the horses, and **wet** his whistle, then **wed** his sweetheart in a suit that **fit** him perfectly.*

We still use *wedded*, but mostly as an adjective (a word that describes people or things): ***Wedded** life is a thrill a minute.*

We also use *fitted* as an adjective (*a **fitted** sheet, a **fitted** suit*). And we use *fitted* when we speak of someone whose clothes are, shall we say, under construction: *Alice was **fitted*** *for a new dress.* But later we would say, *When it was finished, the dress **fit** like a glove.*

HAPPY ENDINGS: BURNED OR BURNT?

He *spilled* the milk, or he *spilt* it? He *burned* the toast, or he *burnt* it? Actually, they're all correct.

Most English verbs form the past tense in the familiar way, by adding *d* or *ed* at the end (for example, *sneeze* becomes *sneezed*). But some past forms end in *t*, including *bent* (except in the phrase *on bended knee*), *crept, dealt, felt, kept, left, lost, meant, slept, spent, swept,* and *wept.*

Still other verbs, like *spill* and *burn,* are in between and can form the past tense with either *ed* or *t*. In some cases, *ed* is more common in the United States, and in other cases *t*, but they're both correct, so the choice is yours. In these examples, the spellings I use are given first and the others, many of which are popular in Britain, follow in parentheses: *bereaved (bereft), burned (burnt), dreamed (dreamt), dwelt (dwelled), knelt (kneeled), leaped (leapt), learned (learnt), smelled (smelt), spelled (spelt), spilled (spilt), spoiled (spoilt).*

WAKE-UP CALLS

Have you *woken*? Or have you *waked*? Some days it's a challenge just to get up in the morning. If you lie awake nights worrying about this one, don't bother. Either form is correct.

The British preference, *have woken*, was once considered obsolete in the United States. But now *have woken* is just as common here as *have waked*.

For the record, the accepted forms of the verb *wake* are *wake*, *woke* (or *waked*), and *have woken* (or *have waked*). Here they are in action: *I usually **wake** at seven. Yesterday, I **woke** [or **waked**] at nine. In the past, I **have woken** [or **have waked**] as early as five.* By the way, it's fine to add *up* to any of the *wake* forms: ***Wake up** and smell the coffee!*

If you're like me, and you think both *have woken* and *have waked* sound weird, try *have wakened* or *have awakened*. Those are past tenses of related verbs, *waken* and *awaken*.

There are lots of ways to greet the morning—maybe more than we need. You can *wake*, or you can *waken*, or you can *awake*, or you can *awaken*. So rise and shine, already!

WHAT'S THE USE?

Choose one: *Pancho [**used to** or **use to**] play great tennis.*

You hit an ace if you picked the first one, *used to*, another way of saying "formerly did." *He **used to** have a killer serve.*

But what if there's already a *did* in the sentence, as in a question or a negative statement?

*Did Pancho [**use to** or **used to**] smile a lot on the court?*
*No, he didn't [**use to** or **used to**] smile a lot on the court.*

This time the call is for *use to*:

*Did Pancho **use to** smile a lot on the court?*
*No, he didn't **use to** smile a lot on the court.*

Why the difference? Because *did use* is another way of saying *used,* just as *did like* is another way of saying *liked.* We don't write *did liked,* and for the same reason we don't write *did used.* Here's what to remember.

- If there's no *did,* choose *used to*: *Pancho **used to** be ruthless on the court.*
- If there's a *did,* choose *use to*: *Did Pancho **use to** argue a little? No, he **didn't use to** argue a little. He **did use to** argue a lot.*

GETTING THE HANG OF HUNG

No, it's not true that *hung* is never right. I would like to impress this on the magazine writer who described somebody's walls as "hanged with handsome black-and-white photographs."

Both past tenses have been around for hundreds of years, but since the sixteenth century it's been customary to reserve *hanged* for referring to executions, and to use *hung* for other meanings.

So, except at the gallows, *hung* is the correct past tense of *hang*: *He **hung** around. They **have hung** around.* This is true whether you've *hung* pictures, *hung* loose, *hung* out, *hung* laundry, or *hung* up.

Anyone who still uses *hanged* in such expressions should be suspended.

THAT'S THAT

There are two kinds of editors. One kind sticks in *that* wherever it will fit. The other kind takes it out.

They're both wrong.

Many verbs (*think, say, hope, believe, find, feel,* and *wish* are examples) sometimes sound smoother—to my ears, at least—when they're followed by *that*: *Carmela believed [**that**] Tony was unfaithful.* You may agree that the sentence sounds better with *that*, or you may not. It's purely a matter of taste. The sentence is correct either way.

Some writers and editors believe that if *that* can logically follow a verb, it should be there. Others believe that if *that* can logically be omitted, it should be taken out. If you like it, use it. If you don't, don't. Sometimes, though, a *that* can make a difference. Here are some cases where adding *that* can sharpen a blurry sentence.

- When a time element comes after the verb: *Wimpy said on Tuesday he would pay me back.* This could mean either: *Wimpy said **that** on Tuesday he would pay me back,* or *Wimpy said on Tuesday **that** he would pay me back.* So why not add a *that* and make yourself clear?
- When the point of the sentence comes late: *Johnny discovered the old violin hidden in a trunk in his attic wasn't a real Stradivarius.* Better: *Johnny discovered **that** the old violin hidden in a trunk in his attic wasn't a real Stradivarius.* Otherwise, we have to read to the end of the

sentence to learn that Johnny's discovering the violin isn't the point.

- When there are two more verbs after the main one: *The pastor thinks the idea stinks and the congregation does too.* What exactly is the pastor thinking? The sentence could mean *The pastor thinks **that** the idea stinks and **that** the congregation does too.* Or it could mean *The pastor thinks **that** the idea stinks, and the congregation does too.* Adding *that* (and a well-placed comma) can make clear who's thinking what.

SPLITSVILLE

Many people seem to believe that there's something sacred about a verb, and that it's wrong to split up one that comes in parts (*had gone* or *would go*, for example). You've probably heard at one time or another that you're cheating if you slip a word (say, *finally*) in between (as in *had finally gone* or *would finally go*). Well, it just isn't so.

The best place to put a word like *finally*—that is, an adverb, a word that characterizes a verb—is directly before the action being described: in this case, *go* or *gone*. It's perfectly natural to split the parts of a verb like *have gone* by putting an adverb between them: *The Bingleys **have finally gone**.* If you prefer to put the adverb either before or after all the parts of the verb (*The Bingleys **finally have gone***, or *The Bingleys **have gone, finally***), that's all right too. But don't go out of your way to avoid the "splits." And keep in mind that adverbs usually do the most good right in front of the action words they describe.

This fear of splitting verb phrases, by the way, has its origins in another old taboo—the dreaded "split infinitive" (*to finally go*, for instance). The chapter on dead rules has more on that one, and on how the myth got started. See pages 238–239 and 242.

THE IS-NESS CYCLE

Isn't *is* a wonderful word? So wonderful is *is* that some people can't get enough of it. Forgetful speakers sometimes use one *is* too many when they begin a sentence with an expression like "The trouble *is*. . . ." or "The thing *is* . . ." or "The point *is* . . ."

The problem is that they repeat themselves. They treat these introductory words as mere throat-clearing with no grammatical significance, then stick in an unnecessary *is* before going on with the rest of the sentence. The result: *The problem* **is, is** *that they repeat themselves.*

If you use one of these introductory phrases, one *is* is enough.

Sometimes, though, twice is nice. A second *is* may be necessary, especially if the sentence begins with *what* or *all*: *What the problem* **is is** *unclear. All it* **is is** *a tempest in a teapot.* Those sentences wouldn't make sense without the second *is*.

Here's what to remember.

- Wherever *is* appears twice, drop one if the sentence reads correctly without it. *The point* **is** *that you're*

> *not supposed to feed wild animals. The trouble **is**,*
> *they hang around the back door.*
>
> - If the sentence makes no sense without both, keep both.
>   *What that **is is** an armadillo. All it **is is** a nuisance.*

THE WILLIES: WILL OR SHALL?

In George Washington's day, schoolchildren on both sides of the Atlantic were admonished to use *shall* instead of *will* in some cases. (Don't ask!) Americans have since left *shall* behind and now use *will* almost exclusively. Although *shall* survives in parts of England, even the British use it less these days.

Shall can still be found in a few nooks and crannies of American English, such as legalese (*This lease **shall** commence on January 1*) and lofty language (*We **shall** overcome*). It's also used with *I* and *we* in some kinds of questions—when we're asking what another person wishes: ***Shall** we dance, or **shall** I fill your glass?*

Shall is one of the "living dead" discussed in the chapter on outdated rules, page 247.

THE INCREDIBLE SHRINKING WORDS: CONTRACTIONS

The contraction—usually two words combined into one, as in *don't* or *I'm*—seldom gets a fair shake from English teachers. It may be tolerated, but it's looked down upon as colloquial or, according to one expert, "dialect" (what a slur!). Yet despite its esteem problem, the humble contraction is used every day by virtually everyone, and has been for centuries. Quaint antiquities like *shan't* (*shall not*), *'tis* (*it is*), *'twas* (*it was*), *'twill* (*it will*), *'twould* (*it would*), and even *'twon't* (*it will not*) are evidence of the contraction's long history.

Today's contractions generally include a verb, along with a subject or the word "not." An apostrophe shows where letters have been dropped (see page 207).

Isn't it time we admitted that the contraction has earned its place in the sun? It has all the qualities we admire in language: it's handy, succinct, and economical, and everybody knows what it means. Contractions are obviously here to stay, so why not give them a little respect? Here's the long and the short of it: the contractions that are respectable, followed by a few that aren't.

FIT TO PRINT

aren't	are not	he'll	he will
can't	cannot	here's	here is
couldn't	could not	he's	he is; he has
didn't	did not	I'd	I would; I had
doesn't	does not	I'll	I will
don't	do not	I'm	I am
hadn't	had not	I've	I have
hasn't	has not	isn't	is not
haven't	have not	it'll	it will
he'd	he would; he had	it's	it is; it has
		let's	let us

mightn't	might not	we've	we have
mustn't	must not	weren't	were not
oughtn't	ought not	what'll	what will
she'd	she would;	what're	what are
	she had	what's	what is;
she'll	she will		what has
she's	she is;	what've	what have
	she has	where's	where is;
shouldn't	should not		where has
that's	that is;	who'd	who would;
	that has		who had
there's	there is;	who'll	who will
	there has	who's	who is;
they'd	they would;		who has
	they had	who've	who have
they'll	they will	won't	will not
they're	they are	wouldn't	would not
they've	they have	you'd	you would;
wasn't	was not		you had
we'd	we would;	you'll	you will
	we had	you're	you are
we'll	we will	you've	you have
we're	we are		

OUT OF BOUNDS

AIN'T. In presentable English, it's not OK and it never will be OK. Get used to it. If you're tempted to use it to show that you have the common touch, make clear that you know better: *Now, **ain't** that a shame!*

COULD'VE, SHOULD'VE, WOULD'VE, MIGHT'VE, MUST'VE.
There's a good reason to stay away from these in your writing. Seen in print, they encourage mispronunciation, which explains why they're often heard as *could of, should of, would of, might of,* and *must of* (or, even worse, *coulda, shoulda, woulda, mighta,* and *musta*). It's fine to pronounce these as though the *h* in *have* were silent. But let's not forget that *have* is there. Write it out.

GONNA, GOTTA, WANNA. In writing, these are substandard English. Unless you're talking to your sister on the phone, make it *going to, got to, want to,* and so on.

HOW'D, HOW'LL, HOW'RE, WHEN'LL, WHEN'RE, WHEN'S, WHERE'D, WHERE'LL, WHERE'RE, WHY'D, WHY'RE, WHY'S. Resist the urge to write contractions with *how, when, where,* or *why,* except that old standby *where's.* We all say things like *"How'm I supposed to pay for this and where'm I gonna put it?"* But don't put them in writing.

IT'D, THAT'D, THERE'D, THIS'D, WHAT'D. Notice how these *'d* endings seem to add a syllable that lands with a *thud*? And they look ridiculously clumsy in writing. Let's use the *'d* contractions (for *had* or *would*) only with *I, you, he, she, we, they,* and *who.*

THAT'LL, THAT'RE, THAT'VE, THERE'LL, THERE'RE, THERE'VE, THIS'LL, WHO'RE. No. These clumsies are fine in conversation, but written English isn't ready for them yet. Do I use *that'll* when I talk? Sure. But not when I write.

ALL TENSED UP

If we used only one verb per sentence, we'd never have trouble choosing the tense—past, present, future, or whatever: *They* **waltzed**. *He* **tangos**. *She* **will polka**. And so on. Many sentences, though, have several things going on in them—actions happening at different times, each with its own verb. You can't just string these verbs together like beads in a necklace. There's some logic to it.

With most sentences, we don't give this much thought, and we don't have to. When all the actions happen at about the same time, we can just put them in the same tense and rattle them off in order: *On Sundays, Elaine* **rises** *at seven,* **makes** *tea,* **showers,** *and* **goes** *back to bed. Last Sunday, Elaine* **rose** *at seven,* **made** *tea,* **showered,** *and* **went** *back to bed.*

When we have different things happening at distinctly different times, sentences get more complicated: *Elaine* **says** *she* **made** *tea last Sunday, but she* **will make** *coffee next week.*

Common sense tells us how to do most of these adjustments in timing. But some verb sequences are harder to sort out than others. The next few pages deal with some of the most troublesome ones.

WHERE THERE'S A WILL,
THERE'S A WOULD

Do you waffle when faced with the choice of *will* or *would*? Take your pick:

> *Dudley said he [**will** or **would**] make waffles for breakfast.*

Follow the lead of the first verb (*said*). Since it's in the past tense, use *would*: *Dudley **said** he **would** make waffles for breakfast.* When the first verb is in the present tense (*says*), use *will*: *Dudley **says** he **will** make waffles for breakfast.*

Now here's an example with three verbs (the same principle applies):

> *Dudley **thought** that if he [**eats** or **ate**] one waffle, he [**will** or **would**] want another.*

Since the first verb (*thought*) is in the past, use the past tense, *ate*, and *would*: *Dudley **thought** that if he **ate** one waffle, he **would** want another.* When the first verb is in the present (*thinks*), use the present tense, *eats*, and *will*: *Dudley **thinks** that if he **eats** one waffle, he **will** want another.*

NOTE: Don't let *would have* creep in where *had* belongs, especially in sentences with *wish* or *if*. See page 64.

IN THE LAND OF IF

Think of *if* as a tiny set of scales. When a sentence has *if* in it, the *will*s and the *would*s have to be in balance. When the *if* side of the scale is in the present tense, the other side calls for *will*. When the *if* side of the scale is in the past tense, the other side gets a *would*.

> If he **shops** [present] *alone, he* **will spend** *too much.*
> If he **shopped** [past] *alone, he* **would spend** *too much.*

Balancing the scales becomes more complicated as the tenses get more complicated. When you use a compound tense with *has* or *have* on the *if* side of the scale, you need a *will have* on the other side. Similarly, when you use a compound tense with *had* on the *if* side of the scale, you need a *would have* on the other.

> If he **has shopped** *alone, he* **will have spent** *too much.*
> If he **had shopped** *alone, he* **would have spent** *too much.*

The *if* part doesn't have to come first, but the scales must stay in balance: *He* **will spend** *too much if he* **shops** *alone. He* **would spend** *too much if he* **shopped** *alone.*

NOTE: Remember, don't let *would have* sneak in where *had* belongs. See page 64.

AFTER THOUGHTS

Some people tense up when one action comes after another in a sentence. Let's test your tension level. Which verbs would be better in these examples?

*I will open the wine after the guests [**arrive** or **have arrived**].*
*I opened the wine after the guests [**arrived** or **had arrived**].*

There's no wrong answer here. I prefer the simpler tenses (*arrive, arrived*): *I will open the wine after the guests **arrive**. I opened the wine after the guests **arrived**.* Those more complicated tenses (*have arrived, had arrived*) aren't wrong, but there's no reason to use them.

No matter what the tense of the main part of a sentence, and no matter how complicated, the verb following *after* can be in either the simple present (*arrive*) or the simple past (*arrived*). Here's how to take the simple route.

- When the main action in a sentence takes place in the present or in a future tense, the verb that follows *after* is in the simple present:
  *I usually open the wine after the guests **arrive**.*
  *I will have opened the wine after the guests **arrive**.*
- When the main action takes place in any kind of past tense, the verb following *after* is in the simple past:
  *I had opened the wine after the guests **arrived**.*
  *I should have opened the wine after the guests **arrived**.*

The advice is the same if the sentence is turned around so the *after* part comes first:

> *After the guests **arrive**, I will have opened the wine.*
> *After the guests **arrived**, I should have opened the wine.*

Often the simple solution is the best. Keep that in mind, and may all your verbs live happily ever after.

TO HAVE OR NOT TO HAVE

Have is a useful word, but we can have too much of it. Which is correct?

> *I would have liked **to go**.*
> *I would have liked **to have gone**.*

The first example is correct. One *have* is enough, though it can go with whichever half of the sentence you want to emphasize: *I would **have** liked to go*, or *I would like to **have** gone*.

Now, here's a case in which even one *have* is a *have* too many.

> Problem: *Two years ago, Whiskers was the first cat **to have googled** on his own smartphone.*
> Solution: *Two years ago, Whiskers was the first cat **to google** on his own smartphone.*

You need to use *have* only if you're talking about two different times in the past:

Until last year, Whiskers was the only cat **to have googled** *on his own smartphone.*

If you find the concept hard to grasp, think of it this way: One of the times was last year and the other was the period before that.

I could go on about the subtleties of *have*, but I suspect that by now you've had it.

CHAPTER 5

VERBAL ABUSE

NO-NOS, YESES, AND MAYBES

The give-and-take of language is something like life itself. A word might flourish for years—vigorous, useful, the life of the party—then falter and die, a casualty of misuse or neglect or simply time. Some struggling words rise again with new meanings, like *decimate* (see the next page). But some are justifiably forgotten. (Quick! What's a *bodkin*?)

Other words are still fighting the good fight, though misuse is creeping in. *Unique* is a good example: a crisp and accurate word meaning "one of a kind," now frequently downgraded to merely "unusual." *Bemused* is another. Because it sounds like "amused," some people think that's what it means. It doesn't— yet (see page 129). Words like these should be handled with care if you don't want to be misunderstood.

Then there are what I call mixed doubles: pairs of words and phrases that are routinely confused, like *affect* and *effect*, *reluctant* and *reticent*. Finally, there are the words that are so stretched out of shape that it's best to avoid them. See *fulsome* on page 94.

What's a reasonable person to do?

First, keep an open mind. Language changes, and maintaining standards means keeping them up-to-date. Yesterday's no-no just might be today's yes (see *hopefully*, pages 95–96) or maybe (see *fun*, page 94). The folks who write dictionaries are forever sniffing the winds of change as they add, subtract, and redefine words. Their job is to reflect the language people use at a particular time—the good, the bad, the indifferent. So a boneheaded word, like "irregardless," may slip into the dictionary as more and more people use it. But that doesn't make it correct (read the fine print).

Now let's take a closer look at some commonly misunderstood words and phrases. Where authorities disagree, I've tried to weigh the best evidence and make decisions that reflect what thoughtful, literate people consider good English today.

WHAT'S THE MEANING OF THIS?

DECIMATE. Who says grammar books don't have sex and violence? To *decimate* once meant "to slaughter every tenth one," although it's rarely used literally these days. It's now used more loosely, to mean "to destroy in part" (*Gomez says the mushroom crop in the cellar has been* **decimated** *by rats*), but don't use it to mean "to destroy entirely." And definitely don't attach a figure to the damage: *The earthquake **decimated** seventy-five percent of Morticia's antiques.* Ouch!

DILEMMA. This is no ordinary problem; the *di* (from the Greek for "twice") is a clue that there's a "two-ness" here. A *dilemma* is a situation involving at least two choices— all of them bad. (This idea is captured neatly in the old phrase about being caught on the *horns of a dilemma*.) *Richie faced a **dilemma**: he could wear the green checked suit with the gravy stain, or the blue one with the hole.* Note the two *m*'s. It's not spelled "dilemna" and it never was.

DISCOMFIT. In olden times, to *discomfit* was to defeat, rout, or overthrow. A *discomfited* enemy may well have been a dead enemy. *Using only a slingshot, David **discomfited** Goliath.* But over the years, that meaning has been lost, and today to *discomfit* is to disconcert, make uneasy, or embarrass. *Deputy Fife was **discomfited** when his gunbelt fell to his ankles.*

ECLECTIC. This word is mistakenly used to mean "discriminating" or "sophisticated"; in fact, it means "drawn from many sources." *Sherman has an **eclectic** assortment of mud-wrestling memorabilia.*

EFFETE. Traditionally, *effete* has meant "barren," "used up," or "worn out." *Frasier considers Abstract Expressionism a tired, **effete** art form.* But dictionaries now accept it in the sense of "effeminate" or "overrefined." *He regards the cravat as an **effete** fashion accessory.*

ENERVATING. Energizing it's not. On the contrary: if something's *enervating*, it drains you of energy. *Frasier's date found his conversation **enervating**.*

ENORMITY. Don't confuse this with *enormousness*, because *enormity* isn't a measure of size alone. It refers to something that's wicked, monstrous, or outrageous on a large scale. *Sleepy little Liechtenstein was shocked by the **enormity** of the crime.*

FORTUITOUS. Originally, this word meant "accidental," not "fortunate." *It was entirely **fortuitous** that Benedict brought candy instead of flowers.* In today's English, however, those notions of good fortune and chance have blended so much that dictionaries also accept a hybrid definition—something *fortuitous* is a lucky accident. *Since Beatrice was allergic to flowers, candy was a **fortuitous** choice.* The upshot? To avoid misunderstanding, use another word to describe an *un*lucky accident.

FULSOME. For traditionalists, it doesn't mean "full"; it means "excessively flattering," even "offensive." *Eddie's cloying and **fulsome** speeches got on Mrs. Cleaver's nerves.* However, some dictionaries now accept a looser meaning: "abundant" or "copious." To avoid being misunderstood, pick a better word. See page 168 for hints on spelling words that contain *ful* and *full*.

FUN. Not so long ago, this word was strictly used as a noun (for a thing), as in *They had **fun*** or *That was **fun***. In standard English today, *fun* is also accepted as an adjective (a word that characterizes a noun): *The Griswolds had a **fun** vacation.* But I wouldn't recommend the adjective for formal occasions. And don't stretch it—*funner* and *funnest* aren't yet legit. *This was a much **more fun** vacation, maybe the **most fun** vacation we've had together.*

HERO. There was a time when this word was reserved for people who were . . . well . . . heroic. People who performed great acts of physical, moral, or spiritual courage, often risking their lives or livelihoods. But lately, *hero* has lost its luster. It's applied indiscriminately to professional athletes, lottery winners, and kids who clean up at spelling bees. There's no other word quite like *hero*, so let's not bestow it too freely. It would be a pity to lose it. *Sergeant York was a* **hero**.

HOPEFULLY. It's hopeless to resist the evolution of *hopefully*. Purists used to insist (and some still do) that there's only one way to use this correctly—as an adverb meaning "in a hopeful manner." *"I'm thinking of going to Spain," Eddie told Mrs. Cleaver. "Soon?" she asked* **hopefully**. If the holdouts had their way, nobody would use *hopefully* to replace a phrase like "it is hoped" or "let us hope," as in *"Hopefully the cuisine in Spain will be as delectable as your own," Eddie said*. But language changes, and upright citizens have been using *hopefully* in that looser way for ages. It's time to admit that *hopefully* has joined the class of introductory words (like *fortunately, frankly, happily, honestly, naturally, regrettably, sadly, seriously*, and others) that we use not to describe a verb, which is what adverbs usually do, but to describe our attitude toward the statement that follows. The technical term for them is sentence adverbs. When I say, *"Sadly*, Eddie stayed for dinner," I don't mean Eddie was sad about staying. I mean, "I'm sad to say that Eddie stayed for dinner." And *"Frankly*, he's boring" doesn't mean the guy is boring in a frank way. It means, "I'm being frank when I say he's boring." Frankly, I see no reason to treat *hopefully* otherwise. But be aware that some still take a narrow view of *hopefully*. Will they ever join the crowd? One can only hope. See also page 220.

IRONY. I hope some TV news reporters are tuning in. A wonderful word for a wonderful idea, *irony* refers to a sly form of expression in which you say one thing and mean another. *"You're wearing the green checked suit again, Richie! How fashionable of you," said Mrs. Cunningham, her voice full of **irony**.* A situation is *ironic* when the result is the opposite—or pretty much so—of what was intended. It isn't merely coincidental or surprising, as when the newscaster thoughtlessly reports, *"Ironically*, the jewelry store was burglarized on the same date last year." If the burglars take great pains to steal what turns out to contain a homing device that leads the police to them, that's *ironic*. (And forget the correct but clunky *ironical*.)

LIKE. *Like* is a cool word. In one sense it means "similar to," so it's handy for comparing things. And as a verb, to *like* is to be fond of someone or something. I like *like*! But it's possible to like *like* a little too much. You probably know what's coming. Many people—and not just kids—incessantly say "I'm *like*" instead of "I say," and "he's *like*" instead of "he said," as in *"This guy's **like**, 'Your fender was already dented.'"* This informal way of using *like* is fine for casual conversation among friends. But when you're writing or giving a speech or talking to your boss, get out your good English. That means using a word such as *say* or *said*, not *like*, to quote somebody. *"So I said, 'You'll be hearing from my lawyer.'"* As for the *like* that's a mere verbal tic (*I could, **like**, use a cigarette*), break the habit.

LITERALLY. By tradition, *literally* means "to the letter" or "word for word." *Martha sprayed a dried bouquet with metallic paint, **literally** gilding the lily.* But dictionaries now accept the looser use of *literally* to emphasize an exaggeration (much like "really," "actually," or "in effect"). *"These fumes are **literally** frying my brain," she said.* But don't create a ridiculous picture. I'm reminded of a news story, early in my editing career in Iowa, about a Pioneer Days celebration, complete with covered wagons and costumed "settlers." Our reporter proposed to say that spectators "were literally turned inside out and shot backward in time." Gee, we should have sent a photographer along.

MOOT. This word has had a complicated history over the years. Traditionally, it has meant "debatable," and that's how the British still use it. But its primary meaning in the United States today is "irrelevant" or "hypothetical." *The question of bridesmaids' dresses became **moot** when the engagement was broken.*

NOISOME. If you think this means "noisy," you're not even close. *Noisome* and *noisy* are as different as your nose and your ear. *Noisome* means "offensive" or "noxious" and is often used to describe foul smells. It's related to *annoy*, so think of it as a clipped form of *annoysome*. *The **noisome** fumes of the stink bomb forced officials to evacuate the school.*

NONPLUSSED. It means "baffled" or "perplexed," not calm and collected. *Tony was **nonplussed** at finding his golf clubs in the driveway*. (Hint: *Non* means "no," and *plus* means "more." A guy who's *nonplussed* is at a loss and can do no more.)

PRESENTLY. If a deadbeat tells his landlord he's *presently* paying his rent, does that mean . . . uh . . . the check is in the mail, or the check really *is* in the mail? The answer is, don't hold your breath. *Presently* is ambiguous. It can mean "currently" or "at present," as in *"It's eight in the morning and I'm **presently** on my way to the post office."* But it also has other senses, like soon, before long, any minute (hour, day) now, forthwith, shortly, keep your shirt on, faster than you can say Jack Robinson, or when I'm darn good and ready. *"You'll get your money **presently**," he promised*. If you don't want to be ambiguous, make sure your meaning is clear.

RESTIVE. Here's another word that now has dual meanings. On one hand, *restive* can mean "impatient" or "fidgety" (think of *restless*). *The Addamses were **restive** after a seven-hour flight*. On the other hand, it can mean "unruly" or "stubborn." *Even on a good day, Pugsley is a **restive** child*.

SCARIFY. Originally, *scarify* wasn't particularly scary. It meant to cut or scratch marks into the surface of something (think of the word *scar*). *Ricky promised that his skateboard wouldn't **scarify** the floor*. But some dictionaries have now accepted the use of *scarify* to mean "scare" or "frighten" (a usage probably influenced by *terrify*). *No move could **scarify** Ricky, even an ollie off the dining room table*. But if that's your meaning, why not use *scare*?

UNIQUE. There was a time when *unique* didn't mean merely "unusual" or "remarkable." In the old days, something *unique* was unparalleled, without equal, incomparable, nonpareil, unrivaled, one of a kind, the one and only. And there were no degrees of uniqueness, because the unique was absolute. So nothing could be described as more, less, sort of, rather, quite, very, slightly, or particularly *unique*. Like *dead*, *unanimous*, and *pregnant*, the word stood alone. *The Great Wall of China is **unique***. But we all know what's happened. Today respected writers, even dictionaries, have loosened up on the uniqueness of *unique*. *This photo of the Great Wall is rather **unique***. You're free to take liberties with *unique* if you want, but be aware that fussier types still frown on anything but the traditional usage. So if you don't mean *unique* in its absolute sense, consider using *distinctive*, *extraordinary*, or *remarkable* instead.

VIA. In modern usage, it can mean either "by way of" or "by means of." *Willa flew from Dubuque to Des Moines **via** Detroit. She should have traveled **via** car.*

MIXED DOUBLES

ABJURE/ADJURE. The first means "swear off." The second means "command." *"**Abjure** cigars or move out of the house!" Ethel **adjured** Fred.*

ABRIDGE/BRIDGE. To *abridge* something is to shorten it (think of the word *abbreviate*). An *abridged* book, for instance, is a condensed version. To *bridge* something means what you'd expect—to connect or to span a gap. *The producers hope to **abridge** Philip's nine-hour opera about an engineer who tries to **bridge** the Grand Canyon.*

ACCEPT/EXCEPT. To *accept* something is to take it or agree to it. *Except* can also be a verb—it means "exclude" or "leave out"—but its usual meaning is "other than." *"I never **accept** presents from men," said Lorelei, "**except** when we've been properly introduced."*

ADVERSE/AVERSE. The longer word is the stronger word. *Adverse* implies hostility or opposition, and usually characterizes a thing or an action. *Averse* implies reluctance or unwillingness, and usually characterizes a person. *Georgie was not **averse** to inoculation, until he had an **adverse** reaction to the vaccine.*

AFFECT/EFFECT. If you mean a thing (a noun), ninety-nine times out of a hundred you mean *effect*. *The termites had a startling **effect** on the piano.* If you want an action word (a verb), the odds are just as good that you want *affect*. *The problem **affected** Lucia's recital.*

The verb *affect* has another meaning. Besides to "change" or "have an effect on" (as above), it can mean "pretend" or "simulate." *Lucia **affects** an intimate knowledge of Italian.* This is how we got the adjective *affected* (artificial). *Her regal mannerisms are **affected**.*

NOTE: Then there's that one time out of a hundred. Here are the less common meanings for each of these words:

- *Affect,* when used as a noun (pronounced with the accent on the first syllable), is a psychological term for "feeling." *Termites display a lack of **affect**.*

- *Effect,* when used as a verb, means "achieve" or "bring about." *An exterminator **effected** their removal.*

AGGRAVATE/IRRITATE. You can't go wrong if you use *irritate* to mean "inflame" or "provoke," and save *aggravate* for when you mean "worsen." *Poison ivy **irritates** the skin. Scratching **aggravates** the itch.* However, *aggravate* is widely used to mean "vex" or "annoy," and dictionaries accept this usage. *Don't **aggravate** your mother by scratching.* Just be aware that a stickler might find this irritating.

AGO/SINCE. Use one or the other, not both. *Fluffy died three days **ago**.* Or: *It's been three days **since** Fluffy died.* Not: *It's been three days **ago since** Fluffy died.*

ALLUDE/REFER. To *allude* is to mention indirectly or to hint at—to speak of something in a covert or roundabout way. *Cyril suspected that the discussion of bad taste **alluded** to his loud pants.* To *refer* to something is to mention directly. *"They're plaid!" said Gussie, **referring** to Cyril's trousers.*

ALLUSION/ILLUSION/DELUSION. An *allusion* is an indirect mention. *Gussie's comment about burlesque was a snide **allusion** to Cyril's hand-painted tie.* An *illusion* is a false impression. *It created the **illusion** of a naked woman.* A *delusion* is a deception. *Cyril clung to the **delusion** that his tie was witty.* *Delusion* is much stronger than *illusion*, and implies that Cyril has been misled or deceived—in this case, by himself.

ALTERNATE/ALTERNATIVE. Use *alternate* if you mean "one after the other." *Walking requires **alternate** use of the left foot and the right.* But use either adjective if you mean "one instead of the other." *If you're wearing heels, make an **alternate** [or **alternative**] plan.*

AMONG/BETWEEN. When only two are involved, the answer is easy: *between. Miss Bennet sensed a barrier **between** her and Mr. Darcy.* With three or more, you have a choice. Use *between* if you're thinking of the individuals and their relations with one another. *There were several embarrassing exchanges **between** Lydia, Kitty, and Jane.* Use *among* if you're thinking of the group. *Darcy's arrival created a stir **among** the guests.*

APPRAISE/APPRISE. *Appraise* means "evaluate" or "size up"; *apprise* means "inform." *Sotheby's **apprised** Mr. Big of the fact that his "Rembrandt" was **appraised** as worthless.*

ARGUABLE/ARGUABLY. To say that a statement is *arguable*, or that it's *arguably* true, can be either positive or negative. *Arguable* can mean either "plausible" (capable of being supported by argument) or "doubtful" (open to challenge by argument). So I would argue that these words are useless. It's true that *arguably* leans toward the positive when used to hedge what's obviously a personal opinion. *Glenn Gould was **arguably** the greatest of Bach's interpreters.* But it's weak, as if the opinion is half formed. If you mean what you say, delete the weak link. *Glenn Gould was the greatest of Bach's interpreters.*

AS IF/AS THOUGH. These mean the same thing and can be used interchangeably. Once upon a time, *if* was one of the meanings of *though*. It's not anymore, except in the phrase *as though*. *Cliff and Norm looked* ***as though*** *they could use a drink.* See also the box on page 64.

ASSUME/PRESUME. They're not identical. *Assume* is closer to "suppose" or "take for granted"; the much stronger *presume* is closer to "believe," "dare," or "take too much for granted." *I can only* ***assume*** *you are joking when you* ***presume*** *to call yourself a plumber!*

> NOTE: *Presume* in the sense of "believe" gives us the adjective *presumptive*. And *presume* in the sense of "take too much for granted" gives us the adjective *presumptuous*. *As her favorite nephew, Bertie was Aunt Agatha's* ***presumptive*** *heir. Still, it was* ***presumptuous*** *of him to measure her windows for new curtains.*

ASSURE/ENSURE/INSURE. All three have their roots in a Latin word for "safe" or "secure." In American English, to *assure* is to instill confidence or certainty. As for *ensure* and *insure*, both can mean to make certain of something, but only *insure* is used in the commercial sense (to issue or take out insurance). *"I* ***assure*** *you,"* *said the grieving widow, "I* ***ensured*** *he was* ***insured*** *to the hilt."*

AVERAGE/MEAN/MEDIAN/NORM. Don't assume they're synonyms. See pages 266–267.

AVERT/AVOID. *Avert* means "prevent," "ward off," or "turn away." *Avoid* means "shun" or "stay clear of." *Mr. Smithers* **avoided** *the open manhole,* **averting** *a nasty fall.*

BAD/BADLY. When you're describing an activity, use *badly*, the adverb (a word that describes a verb; many adverbs, you'll notice, end in *ly*). When you're describing a condition or a passive state, use *bad*, the adjective (a word that describes a noun). *Josh ran the race* **badly***; afterward, he looked* **bad** *and he smelled* **bad***.* If the difference still eludes you, mentally substitute a pair of words less likely to be confused: *Josh ran the race* **honestly***; afterward, he looked* **honest** *and he smelled* **honest***.*

The same logic applies for *well* and *good*. When it's an activity being described, use *well*, the adverb. (As you can see, not all adverbs end in *ly*.) When it's a condition or a passive state being described, use *good*, the adjective. *Donna sang* **well** *at the recital; she looked* **good** *and she sounded* **good***.*

> **NOTE:** There's a complication with *well*. It's a two-faced word that can be an adjective as well as an adverb. As an adjective, it means "healthy" (*Josh feels* **well**).

BEAR/BORE/BORNE/BORN. The verb *bear* has two separate meanings. It can mean (1) "carry" or "endure": **bear** *a burden,* **bear** *insults,* **bear** *a name.* But it can also mean (2) "produce" or "give birth to": **bear** *fruit,* **bear** *results,* **bear** *a child.* And the simple past tense is *bore* for both meanings: **bore** *a burden,* **bore** *a name,* **bore** *fruit,* **bore** *a child.*

Now for the tricky part—*borne* and *born.* These forms of the verb—they're called past participles—are used in more complicated tenses of *bear,* the ones that use auxiliary (or "helping") verbs. Here's how to choose between *borne* and *born.*

- If the helping verb is a form of *have* alone, use *borne* for all meanings. *They* **have borne** *a heavy burden. The family* **had borne** *the name for centuries. The tree* **has borne** *both flowers and fruit. She returned to work after* **having borne** *twins.*

- If the helping verb includes a form of *be* (even if a form of *have* is also present), use *borne* for all senses except birth. *The burden, however heavy, will* **be borne.** *The insult could not have* **been borne.** *The name* **was borne** *on the family crest for centuries. The fruit and flowers* **are borne** *on new wood.*

- If the helping verb includes a form of *be,* and the sense is birth, either literally or figuratively, use *born.* *The twins will* **be born** *in Cincinnati. Children are* **being born** *every day. The baby has* **been born.** *Puppies* **are born** *with their eyes closed. Man* **is born** *of woman. His wisdom* **was born** *of experience.*

BESIDE/BESIDES. These overlap in some uses. Either one can mean "in addition to," "other than," or "except." *Cleo invited no one* **beside** *[or* **besides***] Marcus.* But only *beside* means "by the side of." *She asked him to sit **beside** her.* And only *besides* is used like "also" or "furthermore." *She dismissed the servants **besides**.*

> **NOTE:** *Beside* is the form used in two common expressions, **beside** oneself and **beside** the point. *Octavia was **beside** herself with rage, but her feelings were **beside** the point.*

BI/SEMI. In theory, *bi* attached to the front of a word means "two," and *semi* means "half." *Although Moose says he's **bi**lingual, he's **semi**literate.* In practice, *bi* sometimes means *semi*, and *semi* sometimes means *bi*. You're better off avoiding them when you want to indicate time periods; instead, use "every two years" or "twice a week" or whatever. I don't recommend using the following terms, but in case you run across them, here's what they mean. (You can see why they're confusing.)

BIENNIAL: every two years
BIANNUAL: twice a year *or* every two years
SEMIANNUAL: every half-year
BIMONTHLY: every two months *or* twice a month
SEMIMONTHLY: every half-month
BIWEEKLY: every two weeks *or* twice a week
SEMIWEEKLY: every half-week

BRING/TAKE. Which way is the merchandise moving? Is it coming or going? If it's coming here, someone's *bringing* it. If it's going there, someone's *taking* it. *"**Bring** me my* slippers," said Lady Dedlock, "and **take** away these stiletto heels!" The rules are the same in the past tense. *Hortense* **brought** *the slippers and* **took** *away the heels.*

That much is pretty straightforward, but there are gray areas where the *bringing* and the *taking* aren't so clear. What if you're the one toting the goods? Say you're a dinner guest and you're providing the wine. Do you *bring* it or do you *take* it? The answer depends on your perspective—on which end of the journey you're talking about, the origin or the destination. "What shall I *bring*, white or red?" you ask the host. "*Bring* red," he replies. (Both you and he are speaking of the wine from the point of view of its destination—the host.) Ten minutes later, you're asking the wine merchant, "What should I *take*, a Burgundy or a Bordeaux?" "*Take* this one," she says. (Both you and she are speaking of the wine from the point of view of its origin.)

Clear? If not, pour yourself a glass, take it easy, and say what sounds most natural. You'll probably be right.

CAN/MAY. The old rule was that *can* means "able to," *may* means "permitted to," and never the twain shall meet. "*I* **can** *fly when lift plus thrust is greater than load plus drag,*" *said Sister Bertrille.* "**May** *I demonstrate?*" But dictionaries today accept the use of *can* for both purposes, especially in negative questions. "*You* **can** *show me after you've cleaned your room,*" *said Mother Placido.* "**Can't** *I be allowed a moment to myself?*" In general, though, *may* is still the politer word for asking permission. An even politer word (some would say stiffer) is *might*, the twin sister of may. *"**May** [or **might**] I ask when you plan to clean your room?"*

NOTE: *May* is used in another sense: to indicate possibility. See the sections on *may* and *might*, pages 66–69.

CAN NOT/CANNOT/CAN'T. Usually, you can't go wrong with a one-word version—*can't* in speech or casual writing, *cannot* in formal writing. The two-word version, *can not*, is for when you want to be emphatic (*Maybe you can hit high C, but I certainly **can not***), or when *not* is part of another expression, like "not only . . . but also" (*I **can not** only hit high C, but also break a glass while doing it*). Then there's *can't not*, as in *The diva's husband **can't not** go to the opera.*

CANVAS/CANVASS. A *canvas* is to an artist what a *canvass* is to a pollster. *The van Gogh **canvas** was No. 1 in a Gallup **canvass** of museumgoers.*

CAPITAL/CAPITOL. The important city where lawmakers meet is a *capital*. The building they meet in is a *capitol*. *Denver, the **capital** of Colorado, has a **capitol** with a gold-plated dome.* (Hint: Both *capitol* and *dome* have *o*'s.) And yes, a big letter is called a *capital* because it's important.

CHORD/CORD. A *chord* is a combination of musical notes; it has an *h*, for "harmony," which is what *chords* can produce. *"That **chord** is a diminished seventh," said Ludwig.* A *cord* is a string or cable, like the ones found in the human anatomy: spinal cord, umbilical cord, and vocal cords. *Wolfgang never had to worry about tripping over an electrical **cord**.* A mislaid rope may be called a *lost **cord**,* but the familiar musical phrase is *lost **chord**.*

CLIMAX/CRESCENDO. These once had separate meanings: a *crescendo* was a progressive increase in volume or intensity, leading to a *climax*. *A gradual **crescendo** in the percussion section led to a **climax** that woke the audience.* But modern dictionaries say the *crescendo* can also be the peak. *The snoring had reached a **crescendo**.*

COMPARE WITH/COMPARE TO. Don't lose sleep over this one. The traditional difference is subtle and most people won't notice anyway. *Compare with*, the more common phrase, means to examine for similarities and differences. The less common *compare to* is used to show a resemblance. ***Compared with** Oscar, Felix is a crybaby. He once **compared** his trials **to** those of Job.* The traditional usage is almost forgotten, but if you want to stick with it, here's a tip: Use "compare to" only when you mean "liken to."

COMPLEMENT/COMPLIMENT. To *complement* is to complete, to round out, or to bring to perfection; a *complement* is something that completes or makes whole. (A little memory aid: Both *complement* and *complete* contain two *e*'s.) To *compliment* is to praise or admire; a *compliment* is an expression of praise or admiration. *Marcel loved to **compliment** Albertine. "That chemise **complements** your eyes, my little sparrow," he murmured.*

COMPTROLLER/CONTROLLER. They mean the same thing, the officer in charge of financial affairs. The original word, *controller*, is more likely to be used in business, and the fancier one, *comptroller*, in government. *Ms. Moneypenny, the company* **controller***, left to become* **Comptroller** *of the Currency.* See also page 172.

CONTINUALLY/CONTINUOUSLY. Yes, there is a slight difference (as there is with *continual* and *continuous*, the adjective forms). *Continually* can mean either "unceasingly" or "intermittently." But *continuously* means just one thing—"unceasingly," with no stops. *Heidi has to wind the cuckoo clock* **continually** *to keep it running* **continuously***.* Because people use both to imply "without interruption," it's better to use *periodically* or *intermittently* instead of *continually* to describe something that starts and stops.

CONVINCE/PERSUADE. These once had different meanings. A person was *convinced* to think something and *persuaded* to do something. So the old rule was that *convince* is followed by *of* or *that*, and *persuade* is followed by *to*. *Father* **convinced** *Bud* **that** *work would do him good, and* **persuaded** *him* **to** *get a job.* But dictionaries have dropped the old distinction, and today someone can be *convinced to* and *persuaded that*: **Persuaded that** *Father was right, Bud was* **convinced to** *buy a tie and write a résumé.*

CREDIBILITY/CREDULITY. If you've got *credibility*, you're believable; you can be trusted. *Credulity* is a different quality—it means you'll believe whatever you're told; you're too trusting. The descriptive terms (adjectives) are *credible* (believable) and *credulous* (gullible). The opposites of these, respectively, are *incredible* (unbelievable) and *incredulous* (skeptical). *Councilman Windbag has lost his **credibility**, even among suckers known for their **credulity**.*

> NOTE: Out in left field, meanwhile, is an entirely different player, *creditable* (deserving of credit, or praiseworthy).

DESERTS/DESSERTS. People who get what they *deserve* are getting their *deserts*—accent the second syllable. *John Wilkes Booth got his just **deserts**.* People who get goodies smothered in whipped cream and chocolate sauce at the end of a meal are getting *desserts* (same pronunciation)—which they may or may not deserve. *"For **dessert** I'll have one of those layered puff-pastry things with cream filling and icing on top," said Napoleon.* (As for the arid wasteland, use one *s* and stress the first syllable. *In the **desert**, August is the cruelest month.*) See also page 157.

DIFFER FROM/DIFFER WITH. In general, things *differ from* one another, but people who disagree *differ with* each other. *Seymour insisted that his left foot **differed from** his right in size. His podiatrist, however, **differed with** him.* In either sense, *differ* may be used alone. *Seymour says his feet **differ**. His podiatrist **differs**.*

DIFFERENT FROM/DIFFERENT THAN. What's the difference? The simple answer is that *different from* is almost always right, and *different than* is almost always wrong. However, both are right if what follows is a clause (a group of words with its own subject and verb). So each of these is correct: *Respectability is **different from** what it* *was fifty years ago. Respectability is **different than** it was fifty years ago.* But use *different from* when no clause follows. *Respectability is **different from** reliability.*

DISCREET/DISCRETE. If you're philandering, you'd better be *discreet*, a word that means "careful" or "prudent." The other spelling, *discrete*, means "separate," "distinct," or "unconnected." *Arthur was **discreet** about his bigamy. He managed to maintain two **discrete** households.*

DISINTERESTED/UNINTERESTED. The traditional difference here is that *disinterested* means "unbiased," while *uninterested* means "bored" or "lacking interest." *A good umpire should be **disinterested**, said Casey, but most certainly not **uninterested**.* Today the old distinction has blurred. So for the sake of clarity, you're better off using *impartial* or *neutral* instead of *disinterested*.

DIVED/DOVE. *Dived* is the traditional past tense for what Esther Williams did off a diving board. But dictionaries and usage guides now accept *dove* as standard American English, so take your pick. *With the swamp before him and an angry rhino at his heels, Indiana **dived** [or **dove**] into the murky waters.* See also page 249.

DONE/FINISHED/THROUGH. Consider them interchangeable in uses like this: *"Are you **finished**?" Aunt Polly called. "I'm not **done** yet," said Tom, quickly picking up his paintbrush, "but I'm almost **through**."*

EACH OTHER/ONE ANOTHER. Old usage guides once recommended saving *each other* for two, and using *one another* for three or more. *Nick and Nora found **each other** adorable. Nick and his cousins all heartily despised **one*** *another*. But there was never a good reason for this, and in fact *each other* and *one another* have always been used interchangeably: *Husband and wife should respect **one another** [or **each other**]*. So use them as you like. (Speaking of *other* and *another*, here's a whole other issue. Some people jumble *whole other* with *another* and end up with "a whole nother." Ahem! Not that you or I would ever do such a thing, of course.)

E.G./I.E. Go ahead. Be pretentious in your writing and toss in an occasional *e.g.* or *i.e.* But don't mix them up. Clumsy inaccuracy can spoil that air of authority you're shooting for. *E.g.* is short for a Latin term, *exempli gratia*, that means "for example." *Kirk and Spock had much in common, **e.g.**, their interest in astronomy and their concern for the ship and its crew.* The more specific term *i.e.*, short for the Latin *id est*, means "that is." *But they had one obvious difference, **i.e.**, their ears.* Both *e.g.* and *i.e.* must have commas in front (unless they're preceded by a dash or a parenthesis) and in back.

ELDER/ELDEST and **OLDER/OLDEST**. The *eld* words, *elder* and *eldest*, are used only for people. But the *old* words, *older* and *oldest*, are used for both people and things. *Their **elder** [or **older**] daughter attended the **older** school.* The versions ending in *er* (*elder, older*) are for comparing only two, so that example implies that there are only two daughters and only two schools. The versions ending in *est* are traditionally used for three or more. *Their **eldest** [or **oldest**] relative owns the **oldest** cat in North America.*

NOTE: Words used in making comparisons are either "comparative" (ending in *er*, like *younger, greater, closer, better*, and so on) or "superlative" (ending in *est*, like *youngest, greatest, closest, best*, etc.). The *er* versions are always used in comparing two, and generally the *est* endings are used for three or more. But the *est* forms are becoming more common in comparisons of just two, and this is fine in casual use. *Of the two cars, Jim's classic 1975 Buick Electra convertible was **closest** to his heart.*

EMIGRATE/IMMIGRATE. You *emigrate from* one country and *immigrate to* another. *Grandma **emigrated from** Hungary in 1956, the same year that Grandpa **immigrated to** America.* Whether you're called an *emigrant* or an *immigrant* depends on whether you're going or coming, and on the point of view of the speaker. A trick for remembering:

*E*migrant as in *E*xit.
*I*mmigrant as in *I*n.

EMINENT/IMMINENT/IMMANENT. If you mean "famous" or "superior," the word you want is *eminent*. If you mean "impending" or "about to happen," the word is *imminent*. If you mean "inherent," "present," or "dwelling within," the word is the rarely used *immanent*. *The **eminent** Archbishop Latour, knowing that his death was **imminent**, felt God was **immanent**.*

NOTE: The legal term is *eminent domain*.

ENDEMIC/EPIDEMIC/PANDEMIC. People toss these around as if they were interchangeable. They're not. *Endemic* is an adjective meaning "native to" or "prevalent." *In medieval Europe, poor sanitation was **endemic**.* The other two are nouns as well as adjectives: traditionally, *epidemic* refers to something widespread in a particular community or population, and *pandemic* to something that has spread to an entire country, continent, or beyond. *Messina's **epidemic** became **pandemic**, and the plague wiped out much of Europe.* The prefixes may help you remember: *en* means "in" or "within"; *pan* means "all"; *epi* means "upon" or "close to" (as in *epicenter*).

FARTHER/FURTHER. Use either one for distance, whether actual or metaphorical. *"I'm walking no **farther** [or **further**] than this bench," said Lumpy. "Nothing is **farther** [or **further**] from my mind."* But use only *further* if there's no notion of distance. *He refused to discuss it any **further**. "I have nothing **further** to say," he added.* The upshot is that if you're in doubt, choose *further*.

FAZE/PHASE. To *faze* is to disconcert or embarrass; it comes from a Middle English word, *fesen*, which meant "drive away" or "put to flight." A *phase*, from the Greek word for "appear," is a stage or period of development; the word is used as a verb in the expressions *phase in* and *phase out*, to appear and disappear by stages. *Jean-Paul's infidelity is just a **phase**, says Simone, so she never lets it **faze** her.*

FEWER/LESS. In general, use *fewer* for a smaller number of individual things; use *less* for a smaller quantity of one thing. *The **less** money Mr. Flanders spends, the **fewer** bills he gets.* But when you're down one, use *less*: *After Charlotte's wedding, Lady Lucas had one **less** thing to worry about.* In addition, use *less than* (not *fewer than*) with percentages and fractions: ***Less than** a third of the graduates showed up for the reunion.* Use *less than* for quantities of time and money, too: *He built the bookcase in **less than** two weeks and for **less than** thirty dollars.* Finally, use *less than* when measuring distance (***less than** five miles*), weight (***less than** 150 pounds*), temperature (***less than** 30 degrees*), speed (***less than** 50 miles an hour*), and so on. See also page 36.

FLAMMABLE/INFLAMMABLE. These may look like opposites, but they aren't; both mean "combustible." *Inflammable* came first. Here the prefix *in* is for emphasis, as in words like *incinerate*, *incoming*, and *intense*. *Flammable*, which came along much later, was seen as a way to avoid confusion (which isn't a bad idea). *Dr. Frankenstein thought the castle wasn't **flammable**, but the villagers proved him wrong.* See also the box on page 123.

FLOUNDER/FOUNDER. To *flounder* is to stumble awkwardly or thrash about like a fish out of water. *Harry **flounders** from one crisis to another.* To *founder* is to collapse, fail completely, or sink like a ship. *His business **foundered** when the market collapsed.*

FLOUT/FLAUNT. To *flout* is to defy or ignore. To *flaunt* is to show off. *When Bruce ran that stop sign, he was **flouting** the law and **flaunting** his new Harley.*

GANTLET/GAUNTLET. Once upon a time, combative types ran the *gantlet* (a form of military punishment), but threw down the *gauntlet* (a glove tossed to the ground as a challenge). Over the centuries, however, the differences between *gantlet* and *gauntlet* faded away, and today *gauntlet* is used for both meanings. *Wearing her mink to the ASPCA meeting, Tiffany ran a **gauntlet** of hostile stares. "How dare you!" shouted one animal lover, throwing down the **gauntlet**.*

GOOD/WELL. These two are cousins to BAD/BADLY (see page 104).

HISTORIC/HISTORICAL. If something has a place in history, it's *historic*. If something has to do with the subject of history, it's *historical*. *There's not much **historical** evidence that the Dumbellos' house is **historic**.* And by the way, the *h* is pronounced, not silent, so the article of choice is *a*, not *an*. *The Dumbellos' wedding was **a historic** occasion.* For the scoop on *a* versus *an*, see pages 144–145.

HOME/HONE. As verbs, these are often confused. To *home* in on something is to zero in or concentrate on it. But to *hone* (not "hone in") is to sharpen. *Uncle Bertram **honed** his knife, then **homed** in on the problem: how to carve a roast suckling pig.*

HYPER/HYPO. Added to the front of a word, *hyper* means "over" or "more"; *hypo* means "under" or "less." *I become **hyper**active and get a rash if I forget to use my **hypo**allergenic soap.*

IF/WHETHER. When you're talking about a choice between alternatives, use *whether*: *Richie didn't know **whether** he should wear the blue suit or the green one.* The giveaway is the presence of *or* between the alternatives. But when there's a *whether or not* choice (*Richie wondered **whether or not** he should wear his green checked suit*), you can usually drop the *or not* and use either *whether* or *if*: *Richie wondered **if** [or **whether**] he should wear his green checked suit.* You'll need *or not*, however, if your meaning is "regardless of *whether*": *Richie wanted to wear the green one, **whether** it had a gravy stain **or not**.* (Or, if you prefer, ***whether or not** it had a gravy stain.*) See also page 133.

IMPLY/INFER. Careful writers maintain the difference. To *imply* is to suggest, or to throw out a suggestion; to *infer* is to conclude, or to take in a suggestion. *"You **imply** that I'm an idiot," said Stanley. "You **infer** correctly," said Blanche.* (Memory aid: To *infer* is to make an *inference*, just as to *refer* is to make a *reference*.)

IN BEHALF OF/ON BEHALF OF. Traditionally, *in behalf of* means "for the benefit of" or "in the interest of." *On behalf of* means "in place of" or "as the agent of." *Bertie presented the check **on behalf of** the Drones Club, to be used **in behalf of** the feebleminded.* The traditional difference is worth knowing, but it's becoming weaker, and current dictionaries are beginning to accept *on behalf of* for both uses.

IN TO/INTO. Yes, there is a difference! Don't combine *in* and *to* to form *into* just because they happen to land next to each other. *Into* is for entering something (like a room or a profession), for changing the form of something (an ugly duckling, for instance), or for making contact (with a friend or a wall, perhaps). *Get **into** the coach before it turns **into** a pumpkin, and don't bang **into** the door!* Otherwise, use *in to*. *Bring the guests **in to** me, then we'll all go **in to** dinner.* (You wouldn't go *into* dinner, unless of course you jumped *into* the soup tureen.) And be careful with *tune* and *turn*: *I think I'll **tune in to** my favorite TV show and **turn into** a couch potato, until Dad **turns into** the driveway and **turns** me **in to** Slackers Anonymous.*

> **NOTE:** Still having a hard time with *in to* and *into*? Here's a trick to help keep them straight. If you can drop the *in* without losing the meaning, the term you want is *in to*. *Bring the guests **(in) to** me, then we'll all go **(in) to** dinner.* (Yes, there's also a difference between *on to* and *onto;* see page 122.)

INCIDENCE/INCIDENTS. The first is a singular word meaning "occurrence" or "rate." *There's a high **incidence** of petty crime in Hooterville.* The second is the plural of *incident*. *Detective Horton investigated three **incidents** of vandalism.* (Please, no "incidences.")

INGENIOUS/INGENUOUS. Someone who's *ingenious* (pronounced in-JEEN-yus) is clever or brilliant; the tip-off is the pronunciation of *genius* built right in. Someone who's *ingenuous* (in-JEN-yoo-us) is unworldly, unsuspecting, innocently open, or candid; the term is related to *ingénue*, a word for an inexperienced girl. (Calling people *disingenuous*—insincere—is a roundabout way of saying they lie.)

JIBE/JIVE. When things don't *jibe*, they aren't consistent. The other word, *jive*, is a noun, a verb, and an adjective referring to hot music or to baloney. *All that **jive** doesn't **jibe** with Senator Paine's record.* And there's more. The word *gibe* (sometimes spelled *jibe*) can also be a noun or a verb for taunting or teasing. *Lydia was used to Dad's **gibes** about her tattoos. She often **gibed** him about his hair transplants.*

LAY/LIE. To *lay* is to place something; there's always a "something" that's being placed. To *lie* is to recline. *If you're not feeling well, **lay** your tools aside and **lie** down.* (These two get really confusing in the past tense. There's more about *lay* and *lie*, and how to use them in the past, on pages 72–73.)

LEND/LOAN. Only the strictest usage experts now insist that *loan* is the noun and *lend* is the verb, a distinction that is still adhered to in Britain (***Lend** me a pound, there's a good chap*). American usage allows that either *loan* or *lend* may be used as a verb (***Loan** me a few bucks till payday*). To my ears, though, *lend* and *lent* do sound a bit more polished than *loan* and *loaned*.

LIABLE/LIKELY. They're not interchangeable, but they come mighty close sometimes. Use *likely* if you mean "probable" or "expected." Use *liable* if you mean "bound by law or obligation" (as in *liable for damages*) or "exposed to risk or misfortune." *If Madeline goes skating, she's **liable** to fall, and not **likely** to try it again.*

LIKE/AS. Which of these is correct? *Homer tripped, [**as** or **like**] everyone was expecting.* The answer is *as*, because it is followed by a clause, a group of words with both a subject (*everyone*) and a verb (*was expecting*). If no verb follows, choose *like*: *Homer walks **like** a duck.*

Those are the rules in formal English, but the ground is shifting. In casual usage, *like* is gaining steadily on *as* (*She tells it **like** it is*), and on its cousins *as if* and *as though*, which are used to introduce clauses that are hypothetical or contrary to fact (*She eats chocolate **like** it's going out of style*).

The informal use of *like* to introduce a clause is fine in conversation or casual writing, but for those occasions when you want to be more formal, here's how to remember the "*as* comes before a clause" rule: Just think of the notorious old cigarette ad—"*Winston tastes good **like** a cigarette should*"—and do the opposite. On those more relaxed occasions, join the crowd and do as you like.

LIKE/SUCH AS. Which is correct? *Mrs. Teasdale prefers cool colors, [**like** or **such as**] blue, violet, and aqua.* It's a matter of taste—either is acceptable. To my ear, *like* sounds more natural; *such as* often seems somewhat formal. Of course, there are times when a bit of stiffness is appropriate: "*I've got my reasons for always using '**like**,'*" said Rufus T. Firefly. "***Such as?***" said Mrs. Teasdale.

LOATH/LOATHE. The one without an *e* is an adjective describing somebody who's unwilling or reluctant, and it's usually followed by *to*: *Dmitri is **loath** to eat in Indian restaurants.* The one with an *e* is a verb: *He **loathes** chicken vindaloo.* (The adjective for something you loathe is *loathsome*, and there's no *e* in the middle.)

MAY/MIGHT. These can be tricky. For the story, check out pages 66–69.

NAUSEATED/NAUSEOUS. Traditionally, you were made sick (*nauseated*) by something sickening (*nauseous*). But usage has loosened up. The first, *nauseated*, still means "affected by nausea." But the second, *nauseous*, now covers all the bases; it can mean "affected by nausea," "causing nausea," or simply "disgusting." *Ethel said she was thoroughly **nauseated** [or **nauseous**], thanks to Fred's **nauseous** cigar.* (Another word that means "sickening" or "disgusting" is *nauseating*.)

ON TO/ONTO. If you mean "on top of" or "aware of," use *onto*. *The responsibility shifted **onto** Milo's shoulders. "I'm really **onto** your shenanigans," he said.* Otherwise, use *on to*. *Hang **on to** your hat.* Sometimes it helps to imagine a word like "ahead" or "along" between them: *Milo drove **on** (ahead) **to** Chicago. He was moving **on** (along) **to** better things.* (Confused about *in to* and *into*? Then see pages 118–119.)

ORAL/VERBAL. They're not the same, though the meanings do overlap. *Oral* means "by mouth" or "by spoken word." *Verbal* means "by written or spoken word." That's why *verbal* is so easily misunderstood. What's a *verbal* contract? Written or spoken? It can be either. When it's important to make the distinction, use *oral* when you mean "spoken," *written* when you mean "written." As Sam Goldwyn supposedly said, "A verbal contract isn't worth the paper it's written on."

KEMPT AND COUTH

Some words are sourpusses. They're negative through and through, and have no positive counterparts. I'm thinking of words like *unkempt*, *inept*, *disgruntled*, and *uncouth*. We might joke about looking "kempt" or being "couth," but in fact the negatives have no opposite forms—they're either obsolete rarities or whimsical inventions.

Other negatives with nonexistent or obscure opposite numbers include *debunk*, *disappointing*, *disconcerting*, *disconsolate*, *disheveled*, *dismayed*, *immaculate*, *impeccable*, *inadvertent*, *incapacitated*, *inclement*, *incognito*, *incommunicado*, *incorrigible*, *indefatigable*, *indomitable*, *inevitable*, *insipid*, *misnomer*, *mistake*, *nonchalant*, *noncommittal*, *nondescript*, *nonpareil*, *nonplussed*, *unassuming*, *unbeknownst*, *ungainly*, and *unwieldy*.

Some similar words without opposite versions may look like negatives, but they aren't. Their negative-looking prefixes (*im* and *in*) emphasize or intensify instead. Actually, *intensify* and *instead* are among these words, and so are *impromptu*, *inscribe*, *insure*, and *inflammable* (see page 116).

OUGHT/OUGHT TO. Which is proper? You'll always be correct if you use *ought to*. Omit *to*, if you wish, in a negative statement: *Children **ought** not take candy from strangers. Pigs **ought** never be allowed in the kitchen.*

OVERWHELMING/OVERWEENING. The more familiar *overwhelming* means just what you think it does—"too much!" *Overweening*, a useful word that we don't see very often, means "conceited" or "pretentious." *The arrogance of that **overweening** little jerk is simply **overwhelming**.*

PALATE/PALETTE/PALLET. Maybe you don't have any trouble telling these apart, but I have to look them up every time. The *palate* is the roof of the mouth, and the word also refers to the sense of taste (the letters spell "a plate"). A *palette*, the board a painter mixes colors on, is also a range of colors. A *pallet* is a platform or rustic bed, usually a makeshift mattress of straw or some other humble material. *Vincent painted his supper, then ate it. Having satisfied his **palate**, he cleaned his **palette**, and retired to his **pallet**.*

PERCENT/PERCENTAGE/PERCENTAGE POINT. See page 266.

PORE OVER/POUR OVER. You *pore over* an engrossing book, but it's gross to *pour over* one. *While Charlotte **pored over** a steamy novel, the bathtub **poured over**.*

PRESUME/PRESUMPTIVE/PRESUMPTUOUS. See ASSUME/ PRESUME, page 103.

PRINCIPAL/PRINCIPLE. Still can't keep these straight? A *principal* is a leading figure (the head of a school, for example), and plays a leading, or *principal*, role. A *principle*, on the other hand, is a rule or standard. Here's a tried-and-true memory aid: If you're good in school, the *principal* is your *p-a-l*.

PROPHECY/PROPHESY. The *prophecy* (noun) is what's foretold. To *prophesy* (verb) is to foretell. As for pronunciation, *prophecy* ends in a "see," *prophesy* in a "sigh." *Madame*

*Olga charged $50 per **prophecy**, claiming that she could **prophesy** fluctuations in the commodities market.*

RACK/WRACK. Are you *racked* with guilt, or *wracked*? Is tax time nerve-*racking*, or nerve-*wracking*? Are you on the brink of *rack* and ruin, or *wrack* and ruin? Most of the time, you are *racked* (tortured, strained, stretched, punished). Just think of the *rack*, the medieval instrument of torture. If you're *wracked*, however, you're destroyed— you're *wreckage* on the beach of life (the words *wrack* and *wreck* are related). In sum: *You are **racked** with guilt, you've had a nerve-**racking** time, and you're facing **wrack** and ruin.* You need a less stressful life!

RAISE/RISE. To *raise* is to bring something up; there's always a "something" that's being lifted. To *rise* is to get up. *When they **raise** the flag, we all **rise**.* (There's more about *raise* and *rise*, and how they're used in the past tense, on page 73.)

RAVAGE/RAVISH. When the ocean liner *Queen Elizabeth* caught fire and burned in Hong Kong harbor, a newspaper in Minnesota heralded the news with this headline: "Queen Elizabeth Ravished." What the headline writer intended was *ravaged*, meaning "damaged" or "destroyed." There's an element of lust in *ravish*, which means "carry off" (either by force or by emotion) or "rape." These days we're more likely to use *ravish* in the emotional than in the physical sense. *Though it was **ravaged** by the cleaners, the dress still looked **ravishing**.*

REGRETFULLY/REGRETTABLY. A person who's full of regret is *regretful*, and sighs *regretfully*. A thing that's a cause of regret is *regrettable*, and *regrettably* that's the situation. *Hazel **regretfully** swept up the Ming vase, which **regrettably** had smashed to smithereens.*

RELUCTANT/RETICENT. These aren't even distant cousins. A *reluctant* person is unwilling, but a *reticent* one is silent. *The **reluctant** bride was **reticent** when asked to say "I do."* By the way, *reticent* comes from the same Latin verb (meaning "to keep silent") as *tacit* (unspoken) and *taciturn* (uncommunicative).

SET/SIT. To *set* is to place something; there's usually a "something" that's being placed. To *sit* is to take a seat. ***Set** the groceries on the counter and **sit** at the table.* (There's more about *set* and *sit*, and how they're used in the past tense, on page 73.)

> **NOTE:** Both verbs have other uses. *Set* can mean "sink" or "settle," as in *The Jell-O will **set** by five, long before the sun **sets**.* And *sit* can mean "accommodate" or "seat," as in *The theater **sits** two thousand and there were lots of empty seats, yet the usher **sat** us behind a post.*

SIGHT/SITE. The *sight* is what you see; the *site* is the location. *At Walley World, their favorite vacation **site**, the Griswolds saw all the usual **sights**.*

SNEAKED/SNUCK. The traditional past tense of *sneak* is *sneaked*, but *snuck* is quietly sneaking up. Dictionaries now accept *snuck*, but be aware that purists look down their noses at it. So I don't recommend using *snuck* on formal occasions. *Your Honor, the defendant* *sneaked* into the kitchen and stole Mrs. Crocker's recipe. See also page 249.

SPADE/SPAYED. People who confuse these must drive veterinarians crazy. A *spade* is a skinny shovel. An altered female dog or cat is *spayed*. To *spade* a garden (past tense *spaded*) is to dig it up; to *spay* a pet (past tense *spayed*) is to keep her from having puppies or kittens. *Ashley took up a **spade** and **spaded** the flower bed, while Melanie took Boots to be **spayed**.*

STATIONARY/STATIONERY. If the *stationery* (paper) is *stationary* (fixed or still), you can write on it without its sliding off your desk. (Tip: Both *stationery* and *paper* contain *er*.) *"If you haven't become **stationary**, Barney, please get up and bring me my **stationery**," said Thelma Lou.*

THAN/THEN. Does it make your hair stand on end when someone writes, *"He's taller **then** his brother"*? No? Then go stand in the corner. *Than* and *then* are similar only in the way they sound. Use *than* to compare or contrast things (as in *more **than*** or *less **than***). Use *then* to show that one thing follows or results from another (as in *Look, **then** leap*). *The next morning, Paolo was sicker **than** a dog. He took some aspirin, **then** went back to bed. "If gin disagrees with you, **then** avoid it," said Francesca.* For advice on what to do when *than* comes before a pronoun (*I*, *me*, *he*, *she*, etc.), see pages 12–13 and 241–242.

THERE ARE/THERE IS/THERE'S. See pages 60–61.

THOUGH/ALTHOUGH. These are interchangeable, except in two cases, when only *though* will do:

- in the phrases *as though* or *even though*
- when it's used to mean "however." *Madame Olga pre-dicted it would rain in Brazil; it didn't, **though**.*

TILL/UNTIL. Either of these is correct, but forget about little "til." ***Until** [or **till**] recently, Sluggo's tie was spotless.*

> **NOTE:** Contrary to popular opinion, *till* isn't a shortening of *until*. In fact, *till* came first. The prefix *un* was a later addition, and eventually the final *l* on the old "untill" fell off. That gave us two words for one job: *till* and *until*. The upstart "til" (sometimes preceded by an apostrophe) was formed on the assumption that it was a contraction of *until*. Long considered illegitimate, it's now accepted as a variant in some dictionaries, but I don't recommend it.

TORTUOUS/TORTUROUS. The first means "winding," "crooked," "full of turns." The second is associated with *torture* (the word it comes from), and means "painful." *On the **tortuous** drive through the mountains, Jake developed a **torturous** headache.*

TROOPER/TROUPER. The one in uniform is a *trooper*. A *trouper* is a performer (a member of a troupe) or simply a dependable person. *Lars was a real **trouper** when the touring company's bus was stopped by a state **trooper**.*

TRY AND/TRY TO. The preferred phrase, especially for formal occasions, is *try to*. *Sir Winston insisted the Lord High Chancellor **try to** improve the efficiency of the courts.* But *try and*, which has been around for hundreds of years, is acceptable in casual writing and in conversation. *"**Try and** make me," said the Lord High Chancellor.*

WHILE/WILE. The word *while* has a time element. The old expression "worth your *while*" means "worth your time," and to "*while* away" is to spend time idly. *Moose blew the exam by **whiling** away the hours instead of studying.* Dictionaries now accept "*wile* away," which began as a spelling error, but I don't recommend it. "*While* away" is still much more common. Strictly speaking, to *wile* is to deceive and a *wile* is a trick or an enticement. *Despite all his **wiles**, Moose failed to sway the professor.* For more about *while*, see pages 134 and 248.

WILL/WOULD. See pages 85–86.

USE IT (RIGHT) OR LOSE IT

BEMUSED. In traditional usage, you're *bemused* when you're bewildered, puzzled, or plunged in thought. You're not *amused*. But many people confuse the two words, and at least one dictionary now accepts a new sense of *bemused*— inwardly or wryly *amused*. As a result, *bemused* has become a slippery word, one that might be interpreted in very different ways. My advice: Don't use *bemused* as an exact synonym for *amused*. And when you do use it, be sure the context makes your meaning clear. *"I fail to see why you're amused," whined the **bemused** Mr. Peepers, whose missing spectacles were perched on his head.*

COMPRISE. The old rule was that *comprise* means "include" or "contain" or "consist of." *Vladimir's butterfly collection* **comprises** *several rare specimens.* But today most dictionaries accept two nontraditional uses as standard English. You can safely use *comprise* for "make up" or "constitute," and *comprised of* for "made up of." *Many species of butterflies* **comprise** *the collection. It's* **comprised of** *ordinary specimens as well as rarities.*

COUPLE. In better English, it takes *of* when followed by a noun: *Let's pick up a* **couple of** *hamburgers.* Not: *Let's pick up a* **couple** *hamburgers.* (Similarly, *pair of, plenty of, type of, variety of, breed of, kind of*: *What* **kind of** *fries do they have?*) But *of* is often dropped before a number: *I've probably eaten there a* **couple** *dozen times.* And *of* isn't used before a comparative term like *more* or *fewer*: *It's just a* **couple** *more miles ahead.*

> **NOTE:** Sometimes *couple* is singular and sometimes it's plural. See pages 26 and 57.

DEPEND. It usually takes *on* (or, more formally, *upon*). *"Well," said Buster, "that* **depends on** *what [not* **depends** *what] you mean by housebroken."* But sometimes it's followed by nothing: *It all* **depends**.

DUE TO. When you want to be on your very best grammatical behavior, use *due to* only if you mean "caused by" or "resulting from": *The damage was* **due to** *moths.* In recent years, dictionaries have come to accept a looser usage, meaning "because of" or "on account of": *Richie threw* *the suit away **due to** the hole.* But be warned that some find this grating, especially at the front of a sentence: ***Due to** the hole, Richie threw the suit away.*

EQUALLY AS. Forget the *as*: *Ken and Midge are **equally** obnoxious.* Or: *Ken is **as** obnoxious **as** Midge.*

FORBID. You can use it with either *to* (*I **forbid** you **to** smoke in the house*) or *from* (*I **forbid** you **from** smoking in the house*). As an alternative, use *forbid* with an *ing* word alone: *I **forbid smoking** in the house.* See also PREVENT and PROHIBIT, which are used with *from*, on page 133.

GRADUATED. There are three rights and a "questionable." The last choice is now endorsed by at least one major dictionary, but most still disapprove. So it's best avoided unless you're being informal.

Right: *Lulu **graduated** from college.*
Right: *Lulu **was graduated** from college.*
Right: *The college **graduated** Lulu.*
Questionable: *Lulu **graduated** college.*

HARDLY. Avoid attaching *hardly* to a negative verb, as in *Mr. Peepers **can't hardly** see without his glasses. Hardly* is already a negative word, and you don't need two of them. Either of these is correct: *He **can hardly** see without his glasses.* Or: *He can't see without his glasses.*

HARDLY/SCARCELY/NO SOONER. Watch your *when*s and *than*s with these. Use *when* with *hardly* and *scarcely*: *We had **hardly** begun to cook **when** the smoke alarm went off.* Or: *We had **scarcely** begun to cook **when** the smoke alarm* *went off.* Use *than* with *no sooner*: ***No sooner*** *had we begun to cook **than** the smoke alarm went off.*

HENCE. This means "from here" or "from now," so adding "from" is technically redundant. Despite that, the phrase "from *hence*" has a long history and is considered standard English, so use it if you prefer. *"My birthday is three days **hence** [or **from hence**]," said Griselda, "and I could use a new tiara."* Another meaning of *hence* is "thus": *Griselda had no tact, **hence** the broad hint.* See also WHENCE, another venerable old word, on the next page.

INSIDE OF. Drop the *of* in a sentence like this: *Penelope keeps her hankie **inside** her glove.* But when *inside* is a noun meaning "interior," as when *outside* is a noun meaning "exterior," keep the *of.* *The **inside of** the glove was fleece, like the **outside of** the jacket.* See also pages 147 and 250.

KUDOS. This is a singular noun meaning "praise" or "glory" (*Bart won **kudos** for his skateboarding skill*), not a plural form of some imaginary "kudo." Show me one kudo and I'll eat it.

LIKELY (with a verb). When you use *likely* to describe an action, don't use it all by itself; in better English, precede it with *very, quite,* or *most*: *Algonquin J. Calhoun will **quite likely** lose his shirt at the track* (not "will likely lose"). If you prefer, use *is likely to* instead: *Algonquin **is likely to** lose a bundle, and Mrs. Calhoun **is likely to** kill him.*

MYRIAD. It originally meant "ten thousand," but *myriad* now is an adjective meaning "numerous" (*Little Chuckie has **myriad** freckles*) or a noun meaning "multitude" (*He has **myriads** [or **a myriad**] of them*).

ONLY. Aside from casual usage, don't use *only* in place of *but* or *except* in this kind of sentence: *I would go to Paris,* **but** [not *only*] *I'm broke.* For where to place *only* in a sentence, see pages 142–143.

PREVENT: Use *prevent* with *from*, not *to*. *The storm* **prevented** *Sebastian* **from** *going.* (Not: *The storm* **prevented** *Sebastian* **to** *go.*) As an alternative, you can use an *ing* word. *The storm* **prevented** *his* **going***. A storm often* **prevents going** *by air.*

PROHIBIT. Use *prohibit* with *from*, not *to*. *The sign* **prohibits** *us* **from** *feeding the alligators.* (Not: *The sign* **prohibits** *us* **to** *feed the alligators.*) As an alternative, you can use an *ing* word alone. *The sign* **prohibits feeding** *the alligators.*

WHENCE. This means "from where" or "from which," so it's not necessary to add "from." However, the phrase "from *whence*" has a long and distinguished history, and it's standard English. Feel free to add "from" if you like. *So* **whence** [or **from whence**] *came the vampire craze?* The same is true of *thence* (which means "from there") and *hence* ("from here"; see previous page); they can be used alone or with "from." However, their elderly cousins *whither* ("to where"), *hither* ("to here"), and *thither* ("to there") have "to" built in, and they always stand alone. **Whither** *goest thou, my pretty wench?* When you resurrect a grizzled old word, treat it with respect.

WHETHER OR NOT. You can usually ditch *or not*: *Phoebe always knows* **whether** *Holden is telling the truth.* See also IF/WHETHER, pages 117–118.

WHILE. The classic meaning is "during the time that." *Doc whistles* **while** *he works*. But *while* has also gained acceptance as a substitute for *although* or *whereas* at the beginning of a sentence or clause. **While** *Grumpy can whistle, he prefers not to. Elves are industrious,* **while** *gnomes are merely decorative*. For more about *while*, see below and pages 129 and 248.

> NOTE: If you use *while* in place of *although*, be sure there's no chance it could be misunderstood to mean "during the time that." You could leave the impression that unlikely things are happening at the same time: **While** *Dopey sleeps late, he enjoys vigorous exercise*. Only if Dopey is a sleepwalker! For how to use *a while* and *awhile*, read on.

ONE WORD OR TWO?

A WHILE/AWHILE. People often confuse these. *A while* means "a period of time." *Awhile* means "for a time" ("for" is part of the meaning and shouldn't be added). Here's a hint: Generally, *a while* follows a preposition (like *after*, *for*, or *in*), and *awhile* follows a verb. *Heloise rested* **awhile***; she put her feet up and dozed for* **a while***.* For more about *while*, see above and pages 129 and 248.

ALL READY/ALREADY. They're not the same. *All ready* means "prepared"; *already* means "previously." *Carrie and Samantha are* **all ready** *to boogie; in fact, they've* **already** *started.*

ALL RIGHT/ALRIGHT. In your best English, use two separate words. *"**All right**, Officer, I'll go quietly," said Gussie.* Many dictionaries today accept *alright*, but chiefly as informal English.

ALL TOGETHER/ALTOGETHER. They differ. *All together* means "collectively"—all at once or all in one place: *Bertie's aunts were **all together** in the living room.* The one-word version, *altogether*, means "in sum" or "entirely": ***Altogether** there were four of them. Bertie was **altogether** defeated.*

ANY MORE/ANYMORE. Use *any more* if you mean "any additional"; use *anymore* if you mean "nowadays" or "any longer." *Shep won't be chasing **any more** cars. He doesn't get around much **anymore**.*

ANY ONE/ANYONE. If you can substitute *anybody*, then the single word *anyone* is correct; if not, use two words, *any one*. ***Anyone** can fool Lumpy. **Any one** of his friends is smarter than he is.* See also EVERY ONE/EVERYONE on the next page.

ANY PLACE/ANYPLACE. One word is acceptable if you could substitute *anywhere* (though *anywhere* is usually better). If in doubt, use two. *I can afford to live **anyplace**, but I can't live in **any place** that doesn't accept pets.*

ANY TIME/ANYTIME. Use two words if you mean "any amount of time," one if you could substitute *whenever*. *The boss will see you **anytime** she has **any time**.*

ANY WAY/ANYWAY. It's one word if you mean "in any case." Otherwise, use two words, *any way*. Never "anyways." *I don't know of **any way** to visit the dungeons without* *bumping into Snape. You wouldn't want to see them, **anyway***.

EVERY DAY/EVERYDAY. We mix them up daily (or *every day*). The single word, *everyday*, is an adjective. It describes a thing, so it can usually be found right in front of a noun: *"I love my **everyday** jeans," said Jack*. The time expression *every day* is two words: *"That's why you wear them **every day**," said Ennis*.

EVERY ONE/EVERYONE. If you can substitute *everybody*, then the single word *everyone* is correct; if not, use two words, *every one*. ***Everyone** fears Miu-Miu's kittens. **Every one** of them is a little terror*.

DETOUR—DANGEROUS CONSTRUCTION AHEAD

ALL . . . NOT/NOT ALL. Many sentences that are built around *all . . . not* face backward. Use *not all* instead: ***Not all** the boys are dancing*. Putting *not* next to the verb (***All** the boys are **not** dancing*) could mean they're all sitting it out.

> **NOTE:** Sentences constructed with *both* and *not* can create a similar problem. See pages 138–139.

AS BAD OR WORSE THAN. Stay away from this kind of sentence: *Opie's math is **as bad or worse than** his English*.

Do you see what's wrong with it? There are two kinds of comparisons going on, *as bad as* and *worse than*. When you telescope them into *as bad or worse than*, you lose an *as*. Putting it back in (*Opie's math is **as bad as or worse than** his English*) is correct but cumbersome. A better idea is to put the rear end of the comparison (*or worse*) at the end of the sentence: *Opie's math is **as bad as** his English, **or worse**.* (Another way to end the sentence is *if not worse*.)

AS GOOD OR BETTER THAN. This is a variation on the previous theme. It's better to split up the comparison: *Harry's broom is **as good as** Malfoy's, **or better**.* (Another way to end that sentence is *if not better*.)

AS MUCH OR MORE THAN. Here's another variation on *as bad or worse than* (see previous page). Don't use this phrase all at once; split it up: *Mr. Sousé loves bourbon **as much as** rye, **or more**.* (Another ending is *if not more*.)

NOTE: For a way out of another common trap, see **ONE OF THE . . . IF NOT THE**, pages 141–142.

BEING AS/BEING THAT. These clunkers are sometimes used as alternatives to *because* or *since*: ***Being that** he was starving, he ate a piece of Grandma's fruitcake.* They may squeak by in conversation (not with me, please) but should be avoided in writing. *Being as how* is just as bad. These aren't felonies, but neither is snoring at the ballet. The same goes for *seeing as*, *seeing as how*, and *seeing that*. Don't use them in place of *because* or *since*.

BOTH. The pair (of people, actions, things, ideas, and so on) following *both* should have the same accessories or functions:

- If one of the pair has a preposition (*as*, *by*, *for*, *to*, and so on), so should the other: *Phineas has proposed both **to Mary** and **to Laura***. Or: *Phineas has proposed to both **Mary** and **Laura***.
- If one of the pair is a verb or an adjective, so is the other: *His attentions both **pleased** and **flattered** them*. Or: *His attentions were both **pleasing** and **flattering***.

> NOTE: Don't try to use *both* and *as well as* at the same time. Use one or the other, not both. *Giulietta had **both** a facial and a massage*. Or: *Giulietta had a facial **as well as** a massage*.

BOTH . . . NOT/NOT BOTH. Using *both* and *not* in the same sentence is asking for trouble. That's because saying something negative about *both* can be ambiguous. When you say, ***Both** children did **not** get the flu*, do you mean both escaped it? Or that just one—*not* both—got it? Put the negative part where it belongs: *One of the children, **not both**, got the flu*. Or drop *both* and use *neither* instead: ***Neither** child got the flu*.

In fact, any negative statement with *both* should be looked on with suspicion. A sentence like *There are no symptoms in **both** children* probably won't be misunderstood. But it would be clearer and more graceful to drop *both* and use *either*: *There are no symptoms in* **either** *child.*

NOTE: For a similar problem with *all* and *not*, see page 136.

EITHER/NEITHER. We generally use *either* and *neither* when referring to only two. *Let's invite* **either** *Kitty or Lydia. They're* **neither** *smokers nor vegans.* But *either* and *neither* can refer to three or more when used to introduce a series. *Let's* **either** *make dinner, order in, or go out to eat. My diet allows* **neither** *salt, sugar, nor fats.* Any pedant who insists that the series can't have more than two should memorize the unofficial motto of the Postal Service: "Neither snow nor rain nor heat nor gloom of night stays these couriers from the swift completion of their appointed rounds." You can use the conjunction (*or, nor*) with several items in the series or only the last.

However, there's a "two-ness" in the following situations: (1) When *either* and *neither* are used as adjectives, words that describe nouns. *I'll take* **either** *[or* **neither***] dessert.* (2) When they're used as pronouns, words that stand in for nouns. *I can't have* **either** *of them because* **neither** *is on my diet.* As adjectives and pronouns, *either* and *neither* always mean "one [or none] of two."

Now, what about the verb that goes with *either* or *neither*? Is it singular or plural? This gets two answers.

- If *either* or *neither* is used to introduce a series of two or more, the verb agrees with the closest item in the series (see also pages 56–57). Here the verb is singular: **Either** *checks, credit cards, or cash* **is** *accepted.* Here it's plural: **Neither** *the maître d' nor the waiters* **are** *awake.*

- If there's no series, and *either* or *neither* is used as an adjective or pronoun (see previous page), the verb is singular. **Either** [or **neither**] *restaurant* **is** *affordable, and* **either** [or **neither**] **is** *an easy drive.*

For how to juggle *either* with *or* and *neither* with *nor*, read on.

EITHER . . . OR. Think of the elements joined by *either* and *or* as perfectly matched pearls. Make sure they're alike. If what follows *either* has both a subject and a verb (is a clause, in other words), what follows *or* should, too: **Either** *Reginald forgot* **or** *he didn't care.* If what follows *either* is a verb, then so is what follows *or*: *Reginald* **either** *forgot* **or** *didn't care.* If what follows *either* could be a subject, then what follows *or* should match: **Either** *the kids* **or** *his wife should have reminded him.* If what follows *either* is a descriptive term, then so is what follows *or*: *Reginald is* **either** *forgetful* **or** *thoughtless* **or** *both.* In short, the pearls strung together by *either* and *or* should match grammatically—clause with clause, verb with verb, and so on. If the pearls don't match, you can often fix the problem by moving *either* a few words over. So this blunder, **Either** *his wife is angry* **or** *amused*, becomes *His wife is* **either** *angry* **or** *amused*. For more, see pages 56–57 and 139–140.

NOTE: Several other pairs should also join matching elements: *neither + nor* (see below); *not only + but also*; *both + and*. As with *either + or*, they may take some arranging; all the pearls on the string should match. See pages 56–57.

NEITHER . . . NOR: As with *either* and *or* (see previous page), the elements joined by *neither* and *nor* should match. If *neither* is followed by a noun, then so is *nor*: *Oscar eats* **neither** *peas* **nor** *broccoli*. If *neither* is followed by a verb, then so is *nor*: *Oscar* **neither** *likes* **nor** *eats them*. If *neither* goes with a description, then so does *nor*: *Peas are* **neither** *tempting* **nor** *tasty* **nor** *toothsome*. (Yes, there can be more than one *nor*.) But if each of the parts being joined has both a subject and a verb—if they're clauses, in other words—you can use another negative term instead of *neither*. *Oscar* **never** *eats peas,* **nor** *does he eat broccoli*. For more, see pages 56–57 and 139–140.

ONE OF THE . . . IF NOT THE. Here's another corner you can avoid backing yourself into: *Jordan was* **one of the** *best,* **if not the** *best, player on the team*. Oops! Can you hear what's wrong? The sentence should read correctly even if the second half of the comparison (*if not the best*) is removed, but without it you've got: *Jordan was one of the* *best player on the team.* One of the best *player*? Better to put the second half of the comparison at the end of the sentence: *Jordan was* **one of the** *best players on the team,* **if not the** *best.*

ONLY. This slippery word—meaning "alone," "solely," or "and no other"—can be found almost anywhere in a sentence, even where it doesn't belong. To put *only* in its place, make sure it goes right before the word or phrase you want to single out as the lone wolf. Take this sentence as an example: *The butler says he saw the murder.* By inserting *only* in various places, you can give the sentence many different meanings. Keep your eye on the underlined words—those are the wolves being singled out of the pack:

Only the butler *says he saw the murder.* (The butler, and no one else, says he saw the murder.)

The butler **only** says *he saw the murder.* (The butler says, but can't prove, he saw the murder.)

The butler says **only** he *saw the murder.* (The butler says he, and no one else, saw it.)

The butler says he **only** saw *the murder.* (He saw—but didn't hear—the murder.)

The butler says he saw **only** the murder. (He saw just the murder, and nothing else.)

Remember: *Only* the lonely! It's easy to slip *only* into a sentence carelessly, so get into the habit of using it right in front of the word you want to single out. See also page 133.

NOTE: The whole point of putting *only* in its place is to make yourself clear. In the examples on the previous page, the various locations of *only* make a big difference. But in informal writing and conversation, if no one's likely to mistake your meaning it's fine to put *only* where it seems most natural—usually in front of the verb: *I'm **only** saying this for your own good. This food can **only** be called swill.* The more technically correct versions—*I'm saying this **only** for your own good; This food can be called **only** swill*—only sound unnatural.

REASON ... IS BECAUSE. Here's a redundancy for you, a wording that seems to repeat itself: *The **reason** Rex stayed home **is because** robbers tied him up.* Can you hear the echo effect? *Because* means "for the reason that," so the example says, in effect: *The **reason** Rex stayed home is **for the reason that** robbers tied him up.* For more graceful English, use *reason* with *that*, not with *because*. *The **reason** Rex stayed home is **that** robbers tied him up.* Or drop the *reason*: *Rex stayed home **because** robbers tied him up.*

REASON WHY. This one, on the other hand, is NOT a redundancy, and here's the reason why. It's a venerable English expression in which *reason* means "cause" and *why* means "for which" or "on account of which." Strictly speaking, the *why* is not necessary, but that doesn't make it wrong. While *reason* can be used by itself (*the **reason** we called*), it is also quite properly used with *why* (*the **reason why** we called*), and with *that* (*the **reason that** we called*).

SEEING AS/SEEING THAT. See BEING AS/BEING THAT,
    page 137.

PLUG UGLY

It's usually easy to stretch an adjective (a word that describes
a noun) into an adverb (one that describes a verb). Just add *ly*
to a word like *neat* and you end up with *neatly*: *It's a **neat** trick
to pack a suitcase **neatly***. What could be neater?

But not all adjectives like having *ly* tacked on to them,
especially if they already end in *ly*, like *ugly, friendly, surly*,
and *jolly*. Sure, some dictionaries say we can use lame adverbs
like *uglily, friendlily, surlily*, and *jollily*, but nobody says we
have to.

If a word doesn't want to be stretched out of shape, don't
force it.

Incidentally, an adverb doesn't have to end in *ly*. Check out
slow versus *slowly* in the chapter on myths, pages 250–251.

ET CETERA

A/AN. Sometimes it's the little things that give us away. For
    instance, we all know the rule about using *an* in front of
    words that begin with a vowel (*a, e, i, o, u*), and *a* in front
    of those starting with consonants (letters with a "hard"
    sound, like *b, c, d, f, g, h*, and so on). Well, that "rule" is

misleading. What matters is the sound the word begins with, not the letter. Sometimes *h* sounds like a vowel, and sometimes *u* sounds like a consonant. Here's what to do.

Use *an* in front of words that start with these sounds:

- The *h* that you can't hear, as in *heir, hour, honor,* and *herb.* (No, Americans don't pronounce the *h* in *herb.* See page 175.)
- The "short" *u* (the "uh" variety), as in *uncle, umbrella, underwear,* and *ulcer.*

Use *a* in front of words that start with these sounds:

- The *h* that you can hear (the "ha-ha" variety), as in *hair, horror, hotel,* and *historic* (see page 117).
- The "long" *u* (the "yoo" variety), as in *university, utopia, unisex,* and *unique.*
- The combination *eu* (another "yoo" sound), as in *eulogy, euphemism, European,* and *eureka.*

AND/OR. This ugly wrinkle—*Tubby, would you like apple pie **and/or** ice cream?*—can be smoothed out: *Tubby, would you like apple pie, ice cream, or both?*

AT. Avoid using it unnecessarily with *where,* as in *Where is Waldo **at**? The at* is understood, so all you need is *Where is Waldo?*

BUT. It's common to use *but* to mean "nothing but" or "only"—just don't get tangled in negatives, since *but* in these cases already has a negative sense built in.

> *Tom **is but** a boy.* Not: *Tom **isn't but** a boy.*
> *Aunt Polly **weighs but** 105 pounds.* Not: *Aunt Polly* ***doesn't weigh but** 105 pounds.*

> **NOTE:** The expression "can't help but" means "can only."
> *Huck **can't help but** look silly in those pants.* The expression
> is now considered standard English, but if you prefer, you
> can drop the *but* and use an *ing* word instead. *Huck **can't**
> **help looking** silly in those pants.* Expressions like "can't
> help but" are often called "idiomatic," because we all know
> what they mean even if they don't necessarily make sense
> when examined word for word. English is very rich in
> idiomatic expressions, like "Far be it from me," "You bet,"
> "Don't go there," and "That dress isn't you." Every language
> has peculiarities that people simply accept on faith.

ETC. Since this abbreviation (it stands for *et cetera*) means "and others," it's redundant to say or write "and etc." It's even worse to use "etc., etc." *Tony's business interests are diverse: waste management, luxury auto exports, pharmaceuticals, **etc.*** And if you're one of those people who pronounce it ek-SET-ra, think again. There's no *k* sound (see the box and the **ETC.** entry on page 174).

OF. Don't use it if you don't need it. *Cousin Vinnie says his new TV fell off **of** a truck. The missing warranty is not that big **of** a problem.* Whack the *of*: *Cousin Vinnie says his new TV fell off a truck. The missing warranty is not that big a problem.* See also pages 132 and 250.

CHAPTER 6

SPELLBOUND

HOW TO BE LETTER PERFECT

A spell-checker can be your best friend—and your worst enemy.

I use mine routinely, and I can't count the times it's saved my bacon. For example, I'm incapable of typing the word *substitution* correctly. My fingers simply can't do it. If it weren't for my speller, I'd have to use *replacement* or *stand-in* or *pinch hitter* instead.

I also tend to misspell *the*—it comes out *hte*. Or I write it twice: *the the*. Spell-check bails me out every time.

But good old spell-check doesn't always come through. Turn your back on it, and it'll kick you in the but. There! That's what I mean. My software didn't catch that *but* because, as we all know, it can't tell the difference between sound-alike words: *but* and *butt*, *need* and *knead*, *sew* and *sow*, and so on.

Confidentially, your spell-checker isn't very smart. It doesn't care whether someone's a *guerrilla* or a *gorilla*, lives in a *desert* or a *dessert*, is a *bass* player or a *base* player. It's not picky.

Humans, however, are picky. They notice little differences between words that sound the same (like *way* and *weigh*, or *rain* and *reign*), or words that are similar but not alike (such as *not* and *now*, or *affect* and *effect*, or *how* and *who*). To a real person, one is not just as good as another!

The lesson? Don't expect your computer to think for you. Sure, go ahead and use your checker, but don't depend on it to catch every mistake. Word processors have dictionaries, but not common sense—at least not yet. So don't automatically hit Change or Replace just because a program tells you to (oar Yule bee sari).

The truth is, your spell-checker needs a spell-checker, and that's you! It pays to get familiar with hard-to-spell words before you need them. When in doubt, use a reputable dictionary, digital or not, and (as I'm always saying) read the fine print. When two acceptable spellings are listed for the same word, use the first, because it may be more common.

As for your grammar-checker, it ain't what it's cracked up to be. Grammar software has gotten a lot better lately, but some awful howlers still manage to sneak by. Just for the heck of it, I tested my grammar-checker on this sentence: "After peeing on the rug, Paris scolded her Chihuahua." No comment. Grammar-check didn't get it: The Chihuahua, not Paris, should have been the guilty party. (For the inside story on this kind of mistake, see Chapter 9.)

Now let's get to know some of the most persistent spelling troublemakers. (If there's one you don't see here, sniff around. The word could be lurking in the "Mixed Doubles" section of Chapter 5.)

CASTING A SPELL

A HOLD. I don't hold with the mushed-together "ahold," though some dictionaries accept it. Either make it two words (*"Gal, you've really got **a hold** on me," said Roy*), or use *hold* (*"For heaven's sake, Roy, get **hold** of yourself," said Dale*).

A LOT. It's two words (not "alot"). *Piers hasn't plowed **a lot** lately.* The verb *allot*, by the way, means "parcel out." *He doesn't **allot** enough time to farming.*

ABSENCE. It ends in *ce*, like *fence*. *Wishbone's **absence** was explained by a hole in the fence.*

ACCESS. Double up on the *c*'s and the *s*'s. *The Scouts didn't have **access** to their phones.*

ACCIDENTALLY. There's an *ally* at the end. *Rachel needed an ally when she **accidentally** ruined the dinner.* (I don't recommend "accidently," though you may stumble across it in the dictionary. It still looks like a mistake—which is how it started.) And don't forget the *ally* in *incidentally*, either. ***Incidentally**, the smoke alarms went off.*

ACCOMMODATE. It has two *c*'s and two *m*'s. *"I believe I can **accommodate** you, even without a reservation," said Mr. Fawlty.*

ACHIEVEMENT. The *i* comes before the *e* in *achieve* (see the box on page 154), and you keep the final *e* when *ment* is added. *"Cheer up, Wilbur,"* said Orville. *"Flying five hundred and forty feet is quite an* **achievement***."*

ACKNOWLEDGMENT. In American English, *acknowledge* loses its final *e* when you add *ment*. *"I replied to your reply, but you failed to acknowledge my* **acknowledgment***,"* wrote Miss Hathaway, whose texts were always spelled perfectly.* The other form, *acknowledgement*, is preferred in Britain.

ACQUAINTANCE. Don't overlook the first *c*. *"I don't believe I've made your* **acquaintance***, Mr. Firefly,"* said Mrs. Teasdale.*

ADVERTISE/ADVERTISEMENT/ADVERTISING. There's no *z*. *When Mr. Bernbach got his first job in* **advertising***, he didn't* **advertise** *the fact that he'd never written an* **advertisement***.

ADVISABLE. It ends in *able*, not *ible*. *Rufus learned that it was not* **advisable** *to tease Mrs. Teasdale.* I advise you to check out the box on *ible*s and *able*s, page 159.

ADVISER. This is the preferred spelling for someone who advises or gives advice. But *advisor* is also acceptable. *Warren doesn't need the advice of a financial* **adviser***.

AFICIONADO. Don't be tempted to double up on *f*'s or *c*'s. There's one of each. *Rube Goldberg was an* **aficionado** *of Cuban cigars, mostly Macanudos.*

AGING. There's no *e*. *"***Aging** *is no fun,"* said Dorian.* See also page 171.

AIN'T. Are you sure you want to spell this? ***Ain't*** *is still misbehavin'.* See page 82.

ALL-AROUND. This is the preferred American spelling (the British mostly use *all-round*) for the term that means "versatile" or "well-rounded." *Shep is a good **all-around** dog.*

ALTAR. The religious furniture has no *e*. *"Why, Vicar, that **altar** is just divine!" cried Lucia.* The verb meaning "change" is *alter*. *"I wouldn't **alter** a thing!"*

ANYWHERE. Never "anywheres"! *"The aliens could be almost **anywhere**," said Ripley.*

APPALL. Two *p*'s, two *l*'s. *"Mr. Slope's compliments **appall** me," said Signora Neroni.*

ARCTIC. Don't spell it "artic" (mind the middle *c*). The lower-case *arctic* implies bitterly cold. The capitalized *Arctic* means the region. And it's *Antarctica*, not "Antartica" (a common misspelling). *The **Arctic** expedition reached the North Pole. Next year's goal, **Antarctica**, is in the opposite direction.* I was once astonished to see a big sign from Coors advertising a frosty beverage called Artic Ice. Never trust what you read on the side of a bus. (In pronouncing *arctic*, you can be less picky; see page 171.)

ARTIFACT. It has an *i*, not an *e*, in American usage. *"An 1840 saxophone is a rare **artifact**," said Lisa.* The other spelling, *artefact*, is preferred in Britain.

BATTALION. Think of the word *battle*—two *t*'s, one *l*. *Benito secretly played with a **battalion** of toy soldiers.*

BELIEVE. It has *ie* in the middle, not *ei*. This is an example of the old "*i* before *e*, except after *c*" rule (see the box on the next page). *Would you **believe** that Agent 86 lost his shoe phone?*

I BEFORE E, EXCEPT AFTER C

When I was in school, we had to memorize this little rhyme:

*Use **i** before **e**,*

*Except after **c**,*

*Or when sounded like **a**,*

*As in **neighbor** and **weigh**.*

I still use it to check my spelling when I come across words that have an *e* and an *i* next to each other. Even though it doesn't work a hundred percent of the time, it's a good trick for dealing with a tricky spelling problem.

Of course, there are always weird words that don't co-operate. The most common exceptions to the rule (besides *weird* itself) are *either, foreign, forfeit, height, leisure, neither, seize, sheik, species,* and *their*.

BENEFITED/BENEFITTED. Use one *t* or two. *Nobody in Springfield ever **benefited** [or **benefitted**] from the Merry Widow Insurance Company.*

BUSES/BUSSES, etc. The words formed from *bus* are traditionally spelled with just one *s* in the middle, but today the double-*s* versions are also acceptable. *The Drones and their guests were **bused** [or **bussed**] in two gaily colored **buses** [or **busses**]. They much prefer **busing** [or **bussing**] to going in separate cars.*

CAESAR. I invented a memory trick to help me with this one: What did *Caesar* have for breakfast? Cheese And Eggs Served All Runny. Silly, but it works.

CANCELED/CANCELLED, etc. The words formed from *cancel* can be spelled either way, though one *l* is more common in American English and two in British. *When rain flooded the roads, Pongo **canceled** [or **cancelled**] the Drones' outing, though he hated **canceling** [or **cancelling**] a party. "**Cancelation** [or **cancellation**] is probably wise," said Barmy.*

CEMETERY. If you use three *e*'s, you'll get it right. *The Addamses don't mind living next door to a **cemetery**.*

COLLECTABLE/COLLECTIBLE. The traditional spelling has *ible* at the end, but either one is acceptable today. *A cookie jar once owned by Andy Warhol is a rare **collectible** [or **collectable**].* There's more about *able*s and *ible*s on page 159.

COMMITMENT. The first part, *commit*, has two *m*'s but just one *t*. *Héloïse pressed Peter to make a **commitment**.*

COMPLEXION. The *x* makes this an excellent word for Scrabble. *The wind and sun were hard on Annie Oakley's **complexion**.* Stay away from *complected* except in casual usage; the preferred adjective is *complexioned*. *After years of riding the range, she was no longer smooth-**complexioned**.*

CONCEDE. The ending is the tough part. *"I **concede**," Garry said to Big Blue.* See the box on "seedy" endings, page 164.

CONCEIVE. Remember, *i* before *e*, except after *c*. *"I can't **conceive** why Henry considers it a problem," Anne said.*

CONNOISSEUR. I have trouble with this too. Double *n*, double *s*. *James is a **connoisseur** of fast cars and slow food.*

CONSENSUS. The only *c* is at the front. *The Tudors and the Stuarts never arrived at a **consensus**.*

COUNCIL. This word (note the *cil* ending) means an "assembly," whether official or unofficial. *After Moose was kicked off the student **council**, his parents called a family **council**.* The word for a member of a *council* can be spelled with one *l* (*councilor*) or two (*councillor*).

COUNSEL. The word with *sel* means "advise" when it's a verb. *"I **counsel** you to study harder or get a job and start paying rent," said Moose's father.* As a noun, *counsel* means "advice" or the one who gives it. *"I will seek **counsel** from my legal **counsel**," Moose replied.* Other forms of the word can be spelled with one *l* (*counseled, counseling, counselor*) or two (*counselled, counselling, counsellor*).

CREDIBLE. This is one of the *ibles* (see the box on page 159). *"It's hardly **credible** that the dog ate your homework," said Miss Brooks.*

DECEIVE. It's *e* before *i* this time. *"Don't try to **deceive** me, Ugarte," said Louis.*

DEFENSE/OFFENSE. No *c*'s in American usage. *The Hufflepuffs are weak on **offense** and not so great on **defense**, either.* The versions with *c* are used only in British spelling. For pronunciations, see pages 173 and 180.

DEFINITELY. Don't be tempted to use an *a*. *"It's **definitely** relative," said Albert.*

DESCENDANT. It ends in *ant*, not *ent*. *Diana was the most famous **descendant** of Georgiana.*

DESICCATED. One *s*, two *c*'s. *"A raisin is simply a **desiccated** grape," said Uncle Fester.*

DESIRABLE. There's no *e* in the middle. *Even on her bad days, Odette was **desirable**.*

DESSERT. The extra *s* is for sugar. *Miranda looked around furtively, then had a second **dessert**.* For more on this and similar words, see DESERTS/DESSERTS, page 111.

ECSTASY. Two *s*'s (not "ecstacy"), and there's no *x*. *Young Rona was in **ecstasy** when she spelled "syzygy" correctly.* See also ECSTATIC, page 173.

EMBARRASS. Two *r*'s and two *s*'s. *Spock was not **embarrassed** by his pointy ears.*

ENTREPRENEUR. It's always *re*, not *er* (and remember that second *r*). *In his secret life, Walter was a fabulously wealthy **entrepreneur**.*

EXHILARATE. Don't forget the *h*. *Her husband's fantasies did not **exhilarate** Mrs. Mitty.*

FIERY. This spelling is a holdover from medieval times. Get used to it. *The jalapeño was too **fiery** for Daniel's taste.*

FORESIGHT. Like *foresee*, it has an *e* in the first syllable. *Nostradamus prided himself on his **foresight**.*

FORFEIT. Here's an exception to the "*i* before *e*" rule. *If you lose at strip poker, you **forfeit** your undies.*

FORGO. This means "do without," and it does without an *e*. *People who live in Fargo must **forgo** the beach.* But *forego*, which means "go before," has an *e*, as do its cousins *foregone* and *foregoing*.

FORWARD. Not an *e* in sight. *It takes **forward** thinking to write science fiction.* (A *foreword*, the one with an *e*, is part of a book.) For more on *ward* words, see **TOWARD**, page 167.

FUCHSIA. The good news is that we don't use it every day. *"Cerise is the new **fuchsia**!" said Elle.*

FULFILL. One *l* in the middle, two at the back. *The Terminator was back to **fulfill** his promise.* See also page 168.

GAUGE. Don't put the *u* ahead of the *a*, as in *language*. *The pressure **gauge** has gone haywire!*

GRAFFITI. Two *f*'s, but only one *t*. *Anne kept busy by writing **graffiti** on the Tower walls.*

GRAMMAR. Do I have to say it? No *er* at the end! *Despite his name, Kelsey Grammer uses good **grammar**.*

GUARANTEE. It has *ua* up front, not *au*. *There is no money-back **guarantee** that this cream can reduce cellulite.*

GUERRILLA. Two *r*'s and two *l*'s. *Che raised a **guerrilla** army.* (It's the ape that's a *gorilla*.)

HARASS. Unlike *embarrass*, it has just one *r*. *"Door-to-door salesmen no longer **harass** me," Hannibal said.* See also page 175.

IMPOSTOR. The preferred spelling ends in *tor*, not *ter*. *Ferdinand was a great **impostor**.*

INDISPENSABLE. It ends in *able*, not *ible*. *"Nick, darling, you're **indispensable**," said Nora.* If you confuse your *able*s with your *ible*s, see the next page.

INOCULATE. One *n* is plenty. *He escaped before Dr. Moreau could **inoculate** him.*

INTERCEDE. Another "seedy" ending (see page 164). *Apple decided to **intercede** in the software piracy case.*

END GAMES

Not knowing your *able*s from your *ible*s is contemptible, but the problem is avoidable. The easiest way to get the *able*s and the *ible*s right is to look them up. But if your dictionary isn't available, go with *able*, since the *able*s far outnumber the *ible*s. Here's a sensible sampling.

- **able:** *accountable, advisable, agreeable, allowable, believable, bendable, blamable, breakable, buildable, changeable, commendable, correctable, definable, delectable, desirable, detectable, doable, electable, enforceable, expandable, fixable, forgivable, indispensable, inimitable, irreparable, irritable, movable, noticeable, objectionable, passable, perishable, portable, preferable, preventable, reliable, retractable, salable, transferable, variable, venerable, washable*

- **ible:** *accessible, admissible, audible, collapsible, combustible, compatible, contemptible, convertible, credible, deductible, defensible, destructible, digestible, discernible, divisible, edible, eligible, fallible, flexible, gullible, horrible, incorrigible, invincible, irresistible, legible, negligible, ostensible, perceptible, permissible, plausible, possible, reprehensible, responsible, reversible, sensible, suggestible, susceptible, terrible, visible*

- **ible** or **able:** *collectible, collectable*

IRRESISTIBLE. It ends in *ible*, not *able*. "*Nora, darling, you're* **irresistible**," *said Nick*. For more, see the previous page.

JUDGMENT. The preferred American spelling has no *e* right after the *g*. (The same goes for *acknowledgment*, but not *knowledgeable*.) "*I never make snap* **judgments**," *said Justice Holmes*.

KNOWLEDGE. Knowledgeable people know there's a *d*. "**Knowledge** *and wisdom are not the same*," *said Professor Morgenbesser*.

LIAISON. Don't leave out the second *i*. *Bonnie and Clyde had a dangerous* **liaison**. See also page 179.

LIGHTNING. Flash! There's no *e* in *lightning*, the kind that leaves us thunderstruck. *A bolt of* **lightning** *split the sky*. The word with an *e* (*lightening*) comes from *lighten*. *She's started* **lightening** *her hair*.

LIQUEFY. Notice the *e*. *Dorothy didn't realize the Wicked Witch would* **liquefy** *when drenched with water*.

MARSHAL. One *l* is enough for both the noun and the verb. **Marshal** *Dillon told Chester to* **marshal** *a posse*. The same is true for *marshaled* and *marshaling*. When the military takes charge, that's *martial* law.

MARVELOUS. One *l*. (The British spell it with two, but never mind.) "*Gertrude, that's a* **marvelous** *haircut!*" *said Alice*.

MEMENTO. It's not spelled—or pronounced—"momento." Think of the *mem* in *memory*. *The embroidered pillow was a* **memento** *of Niagara Falls*.

MILLENNIUM. Be generous with the *l*'s and *n*'s. *The new* **millennium** *began with a whimper, not a bang*.

MINUSCULE. It's not spelled "miniscule." Think of *minus* as the root, not *mini*. *Barbie's accessories are **minuscule.***

MINUTIAE. Note the tangle of vowels at the end. *Marcel loved writing about **minutiae.*** The word means "trivia" or "small details," and it's pronounced mi-NOO-shee-ee. (The singular, *minutia*, is pronounced mi-NOO-shee-uh.)

MISCHIEVOUS. This is often misspelled (and mispronounced) with an extra *i*. *Pugsley isn't a bad boy, just **mischievous.*** See also page 180.

NIECE. Here's a good reminder of the "*i* before *e*" rule. *"Depend upon it," Jane wrote to her **niece** Fanny, "the right man will come at last."*

NOTICEABLE. Keep the *e* in *notice* when you add the *able* ending. *Greta always worried that her big feet were too **noticeable.*** But drop the *e* with an *ing* ending. *Was everybody **noticing?*** See also the box on page 159.

OCCASION. People often use one too many *s*'s. *On **occasion**, Emma dabbled in matchmaking.*

OCCUR. Two *c*'s but only one *r*. *It didn't **occur** to Santiago to let the marlin go.* But we gain an *r* in *occurrence, occurred,* and *occurring.*

ORIENT. The extra syllable in *orientate* is ugly and unnecessary, though not a federal offense. *Orient* is sufficient. *Indiana had to **orient** himself without a compass.*

PANICKY. *Nicole gets **panicky** before a screen test.* Do you panic around "icky" words? Then see page 163.

PARALLEL. The only double letters are the twin *l*'s inside. *Annie's brother, Duane, lives in a **parallel** universe. His driving is **unparalleled.***

PASTIME. No double letters here. *Badminton is not Rafael's favorite* **pastime**.

PHILIPPINES. The only double letters are the *p*'s in the middle. *The crème de la crème of Imelda's footwear collection is in the* **Philippines**. The adjective *Filipino* comes from Spanish. *Many of her shoes are in a* **Filipino** *museum*.

PLAYWRIGHT. There's no "write" (a *wright* builds or repairs something). *"A wheelwright or a shipwright makes more money than a* **playwright**," *Anne told William*.

PNEUMONIA. The *p* is silent. *Calamity Jane's* **pneumonia** *was fatal*.

PORTUGUESE. Don't forget the second *u*. *Robert's pet name for Elizabeth was "my little* **Portuguese**."

PRAIRIE. It has two *i*'s. *Winter on the* **prairie** *was no picnic for the Ingalls family*.

PRECEDE. The "cede" is what throws people off (see page 164). *Did the chicken* **precede** *the egg, or vice versa?*

PRETENSIONS. Like *tension*, it has *sion*, not *tion*. *Wishbone is a little dog with big* **pretensions**.

PREVENTIVE. The extra syllable in *preventative* isn't wrong, but it's unnecessary. Choose *preventive* and fight inflation. *Sunscreen is a* **preventive** *measure*.

PRIVILEGE. Tip: Two *i*'s, then two *e*'s. *"It is my* **privilege** *to serve you, sir," said Jeeves*.

PROCEED. This is one of the few words ending in "ceed" (see page 164). *"You may* **proceed**, *Counselor," said Judge Burke*.

PROTESTER. It ends with *ter*, not *tor* (the word *tester* is built in). *The* **protesters** *were testing the mayor's patience*.

ICKY ISSUES

If you like garlic, then you like your food garlicky. But have you ever wondered why there's a *k* in *garlicky* when there isn't one in *garlic*? Or why there's a *k* in *politicking* when there isn't one in *politics*? Wonder no more!

If a word ends in a hard-sounding *c*, we often stick in a *k* to keep the sound "hard" when we add an ending (like *ed*, *er*, *ing*, or *y*). If we didn't, the *c* might go "soft" on us. For example, we say a baby with *colic* is *colicky*. If we spelled it "colicy," without the *k*, the word would rhyme with *policy*. Here's how to finish off some "icky" words.

COLIC: *colicky*
FROLIC: *frolicked, frolicker, frolicking*
GARLIC: *garlicky*
MIMIC: *mimicked, mimicking*
PANIC: *panicked, panicking, panicky*
PICNIC: *picnicked, picnicker, picnicking*
POLITICS: *politicker, politicking*
TRAFFIC: *trafficked, trafficker, trafficking*

PUBLICLY. Not "publically." *Violetta was **publicly** humiliated by her wardrobe malfunction.*

PURSUE. The only *e* is at the end. *She hoped to **pursue** an operatic career.*

QUESTIONNAIRE. Double up on the *n*'s. *The dating service asked Mr. Gallup to fill out a **questionnaire**.*

RAREFIED. Use only one *i* (not "rarified"). If in doubt, remember that it starts with its relative, *rare*. *McCoy feared that the* **rarefied** *air in the* Enterprise *was enervating the crew.* If you don't know what *enervating* means, see page 93.

RECEDE. Three *e*'s, and none of them together. *Marc expects hemlines to* **recede** *next year.* For hints about spelling "seedy"-sounding words, see below.

RECOMMEND. Only one *c*. *"I can't* **recommend** *the fruit salad," said Gustav.*

REGARDLESS. If you think this word should start with an *i*, go sit in the corner. **Regardless** *of what you may have heard, "irregardless" is irredeemable.* (The stem word, by the way, is the noun *regard*, which is singular in office jargon like *in* **regard** *to* and *with* **regard** *to*. It's plural, though, in the *Regards* at the end of a letter or in a sentence like *Give my* **regards** *to Broadway!*)

"SEEDY" ENDINGS

Words that end with a "seed" sound are notoriously hard to spell. It helps to keep in mind that all but four end with *cede*. Three end with *ceed*, and only one ends with *sede*.

- **cede:** *accede, antecede, cede, concede, intercede, precede, recede, secede* (and others)
- **ceed:** *exceed, proceed, succeed*
- **sede:** *supersede*

REMINISCE. The *sce* at the end should linger in your memory. *Marcel loved to **reminisce** about the past.*

RENAISSANCE. There's no need to double that first *n*. *We're seeing a **renaissance** in vinyl records.* Capitalize the word if you're referring, even metaphorically, to the historical period. *Leo is a **Renaissance** man.*

RESTAURATEUR. This comes from a root meaning "restore," and the preferred spelling has no *n*. The *restaurateur* (the person who restores you) runs the *restaurant* (where you go to get restored). Dictionaries these days accept "restauranteur" as a lesser variant, but why use a lesser variant? *When Sanjeev became a **restaurateur**, he called his restaurant Curry in a Hurry.*

RÉSUMÉ. The preferred spelling for the noun (it means a "curriculum vitae") has accent marks. *"Bud, have you finished that **résumé** yet?" said Father.* But the verb *resume*, meaning "continue," has none. *"Not yet," said Bud, "but I'll **resume** after the ball game is over."*

RHYTHM. This word gave me fits until a teacher taught me a memory trick: Rhythm Helps Your Two Hips Move. The first letters spell *rhythm*. Hey, whatever works! *"I got **rhythm**," said Ira. "Who could ask for anything more?"*

SACRILEGIOUS. We're tempted to spell it like *religious*, but *sacrilege* is the root. *"Adding salt to my veal medallions is **sacrilegious**," said Daniel.*

SCISSORS. Four *s*'s—two in the middle and one at each end. *"Now, where did I put the **scissors**?" said Edward.*

SEIZE. Here's an exception to the "*i* before *e*" rule. *Tommy never managed to **seize** the day.*

SEPARATE. Spell it with *par*, not *per*. *Major Pollock and Sibyl sat at **separate** tables.*

SERGEANT. The first syllable sounds like "sar," but it isn't spelled that way. *"Carry on, **Sergeant**," said Inspector Craddock.*

SHERBET. This is the right spelling. Most dictionaries consider "sherbert" an error. *Miss Marple detected traces of arsenic in the **sherbet**.* See also page 181.

SIEGE. Here's the "*i* before *e*" rule at work. *Paolo and Francesca were under **siege** by the paparazzi.*

SKILLFUL. Two *l*'s in the middle, one at the end. *Tex was **skillful** with a lasso.* For more about words containing *ful* and *full*, see page 168.

SPRIGHTLY. The word meaning "energetic" has a *gh*; it's not "spritely": *Ed and Trixie were feeling **sprightly**.* Someone who's like a sprite, a little imaginary creature resembling a pixie or an elf, is *spritelike. Ed looked **spritelike** in his leprechaun costume.*

STRAITJACKET/STRAITLACED. There's no *gh* in either—not "straightjacket" or "straightlaced." ***Straitlaced** people who go over the edge may find themselves in **straitjackets**.* The word *strait* is from the Latin *strictus*, which means "constricted" or "tight." *Straight*, from an Anglo-Saxon word for "stretch," means "uncurved." The word you run across in geography, by the way, is *strait*, referring to a tight waterway: the *Strait* of Gibraltar, the Bering *Strait*.

SUBTLY. We drop the *e* in *subtle* when we add *ly. Anna's motto is "Apply makeup **subtly** and carry a big purse."*

SUPPOSED. The word that means "intended," "required," "permitted," or "expected" has a *d* at the end, even if you don't hear it. *Where in heaven's name are we **supposed** to park?*

SURVEILLANCE. This time, *e* before *i*. *Smiley was pretty sure he was under **surveillance**.* (Hint: This word wears a *veil*.)

SUSCEPTIBLE. Here's one of the *ible*s (and don't forget the *c*). *Howard felt he was **susceptible** to colds.* See page 159.

TEMPERAMENT. Remember the second *e*, even if you don't pronounce it. *Mr. Quilp had a terrible **temperament**.*

THRESHOLD. It can sound as though it has two *h*'s in the middle ("thresh-hold"), but it's not spelled that way. *Distracted by his earworm, Wolfgang tripped over the **threshold**.*

TOWARD. Americans commonly spell it without a final *s*; the British prefer "towards." Similarly, in American English, the usual practice is not to add a final *s* to *backward, downward, forward, onward, upward,* and so on. *George was last seen heading **toward** the buffet.*

UKULELE. Two *u*'s. *Arthur played "For Me and My Gal" on the **ukulele**.*

UNNECESSARY. Double *n*'s and *s*'s. *"Baldness is in," said Vin's girlfriend. "A toupee is **unnecessary**."*

UNWIELDY. This does not end in *ly*. *Biff's Hummer was **unwieldy** in the parking lot.*

WEIRD. It's spelled *ei*, not *ie*. *"You're looking particularly **weird** this evening, Morticia, my love," said Gomez.*

WHOLLY. The root word, *whole*, loses an *e* but gains a second *l*. *Daryl ordered the **wholly** vegetarian refried beans.*

WITHHOLD. Use both *h*'s. *"You can **withhold** the side of hot chile peppers," Daryl told the waitress.*

YIELD. It rhymes with *shield* and is spelled like it too. *"What's the **yield** on a T-bill?" said Mr. Moneybags.*

A FULL HOUSE

You can always tell skillful spellers by the way they handle full-bodied words—the kind that contain *ful* or *full*. One *l* or two? Here's the full story.

- When the tricky part comes at the end of the word, there's just one *l*.

  ful: *armful, awful, beautiful, boastful, bountiful, careful, colorful, cupful, doleful, doubtful, dreadful, graceful, handful, harmful, helpful, hopeful, houseful, lawful, meaningful, mindful, mournful, mouthful, painful, peaceful, playful, powerful, rightful, shameful, sinful, skillful, spiteful, spoonful, stressful, tearful, teaspoonful, thoughtful, useful, wakeful, watchful, wonderful,* and many more. If you add *ly*, you end up with double *l*'s: *awfully, carefully, usefully, wonderfully,* etc. For advice about making the nouns above plural, see pages 23–24.

- When the tricky part comes at the beginning, it can go either way, *full* or *ful*.

  ful: *fulcrum, fulfill, fulminate, fulsome*

  full: *fullback, fullness.* Some phrases beginning with *full* are hyphenated: *full-blooded, full-blown, full-bodied, full-bore, full-fledged, full-scale, full-service, full-size, full-time,* and so on. Others are two separate words, like *full circle* and *full house.*

CHAPTER 7

SO TO SPEAK

TALKING POINTS ON PRONUNCIATION

Does it really matter if I say tuh-MAY-toh and you say tuh-MAH-toh? As a matter of fact, it doesn't. They're both OK. But no dictionary that I know of will tell you it's standard English to say LIE-berry for *library*, or AXED for *asked*. And if you don't care what you sound like, let's call the whole thing off.

Mispronouncing a word—or worse, mistakenly "correcting" someone else—may not be a hanging offense (for how to pronounce *offense*, see later in this chapter), but a pronunciation error can be an embarrassing faux pas (not to be pronounced FOX PAWS).

Your dictionary can tell you how a word is pronounced, and very often there are more correct ways than one. The first pronunciation given won't necessarily be more correct than those that follow, but it may be more common. Different publishers have different ways of doing things, though. The pronunciations I recommend are those that are more widely accepted.

So whichever dictionary you choose, read the user manual in the front to see how yours handles multiple or variant pronunciations. There's usually a pronunciation key at the bottom of each right-hand page, explaining the symbols for the various sounds. Many online dictionaries include audio icons that you can click to hear the words spoken. Of course, you're seldom at Dictionary.com while having a conversation, so become familiar with hard-to-pronounce words before you need them. In the pronunciation advice below, accented syllables appear in capitals.

Now, what do you say we get started?

WOULD YOU MIND REPEATING THAT?

ACCEPTABLE. The first part of the word ends with an *x* sound (as in AXE), not an *s* sound. *Bridget learned that cell-phone conversations were not **acceptable** in church.* For more on *s* and *x* sounds, see the box on page 174.

ACCESSORIES. Here, too, the first syllable ends with an *x* sound, not an *s* sound. *Carmen's **accessories** were excessive: a pineapple headdress and platform sandals.* There's more about *s* and *x* sounds in the box on page 174.

ADULT. This word comes in two varieties, and both are correct: a-DULT and AD-ult. *When he's not fighting crime, Bruce dresses like a normal **adult**.*

ADVOCATE. The last syllable is different in the verb and the noun. The verb is AD-vuh-kate and the noun is AD-vuh-kut. *"I don't **advocate** becoming an **advocate**," said Denny.*

AFFLUENT. Stress the first part: AFF-loo-ent. *Little Cornelius wasn't born into an **affluent** family.*

AGED. This has one syllable, except when it's an adjective meaning "elderly." Here, only the first *aged* has two syllables: *My **aged** grandmother, who **aged** gracefully, took a liking to **aged** cheese when she was a child **aged** ten.*

ALLY. The noun is accented on the first syllable (AL-eye) and the verb on the second (a-LYE). *Vinnie learned the hard way that an **ally** needs to **ally** himself with his friends.*

ALMOND. This can be pronounced with or without the *l* sound. *Not even Julia could make marzipan without **almonds**.*

ALUMNAE. It ends with NEE. *Helena and her friend Pokey were **alumnae** of Vassar.* See also page 33.

APPLICABLE. Stress either the first syllable or the second. *Sean's policy is to flout all **applicable** rules and regulations.*

ARCTIC. You can say this the traditional way and pronounce both *c*'s (ARK-tik), or ignore the one in the middle (AR-tik). *The **Arctic** trip was interesting, but there weren't many gift shops.* (There's no wiggle room in the spelling, though; see page 153.)

ARGENTINE. The last syllable of both the noun and the adjective can be either TEEN or TYNE. *Jorge, a literary **Argentine**, did much to spread **Argentine** culture.*

ASKED. The standard pronunciation is ASKT (not AST or AXED). *Miss Bunting never married, largely because she wasn't **asked**.*

ATE. The British can say ET if they like, but we aren't allowed. Pronounce it EIGHT. *The tourists **ate** their steak-and-kidney pie under duress.*

ATHLETE. Use two syllables, and only two: ATH-leet. *Babe was an **athlete's athlete**.*

BANAL. You'd have to work pretty hard to mess this up, since there are three acceptable pronunciations. One rhymes with *canal,* one with *anal,* and one with *an awl. To Hannah, evil was **banal**.*

BASIL. There are two ways to say it: BAY-zel (with a long *a*) or BAZZ-el (with a short *a,* as in *jazz*). *"Pass me the **basil,** Basil," said Mrs. Fawlty.*

CACHET. See the box on page 182.

CARAMEL. It can be either three syllables or two, and the first can be CARE or CAR. *"This color isn't butterscotch,"* insisted Narciso, *"it's **caramel!**"*

CEMENT. The second syllable gets the stress: si-MENT. *Dennis left a handprint in Mr. Wilson's **cement**.*

COMPARABLE. Stress the first syllable: COM-per-uh-bul (it rhymes with *conquerable*). *Des Moines and Barcelona are **comparable** in latitude.*

COMPTROLLER. This word started out as *controller* (con-TRO-ler), and that's the way I say it. The other acceptable pronunciations are comp-TRO-ler and COMP-tro-ler. *The **Comptroller** of the Currency controls the national banking system.* See also pages 109–110.

COUPON. Say either KOO-pon or KYOO-pon. *Isabella, a personal trainer, threw away a **coupon** for a free Big Mac.*

CUMIN. There are three ways to pronounce this: KYOO-min or KOO-min or KUM-in. *Bob's chili rub could use more **cumin**.*

DEFENSE. The usual pronunciation is dih-FENSE, but in sports terminology it's often DEE-fense. *In their **defense**, it must be said that the rowdy fans were justifiably upset at the Celtics' lackluster **defense**.* See also OFFENSE, page 180.

DETRITUS. Stress the middle syllable (de-TRY-tus). *Hacker's salamander buried itself in the **detritus** at the bottom of the pond.*

ECCENTRIC. It begins with EX, not ESS. *The octopus often displays **eccentric** behavior.* There's more on *s* and *x* sounds in the box on the next page.

ECSTATIC. It starts with EX, not ESS. *Even when excited, Mr. Casaubon was never **ecstatic**.* See also ECSTASY, page 157. And for more on *s* and *x* sounds, see the next page.

ENDIVE. You may say either EN-dive or the more French-sounding on-DEEV. *Julia served her guests caramelized **endive** with poached lobster.*

ERR. The usual pronunciation is UR, but the upstart AIR, long considered a mistake, is now acceptable too. *To **err** is human; to forgive, divine.*

ESCAPE. There's no *x* in *escape*. *John helped Lorna **escape** from the Doone Valley.* See the box on the next page.

ESPRESSO. No, there is no *x*. The standard pronunciation is es-PRESS-o. *Espresso, according to Dr. Glossop, has*

HISSY FITS

People often put an *s* sound where an *x* sound belongs. They get all hissy. They say "asseptable" for *acceptable*, "assessories" for *accessories*, "essentric" for *eccentric*, "estatic" for *ecstatic*, and "estraordinary" for *extraordinary*. This is definitely unacceptable!

Sometimes speakers do the reverse, putting an *x* sound where it doesn't belong. They say "excape" for *escape*, "expecially" for *especially*, "excetera" for *et cetera*, and "expresso" for *espresso*. This gives me fits.

three times the caffeine of regular coffee. For more, see the box above.

ETC. Use three syllables (et-CET-ra) or four (et-CET-er-a), but there's no *k* or *x* sound. *Skink's diet included squirrels, snakes, possums, etc.* See also page 146 and the box above.

EXQUISITE. Stress either the first syllable or the second. *"The Camembert is exquisite,"* said Remy.

FAUX PAS. See page 183.

FLACCID. This is correctly pronounced either FLAK-sid or FLASS-id. *Buzz's muscles were flaccid after the Apollo 11 mission.*

FORTE. See page 183.

GROCERY. There are several choices on the shelves. Say it with or without a "sh" in the middle, and use three syllables or two. *Saul and Eli opened grocery stores in Manhattan.*

HARASS. Accent whichever syllable you like, but the preference on this side of the Atlantic is to stress the second. *"Wally, stop **harassing** your brother," said Ward.* See also page 158.

HEIGHT. It's pronounced HITE, though many people mistakenly end it with a "th" sound (perhaps confusing it with *length*). *Henri would go to great lengths to increase his **height**.*

HEINOUS. No "hee." The right pronunciation is HAY-nus. (A tip for remembering the long *a*: *heinous* comes from an Old French word for *hate*.) *Truman wrote a bestseller about a **heinous** crime.*

HERB. In US English, the *h* is silent: ERB. The same is true with *herbal*. But Americans pronounce the *h* in *herbaceous*, *herbicide*, and *herbivore*. *The ratatouille contained an **herb** that Anton couldn't identify.*

HOMAGE. See page 183.

HOMOGENEOUS. It's pronounced ho-muh-JEE-nee-us or ho-muh-JEEN-yus, and means "uniform" or "similar in nature." The mispronunciation huh-MODJ-uh-nus was no doubt influenced by the word *homogenized* or the lesser-known scientific term *homogenous*. *The architecture in Nantucket is **homogeneous**.*

HYPERBOLE. It is not pronounced like the name of a sporting event, the Hyper Bowl; it's high-PER-buh-lee. It means "exaggeration" or "overstatement." *Buster's claim that his dog could read was **hyperbole**.*

> **NOTE:** If you've read about *hyper* and *hypo* on page 117, you may wonder whether there's such a word as *hypobole*. As a matter of fact, there is; it means something like "suggestion" and is pronounced high-PAH-buh-lee. But nobody uses it.

HYPNOTIZE. No *m* whatsoever! It's HIP-nuh-tize. *"Mimi, you **hypnotize** me," said Rodolfo.* In the adjective, *hypnotic*, the middle syllable is stressed: hip-NOT-ik.

INFLUENCE. Stress the first syllable, not the second. *Did Elvis have much of an **influence** on Buddy?*

INGENIOUS/INGENUOUS. See page 119.

INTERESTING. This can be pronounced with three syllables or four, but don't forget the first *t* (not "inneresting"). *"This is a most **interesting** cigar," said Sigmund.*

IRAN, IRAQ. The first can be pronounced ih-RON, ih-RAN, or eye-RAN. The second is usually either ih-RACK or ih-ROCK. *Ancient Persia and Mesopotamia are now **Iran** and **Iraq**.*

JAGUAR. There are two ways to say the name of the cat (and the car): JAG-wahr and JAG-yoo-ahr. *"My **Jaguar** is in the shop," Darrel said as he helped his date into the pickup truck.*

WHY A DUCK?

When I was about twelve, I learned that what I heard as "duck tape" was actually "duct tape." My ears had been playing tricks on me, and I'd misunderstood what I was hearing. Here are some more mangled phrases that only resemble the real thing. Meanwhile, don't step on any quacks in the sidewalk.

BAITED BREATH. Not quite. A fishing line is *baited*, but breath is *bated* (held in). *Weegee listened to the police radio with* **bated breath**.

BLESSING IN THE SKIES. It's *disguise*, not *the skies*. *The gangland rubout on the Lower East Side was a* **blessing in disguise** *for Weegee*.

CARD SHARK. Not *shark* but *sharp*, and it's spelled as one word, *cardsharp*. *The victim, a notorious* **cardsharp**, *was taken to the morgue*.

DEEP-SEEDED. Don't let your ears fool you. It's *deep-seated*. *Weegee had a* **deep-seated** *loyalty to truth in journalism*.

DOGGY-DOG WORLD. It may be, but only at the dog park. *Life on the streets was a* **dog-eat-dog world**.

ESCAPE GOAT. Well, goats are escape artists, but that's not the point. Make it one word, *scapegoat*. *The cops pinned the killing on a small-time hoodlum, but Weegee thought he was a* **scapegoat**.

FOR ALL INTENSIVE PURPOSES. Nope, it's *intents and purposes*. **For all intents and purposes**, *his beat was the Naked City.*

FREE REIGN. The word is *rein*, and it comes from riding, not royalty. *The police gave Weegee* **free rein** *at the crime scene.*

HEART-RENDERING. Make that *rending*, not *rendering*, and it's one solid word. *When he discovered there was no film in his Speed Graphic, he uttered a* **heartrending** *groan.*

LAST-STITCH EFFORT. Try *ditch*, not *stitch*. *In a* **last-ditch effort**, *he managed to load the camera before the paddy wagon drove off.*

PASS MUSTARD. Only at the table. To *pass muster* is to pass inspection or meet a standard. *Only one of his shots would* **pass muster** *with the photo editor.*

RUN THE GAMBIT. No, not *gambit*. It's *gamut*, a word derived from an Italian term for the notes on a scale. *His subjects* **ran the gamut** *from Hell's Kitchen junkies to Park Avenue socialites.*

SHOE-IN. That's *shoo*, not *shoe*. *Weegee was a* **shoo-in** *for Photographer of the Year.*

STATUE OF LIMITATIONS. The legal term is *statute*, not *statue*. *There's no* **statute of limitations** *on murder.*

TAKE FOR GRANITE. Your ear may hear *granite*, but it's *granted*. *"Luck is something I never* **take for granted**," *Weegee said.*

TOW THE LINE. Close, but no cigar. *Toe the line*, like *come up to the mark*, originally referred to the starting line in athletics. *Weegee made his darkroom assistant* **toe the line**.

TRITE AND TRUE. *Trite* isn't right—it's *tried*. *His boxy old Speed Graphic was* **tried and true**.

LACKADAISICAL. Don't be lax about this pronunciation. The first two syllables are LAK-uh, not LAX-uh. *It's typical of Moose to be* **lackadaisical** *about his studies.*

LIAISON. The usual pronunciations emphasize either the first or the second syllable: lee-AY-zun or LEE-eh-zon. *This* **liaison** *is getting dangerous, thought Marie.* See also page 160.

NOTE: In case you're wondering, *liaise* is a real word (pronounced lee-AYZE). It means "to form a liaison" and was coined during World War I. *Captain Rickenbacker planned to* **liaise** *with the other squadron commanders.*

LIBRARY. There's no "berry" in *library*. Pronounce that middle *r*! *Jeff's* **library** *is in his Kindle.*

LONG-LIVED. How do you pronounce the *i*—like the one in "life," or the one in "to live"? Either way, you're right. *The* **long-lived** *Himalayan hermit credits his longevity to raw yak meat.*

MEMENTO. See page 160.

MINUTIAE. See page 161.

MISCHIEVOUS. It has only three syllables: MIS-chuh-vus. No, it doesn't rhyme with *devious*. *Gollum always had a* **mischievous** *look in his eye.* See also page 161.

NICHE. See pages 183–184.

NUCLEAR. Pronounce it NOO-klee-ur (not NOO-kya-lur). *Some say the energy of the future is likelier to be* **nuclear**.

OFFENSE. The second syllable usually gets the accent (uh-FENSE), except in sports and military terminology (OFF-ense). *Johnny took* **offense** *when the coach criticized his* **offense**. See also DEFENSE, page 173.

OFTEN. You can say this with or without the *t* sound, but the more common pronunciation is OFF-en. *No matter how far apart they are, Kit* **often** *thinks of Nell.*

PATENT. The glossy leather on your shoes, or the document that protects your invention, is pronounced PAT-ent. But the adjective that means "apparent" or "obvious" can be pronounced either PAT-ent or PAY-tent. *"I own the original* **patent** *for making* **patent** *leather," Fletcher said in a* **patent** *lie.*

PENALIZE. The first syllable can be PEN (as in *penalty*) or PEEN (as in *penal*). *"I'm going to* **penalize** *you fifty dollars for sleeping on the job," said Mr. Burns.*

PREFERABLE. Whether you say it as three syllables or four, stress the first one: PREF-ruh-bul or PREF-er-uh-bul. *Those are the* **preferable** *pronunciations.*

PRONUNCIATION. There's a "nun," not a "noun," lurking inside. *"**Pronunciation** rhymes with renunciation," said Sister Mary Ignatius.*

PROPHECY/PROPHESY. See pages 124–125.

QUIXOTIC. The *x* is pronounced here, though it sounds like an *h* in the name it comes from, Don Quixote. *A **quixotic** hero dreams the impossible dream.*

REALTOR. Use two syllables (REEL-ter) or three (REE-ul-ter), but there's no "luh" sound in the middle. And though it's often seen with a small initial *r*, it's supposed to be capitalized as a registered service mark owned by the National Association of Realtors. *Bruce thought the cave was worth at least five million, but his **Realtor** offered a reality check.*

SCHISM. Fifty years ago, the only correct pronunciation was SIZZ-em. But a mispronunciation, SKIZZ-em, became so common that it's now standard English and preferred by most people. *The Brownings' elopement created a **schism** in Elizabeth's family.*

SHERBET. One *r* sound is enough. See page 166.

STRIPED. Choose one syllable (ending with a *t* sound) or two (STRY-ped). *Mr. Collins looked dashing in his **striped** smoking jacket.*

TEMPLATE. Don't be misled by the "plate" spelling. The correct pronunciation is TEM-plit. *Hackers altered the **template** of the emperor's blog.*

TUESDAY. Most Americans say TOOZ-day, though some say TYOOZ-day. Both pronunciations are fine. *"I will gladly pay you **Tuesday** for a hamburger today," Wimpy said.*

VEGAN. The more common pronunciation is VEE-gun, though VEDJ-un is also acceptable. *A **vegan** avoids all animal products, sometimes even leather.*

WASH. Don't let an *r* sound slip in. *"I'm not worried about the money-laundering charge," said Fat Tony. "It will all come out in the **wash**."*

MAY WE? MAIS OUI!

There's no need to stumble over words that come from foreign languages. After all, every word is "foreign" until you get used to it. So here are a few pronunciations you should get used to. Don't let the words intimidate you. They may have been foreign terms at one time, but today they're bona fide (see pronunciation below) members of the English family. While many have kept their foreign flavor, others have adopted distinctly English pronunciations.

BONA FIDE. This means "genuine" or "sincere" (it's Latin for "in good faith"). There are several ways to say it, but the most common is BONE-uh-fied. *Veronica owns a **bona fide** pebble from Graceland.*

CACHET. It means "distinction" or "prestige," and it's pronounced ka-SHAY. *Loulou's beret has a certain **cachet**.* Don't mix this up with another word from French, *cache*, which sounds like "cash" and means something like "stash." *She has a whole **cache** of funky hats.*

CHAISE LONGUE. The French means "long chair," and the standard English pronunciation is shays-LONG. (The folksy "chase lounge" hasn't yet arrived.) *It was a mistake to eat pizza on the **chaise longue**.*

CONCIERGE. This word doesn't end in thin "air" (not: con-see-AIR). Remember the consonant sound at the end: con-SYAIRZH. *The **concierge** left a dozen roses in Rosie's room.*

FAUX PAS. We pronounce this phrase (from the French for "misstep") as foh-PAH. *The Reverend Spooner made an embarrassing **faux pas**.* The plural is spelled the same but pronounced foh-PAZ. *Then he made three more **faux pas** in succession.*

FORTE. This means "strong point," and it can be pronounced as one syllable or two: FORT or FOR-tay. *Bertie is a whiz at checkers, but backgammon is not his **forte**.*

HOMAGE. This word entered English in the 1200s, so there's no reason to say it as if it were French. But it's acceptable to drop the *h* sound if you like: HOM-idj or OM-idj. (The Frenchified oh-MAHZH is unnecessary.) *Jerry Lee's performance was a **homage** to Moon Mullican.* Note that the article you use depends on the pronunciation you prefer: say "*a* HOM-idj" or "*an* OM-idj."

LINGERIE. The most common English pronunciation is lon-zhuh-RAY, but American dictionaries also accept LON-zhuh-ree and lan-zhuh-REE. Or you could forget it and say "undies." *As the elevator rose, a disembodied voice announced, "Fourth floor: shoes, accessories, **lingerie**."*

NICHE. The traditional pronunciation is NITCH. But the newer, French-sounding NEESH has also become acceptable in recent years. *"I found my **niche** in the nick of time,"* said Grandma Moses.

PRIX FIXE. You don't pronounce the first *x* (it's PREE FEEKS). *The **prix fixe** dinner at Chez Panisse included a pork terrine and steamed wild salmon.*

SUI GENERIS. This means "one of a kind" and it's from Latin, so don't pronounce it as if it were French. In English, we say SOO-ee (or SOO-eye) JEN-er-is. *Melinda is **sui generis**, and so generous too.*

VICHYSSOISE. There's a *z* sound at the end: vee-shee-SWAHZ (not SWAH). *"It's kale and potato soup,"* Alice said, *"not **vichyssoise**!"*

VOILÀ. This French attention-getter still has its Parisian flavor: vwa-LAH! *Harry sawed the woman in half and then—**voilà**—put her back together again.*

CHAPTER 8

COMMA SUTRA

THE JOY OF PUNCTUATION

An editor I knew at *The New York Times* once received a gift from a writer friend. It was the tip of a lead pencil, broken off and wrapped up and presented along with a card that said, "A gross of commas, to be used liberally throughout the year as needed." Now, that writer understood the gift of punctuation! When you talk, your voice, with its pauses, stresses, rises, and falls, shows how you intend your words to fit together. When you write, punctuation marks are the travel aids and road signs (stop, go, yield, slow, detour) that guide the reader, and you wouldn't be understood without them.

If you don't believe me, try making sense out of this pile of words:

*Who do you think I saw the other day the Dalai Lama said
my aunt Minnie.*

There are at least two possibilities:

"Who do you think I saw the other day?" the Dalai Lama
    said. "My aunt Minnie."
"Who do you think I saw the other day? The Dalai Lama!"
    said my aunt Minnie.

(I know, I know. I've taken liberties with *who* and *whom*. You can, too, in conversation and informal writing. See the box on page 10.)

Punctuation isn't some subtle, arcane concept that's hard to manage and that probably won't make much of a difference one way or another. It's not subtle, it's not difficult, and it can make all the difference in the world.

THE LIVING END: THE PERIOD (.)

The period is the stop sign at the end of a sentence. When you reach the period, it's all over. Whatever thought you were trying to convey has been delivered. A straightforward sentence that states rather than asks or exclaims something starts with a capital letter and ends with a period.

But what if there's a dot there already, as when a sentence ends with an ellipsis (. . .) or an abbreviation that has a final period (like *St.* or *p.m.*)? And what if a sentence has a smaller sentence within it? Here's what you do:

- If a sentence ends with an abbreviation that has a final period, don't add another period. *Mrs. Hubback's nephew, whose only interest was community theater, stayed out until 4 a.m.* For more about abbreviations, see the box on the next page.

- If a sentence ends in an ellipsis (three dots that indicate an omission), put a period first to show that the sentence is over. *"You'd like to borrow fifty dollars?" said Mrs. Hubback. She reflected on the old saying, Neither a borrower nor a lender be. . . .*

  However, if you want to emphasize grammatical incompleteness or a deliberate trailing off, omit the period. End the sentence with a space, then the three dots. *"Well . . ."*

- If a sentence concludes with the title of a work that ends in a question mark or an exclamation point, don't add a final period. *Her nephew did the lighting for* Who's Afraid of Virginia Woolf? *Next, he hoped for a role in* Oklahoma!

- If a sentence has a smaller sentence within it (surrounded by dashes or parentheses), don't use a period to end the smaller, "inside" sentence. *When Mrs. Hubback made him an offer—"I could use some help around the shop"—he accepted.*

NOTE: This last point doesn't apply to question marks or exclamation points: *She criticized her nephew's manners ("Speak up! How are the customers supposed to hear you?") and his grooming ("Do you call that a beard?").*

UNCOMMONLY USEFUL: THE COMMA (,)

There's nothing much to punctuating a sentence, really, beyond a little comma sense. Get the commas right and the rest will fall into place.

Yeah, yeah, I hear you saying, What's a comma or two—or three? How can something so small, so innocuous, be important? Well, that attitude can get you tossed into grammatical purgatory. You don't believe it? Take a look:

Cora claimed Frank planned the murder.

Without commas, the finger of guilt points to Frank. But add a pair of commas, and Cora becomes the suspect:

Cora, claimed Frank, planned the murder.

Here's another pair of examples with completely different meanings:

Augie quit saying he was looking for another job.
Augie quit, saying he was looking for another job.

In the first sentence, Augie quit talking; in the second, he quit his job.

The lesson: Don't take commas for granted. They're like yield signs that help separate your ideas and prevent pileups. If you ignore one, you could be in for a bumpy ride.

Most problems with commas have to do with dividing a sentence into parts—larger parts like clauses (each with its own subject and verb), or smaller ones like items in a series. Commas are also used to interrupt a sentence and insert another thought.

Here's how to get out of some of the most common comma complications.

LONG DIVISION

- Use a comma to separate clauses (big chunks of a sentence, each with a subject and a verb) joined by *and* or *but*. *Tina hadn't left the city in months, and by Friday she was climbing the walls.* In general, if there's no *and* or *but* in between, use a semicolon instead. *Tina hadn't left the city in months; by Friday she was climbing the walls.*

NOTE: Even when there's no *and* or *but*, you can use a comma instead of a semicolon to separate closely related clauses in cases like this:

1. When the first clause is negative—it has a phrase like "not only" or "not just" or "not simply"—and the second is positive. *She wasn't just antsy, she was frantic. A vacation wasn't merely optional, it was crucial.*

2. When the clauses are simple and parallel. *Some friends suggested Cancún, others favored Puerto Vallarta.*

SHORT DIVISION

- Use commas to separate a series of things or actions. *She packed a toothbrush, a hair dryer, her swimsuit, and three pairs of shoes. But she didn't remember to pay her bills, shut off the lights, or water the plants.*
- Use commas to separate a series of adjectives (words that describe things) or adverbs (words that describe actions). *Tina's biggest suitcase had yellow, blue, and green stripes. She wondered whether she could easily, safely, or gracefully get it downstairs by herself.* For exceptions, see the box beginning on the next page.

NOTE: You can leave out the last comma, the one just before *and* or *or*, but my advice is to use it. The final comma in a series, sometimes called the "serial comma," can't do any harm, but its absence can sometimes create ambiguity. The classic example: *I'd like to thank my parents, Ayn Rand and God.*

HOLD THE COMMAS

You've probably noticed that some bunches of adjectives don't need commas to separate them: *a* **busy young** *woman* . . . **cute little black** *dress* . . . **shiny new alligator** *pumps* . . . **tall red brick** *building* . . . **three distinguished French** *diplomats* . . . **large yellow** *balloon* . . . **battered old brown leather** *briefcase.*

Reading aloud, we don't feel a need to pause between those adjectives. And in writing, we wouldn't feel a need to use commas. Why is this? Why use commas in **yellow, blue, and green** *stripes* but not in **battered old brown leather** *briefcase*?

The reasons have to do with the kinds of descriptions you're combining and whether their order makes any difference. Here's all you need to know.

- If you wouldn't use *and* between the adjectives, don't use commas. *Steffie's favorite toy is a* **big old blue velvet** *rabbit.* (You wouldn't say **big and old and blue and velvet** *rabbit.*)
- If the adjectives always occur in a certain order, don't use commas. *Her favorite babysitters are* **two**

> **elderly Presbyterian** *ladies who live down the block.*
>
> (We wouldn't say **Presbyterian elderly two** *ladies.*)
>
> Certain kinds of adjectives have a special order when combined with dissimilar ones. These include, in this order, adjectives for number (*two*, *three*), size (*little*, *tall*, *large*, *big*), age (*young*, *new*, *old*, *elderly*), color (*black*, *red*, *yellow*, *blue*), and composition (*alligator*, *brick*, *leather*, *velvet*, *suede*). This explains why Elvis was protective of his "blue suede shoes," not his "suede blue shoes."

AS I WAS SAYING

- Use commas before and after the names of people being addressed. *"Good-bye, Mom. Dad, be good," she said, and hung up the phone.* You can skip the comma before the name if all that precedes it is *and* (*"And Mom, don't worry"*) or *but* (*"But Dad, you promised"*).

- Use commas before or after a quotation. *Tina said, "Let's see."* Or: *"Let's see," said Tina.* But don't use a comma after a quotation that ends with an exclamation point or a question mark. *"Have I forgotten anything?" she wondered. "Sunscreen!" she exclaimed.*

MAY I INTERRUPT?

- Use a comma after an introductory phrase if a pause is intended: *As usual, she checked to make sure the stove was turned off. Of course, it always was. You see, Tina was a bit compulsive.*
- Use commas around an aside—information that could just as well go in parentheses. *Her upstairs neighbor, the one with the tattoos, promised to feed her cat.*
- Use a comma when you want to emphasize *too* (meaning "also"). *Lydia offered to clean the litter box, too.* If you don't want the emphasis, leave out the comma. *The tattooed lady had a Siamese too.*
- Use commas if you want to set off a *which* clause that isn't essential. *The airport bus, which was usually on time, never came.* You need only the first comma if the clause comes at the end. *So she took a taxi, which cost her an arm and a leg.*

   But don't use commas around *that* clauses. *The bus that she had planned to take never came, so she grabbed the first taxi that she saw.* (Notice how those two *that*s could easily be dropped.)

   For more about commas with *which* and *that*, see pages 2–4.

SEMI-AVOIDANCE:
THE UNLOVED SEMICOLON (;)

The semicolon is one of the most useful but least used punctuation marks. For whatever reason, many of us avoid it. Maybe it intimidates us; it shouldn't. (See, wasn't that easy?) If a comma is a yield sign and a period is a stop sign, the semicolon is a flashing red—one of those lights you drive through after a brief pause. It's for times when you want something stronger than a comma but not quite so final as a period. Here's when to use it.

- Use a semicolon to separate clauses when there's no connecting *and* or *but* between them and each could be a sentence in itself. *Andy's toupee flew off his head; it sailed into the distance.*
- Use semicolons to separate items in a series when there's already a comma in one or more of the items. *Fred's favorite things were his robe, a yellow chenille number from Brooks Brothers; his slippers; his overstuffed chair, which had once been his father's; murder mysteries, especially those by John D. MacDonald; and single-malt Scotch.*

LET ME INTRODUCE YOU: THE COLON (:)

Think of the colon as a traffic cop that alerts you about road conditions up ahead. Use it to present something: a statement, a series, a quotation, a question, or instructions. But remember that a colon stops the flow of traffic. Use one only if you want to step on the brake. Keep these guidelines in mind.

- Use a colon instead of a comma, if you wish, to introduce a quotation. *I said to him: "Harry, please pick up a bottle of wine on your way over. But don't be obsessive about it."* Many people prefer to introduce a longer quotation with a colon instead of a comma.
- Use a colon to introduce a list, if what comes before the colon could be a small sentence in itself (it has both a subject and a verb). *Harry brought three wines: a Bordeaux, a Beaujolais, and a Burgundy.*
- Don't use a colon to separate a verb from the rest of the sentence, as this example does. *In Harry's shopping bag were: a Bordeaux, a Beaujolais, and a Burgundy.* If you don't need a colon, why use one? *In Harry's shopping bag were a Bordeaux, a Beaujolais, and a Burgundy.*

NOTE: If what comes after the colon is a complete sentence, you may start it with a capital or a lowercase letter. I use a capital when I want to be more emphatic: *My advice was this: Bring only one next time.* (This is a matter of taste, and opinions differ. Whatever your choice, be consistent.)

HUH? THE QUESTION MARK (?)

The question mark is the raised eyebrow at the end of a sentence. It's used with a question, of course (as when you ask for directions). But it can also show skepticism or surprise. *"Lost? My luggage got lost on a direct flight?"* Here are some of the most common questions about questions.

- What do you do when a sentence has a series of questions? This gets an either/or answer.

   You can put the question mark at the very end. *Would Tina have to buy a new hair dryer, toothbrush, swimsuit?*

   Or, for emphasis, you can put a question mark after each item (you don't need capital letters for each item, since it's still one sentence). *Would Tina have to buy a new hair dryer? toothbrush? swimsuit?*

- How do you introduce a question within a longer sentence?

   The simplest way is to use a comma and start the question with a capital letter. *The question was, How long should she wait for her luggage?*

   The same is true if the question is a quotation: Introduce it with a comma. *Tina cried, "What next?"* See also the note on the next page.

   But if the introduction is a complete sentence, especially if it's a long one, a colon works better. *The question she asked herself was this: How long should she wait for her luggage?*

- What comes after a question mark?

    If the sentence continues after the question, don't use a comma after the question mark. *What will I do without my hair dryer? she asked herself.* "*What more can go wrong?*" *she said to the ticket agent.*

THE SILENT SCREAM:
THE EXCLAMATION POINT (!)

The exclamation point is like the horn on your car—use it only when you have to. A chorus of exclamation points says two things about your writing: First, you're not confident that what you're saying is important, so you need bells and whistles to get attention. Second, you don't know a really startling idea when you see one.

When you do use an exclamation point, remember this:

- Use it alone (don't add a comma afterward). *"Holy cow!" said Phil.*

And keep your voice down.

NOTE: Sometimes a sentence that's technically a question behaves more like an exclamation. If an exclamation point seems more appropriate than a question mark, use it: *What were you thinking! How could they do such a thing! "Good grief," the general grumbled, "what next!"*

BRIEF INTERLUDE: PARENTHESES ( )

Once in a while you may need a brief side trip, a gentle interruption to tuck information into a sentence or between sentences. One way to enclose this interruption is with parentheses
(the end rhymes with *cheese*), and you just now saw a pair.

The thing to know about parentheses is that they can enclose a whole sentence standing alone, or something within a
sentence. The tricky part is determining where the other punctuation marks go: inside or outside the closing parenthesis.
Punctuation never immediately precedes an opening parenthesis (not in the same sentence, anyway).

- When the parenthetical aside is a separate sentence, put
  punctuation inside the closing parenthesis, and start
  with a capital letter. *Jimmy thinks he has won the lottery.
  (He is mistaken, however.)*
- When the aside is within a sentence, put punctuation
  outside the closing parenthesis, and start with a small
  letter. *Jimmy thinks he has won the lottery (fat chance).*

Sometimes, though, the remark inside parentheses is an
exclamation (*wow!*) or a question (*huh?*). In that case the exclamation point or question mark goes inside the parentheses,
but any accompanying punctuation marks go outside: *Jimmy
has already made plans for the money (poor guy!), but his wife is
skeptical. He may have misread the numbers on his lottery tickets
(how dumb can you get?).*

TOO MUCH OF A GOOD THING:
THE DASH (—)

We could do with fewer dashes. In fact, the dash is probably even more overused these days than the exclamation point—and I admit to being an offender myself (there I go again).

The dash is like a detour sign; it interrupts the sentence and inserts another thought. A single dash can be used in place of a colon to emphatically present some piece of information: *It was what Tina dreaded most—fallen arches.* Or dashes can be used in pairs instead of parentheses to enclose an aside or an explanation: *Her new shoes had loads of style—they were Ferragamos—but not much arch support.*

Dashes thrive in weak writing, because when thoughts are confused, it's easier to stick in a lot of dashes than to organize a smoother sentence. Whenever you are tempted to use dashes, remember this:

• Use no more than two per sentence. And if you do use two, they should act like parentheses to isolate a remark from the rest of the sentence. *After the flight, Tina looked—and she'd be the first to admit it—like an unmade bed.*

• If the gentler and less intrusive parentheses would work as well, use them instead. *Tina's luggage (complete with her return ticket) appeared to be lost.*

By the way, don't confuse the dash with the hyphen (see below). The dash is longer. If you want a dash but your keyboard doesn't have one, use two hyphens (--).

BETWIXT AND BETWEEN:
THE HYPHEN (-)

A hyphen is not just a stubby version of the dash. The two of them do very different things. While the dash separates ideas or big chunks in a sentence, the hyphen separates (or connects, depending on how you look at it) individual words or parts of words. *My mother-in-law works for a quasi-official corporation that does two-thirds of its business with the government.*

When a word breaks off at the end of a line of print and continues on the next line, a hyphen is what links the syllables together. But the hyphen most of us have problems with is the one that goes (or doesn't go) between words, as in terms for some family members (*mother-in-law*), or in descriptions (*quasi-official*), or in fractions (*two-thirds*). Here are some guidelines for when you need a hyphen and when you don't.

THE PART-TIME HYPHEN

One of the toughest problems with hyphens is how to use them in descriptions. When two or more words are combined to describe a noun, sometimes you use a hyphen between them and sometimes you don't.

The first question to ask yourself is whether the description comes before or after the noun.

- If it's after the noun, don't use a hyphen. *Father is* **strong willed**. *My cousin is* **ten years old**. *This chicken is* **well done**. *Ducks are* **water resistant**. *As a baby he was* **four pounds two ounces** *but now he's* **six feet eight**.
- If it's before the noun, use a hyphen between the words in the description. *He's a* **strong-willed** *father. I have a* **ten-year-old** *cousin. This is* **well-done** *chicken. Those are* **water-resistant** *ducks. The* **four-pound-two-ounce** *baby is now a* **six-foot-eight** *man.* But see the exceptions below.

> **NOTE:** You may have wondered why we say *six-**foot**-eight man* instead of *six-**feet**-eight man*. This is because we almost always use singular words in descriptions that come before a noun: *three-**car** garage, four-**story** building, six-**month** lease, nine-**year**-old boy*. However, we use plurals in fractions with *two* or more: *two-**thirds** majority, three-**fourths** share, nine-**tenths** margin*.

EXCEPTIONAL SITUATIONS

Here are some exceptions to the "before or after" rule for hyphens in multiple-word descriptions:

- If the descriptive words could be used separately and still make sense, don't use a hyphen even if they come before a noun. *Hodge was a **naughty old** cat. Alicia is a **sweet young** thing.*

- If *self* or *quasi* is one of the words, always use a hyphen. *Robert is **self-effacing**; still, he's a **self-confident** person. He's our **quasi-official** leader; the position is only **quasi-legal**.*

- If *very* is one of the words, forget the hyphen: *That Hepplewhite is a **very expensive** chair.* If *very* is added to a description that would ordinarily take a hyphen (**much-admired** architect, for example), drop the hyphen. *Sam's a **very much admired** architect.*

- If one of the words ends in *ly*, you almost never need a hyphen. *That's a **radically different** haircut. It gives you an **entirely new** look.*

- If the first word is *least, less, most,* or *more,* leave out the hyphen. *The **least likely** choice, and the **less costly** one, is the **most preposterous** hat I've ever seen. The one I bought is a **more dignified** chapeau.*

- If *percent* is part of a description, don't use a hyphen. *Bibi's gross income suddenly showed a **10 percent** increase.* Even when *percent* is part of a longer description, hyphens aren't required if the meaning is clear. *"I'd love a **ten percent a year** increase," she said.*

- If the second word is *looking,* use a hyphen whether the description comes before or after the noun. *As a puppy Cosmo was **good-looking**, but he grew into a **weird-looking** dog.*

- If two words form a common expression and a hyphen isn't needed for clarity, leave it out. *The **civil rights** advocates were **high school** sweethearts.*

IS YOUR HYPHEN SHOWING?

Here are some cases where you must use hyphens:

- With fractions. ***Three-quarters*** *of the brownies and **two-thirds** of the cookies are gone.* For how to go halves, see the box below.
- With *ex* (meaning "former"). *Hal is the **ex-president** of the company.*
- When adding a beginning or an ending to a word that starts with a capital (*anti-Nazi, Trollope-like*). Exceptions: *Runyonesque, Christlike, Antichrist.*
- When adding *like* would create a double or triple *l* (*shell-like*) or an unwieldy word (*needle-like*).
- When adding a beginning or ending would create a double vowel (*ultra-average, anti-isolationist*). But *pre* and *re* are often exceptions to this (*preempt, reenter*), so when you have a duplicate vowel, look up the word in the dictionary. (The vowels are *a, e, i, o, u*, and sometimes *y*.)

HALF MEASURES

I wish there were a rule for *half*, but it's all over the map. Some formations involving *half* are one word (*halfhearted, halfway*), some are two words (*half note, half sister*), and some are hyphenated (*half-hour, half-moon*). Check the dictionary.

HEADS OR TAILS

Many of us can't add a beginning or an ending to a word without sticking in a hyphen for good measure. If we put *mini* in front of *van*, it inexplicably becomes *mini-van* instead of *minivan*; if we put *like* after *life*, it unaccountably becomes *life-like*, not *lifelike*. Many hyphens show up where they're not wanted. Here are some common endings and beginnings that don't usually need them:

ENDINGS

ACHE: *I'll trade my **toothache** for your **headache**.*

ESQUE: *Her poetry is **Audenesque**.*

LESS and MOST: *The **ageless** soprano still manages to hit the **uppermost** notes.*

LIKE: *What a **lifelike** Gainsborough.*

WIDE: *Sewer rats are a **citywide** menace.*

BEGINNINGS

ANTI: *Elmer was **antifeminist**.*

BI: *They're conducting a **bicoastal** romance.*

CO: *This celebrity autobiography has no **coauthor**.*

EXTRA: *His **extracurricular** schedule is full.*

INTER: *Luke has **intergalactic** ambitions.*

MICRO, MINI, and MULTI: *Excuse me for a moment while I **micromanage** a **minicrisis** among these **multitalented** children.*

MID: *Our raft sank **midstream**.*

NON: *Hubert is a **nonperson**.*

OVER and **UNDER:** *It pays to be **overcautious** about eating **undercooked** meat.*

POST: *He lives in a **postwar** building.*

PRE and **PRO:** *The **prenuptial** atmosphere was definitely not **promarriage**.* But see the note below.

RE: *They have **reexamined** their situation.* But see the note below.

SEMI: *I wish I'd invented the **semiconductor**.*

SUB and **SUPER:** *Our **subbasement** got **supersaturated** in the flood.*

TRANS: *Leslie is a **transsexual**.*

ULTRA: *That Nancy is **ultrachic**.*

UN: *Argyle socks with sneakers are **uncool**.*

NOTE: There are exceptions, cases when you'll want to use a hyphen in words starting with *pre*, *pro*, and *re*. If a word starting with *pre* or *pro* is just too hard to read without a hyphen, add one (*pre-iron*, *pro-am*). And if a word starting with *re* could be confused with one that's spelled the same but means something else, add a hyphen. For instance, use *re-cover* (for "cover again") to avoid confusion with the word *recover*. Other examples include *re-creation*, *re-petition*, *re-press*, *re-sent*, *re-serve*, *re-sign*, *re-sort*, *re-treat*. (When the boss asks to renew your employment contract, it makes a big difference whether your reply memo says, "I'm going to re-sign" or "I'm going to resign.")

HYPHENS IN THE FAMILY

Some family members get hyphens and some don't. Here's how to keep them straight.

USE A HYPHEN

- With *ex. Meet my* **ex-husband**.
- With *in-law. Fred's my* **brother-in-law**.
- With *great. There goes my* **great-aunt**.

DON'T USE A HYPHEN

- With *step. His* **stepson** *Charlie is a doctor.*
- With *half. Bob's* **half brother** *is a thug.*
- With *grand. She can't be a* **grandmother**!

A MULTITALENTED MARK:
THE APOSTROPHE (')

That little airborne mark that dangles over some words (including last names like O'Conner) is called an apostrophe. This is the punctuation mark that has many sign painters mystified. Store awnings and windows, sides of trucks, even neon signs, are peppered with wayward apostrophes that either don't belong at all or are in the wrong position. Beware, especially, of the unusual apostrophe in a plural word.

Here's how to use an apostrophe with . . .

- **POSSESSIVES.** To indicate ownership, add *'s* to a singular noun (even if it ends in *s*) or to a plural noun that does not end in *s*. ***James's** chameleon escaped in the **children's** room.* Add the apostrophe alone to a plural noun that ends in *s*. *This was the **boys'** fault.* Chapter 3 is all about possessives, in case you need to know more.

- **MISSING LETTERS.** An apostrophe can show where letters have been dropped in a shortened word or phrase. For example, *shouldn't* is short for *should not*; the apostrophe shows where the *o* in *not* was dropped. Some other clipped words are quite irregular, like *won't* and the disreputable *ain't*. Shortened words and phrases are called contractions; there's a list of them on pages 81–82. They're also in the dictionary. When in doubt, look it up.

- **A COMMA OR PERIOD.** When you need a comma or period (or any other punctuation, for that matter) after a possessive word that ends with an apostrophe, the punctuation goes after the apostrophe. *The idea was the **boys'**, but the responsibility was their **parents'**.*

- **SOME UNUSUAL PLURALS.** Add *'s* to make plurals of individual letters easier to read. *At Swarthmore, Libbi got all **A's** and **B's** and started to spell her name with two **i's**.* For more on apostrophes with plural letters, see pages 31–32.

ENOUGH SAID: QUOTATION MARKS (" ")

Think of quotation marks as the road signs that tell you when you're entering and leaving a city. Just as the signs define the city limits, quotation marks show where speech begins and ends.

The opening quotation marks always go right before the first word of the quotation: *"Can we talk?"* The trick is at the other end, where the closing quotation marks go. You'll have to decide whether the punctuation (period, comma, question mark, or whatever) that follows the quoted material goes inside or outside the closing quotation marks. Here's what's in and what's out.

THE INS

- **PERIOD.** *"I think I'm going to be sick."*
- **COMMA.** *"I shouldn't have eaten those strawberries,"* *Gustav said.*

THE OUTS

- **COLON.** *There are two reasons she hates the nickname "Honey": It's sticky and it's sweet.*
- **SEMICOLON.** *Frank's favorite song was "My Way"; he recorded it several times.*

SOMETIMES IN, SOMETIMES OUT

- **QUESTION MARK.** In most cases, a question mark should be inside the quotation marks. *"Who goes there?" said the sentry. "What is the password?"* But the question mark must be outside if it's not part of the actual quotation. *Who first recorded "Lydia, the Tattooed Lady"?*

- **EXCLAMATION POINT.** In most cases, an exclamation point goes inside the quotation marks. *"Captain!" said Sulu. "We're losing speed!"* But the exclamation point goes outside if it's not part of the quotation. *My God, the screen just went blank after reading "Situation Normal"!*

- **PARENTHESES.** If the entire quotation is in parentheses, then the closing parenthesis should go outside the quotation marks. *Uhura had the last word ("I told you so").* If only part of the quotation is in parentheses, then the closing parenthesis goes inside the quotation marks. *She added, "Maybe next time you'll listen to me (if there is a next time)."*

- **APOSTROPHE.** How do we get ourselves into messes like this one? To create the possessive of something that's normally in quotation marks—for example, the title of a poem, "The Raven"—you would have to put the apostrophe outside. *"The Raven"'s first stanza is the best.* Pretty awful-looking, isn't it? It's so awful that many publications even cheat to avoid it, and write *"The Raven's"*— definitely incorrect, although much prettier. My advice is to avoid this problem entirely. Instead of writing *"The Raven"'s author was Poe*, rearrange it. *Poe was the author of "The Raven."*

NOTE: When one quotation appears within another, enclose the interior one in single quotation marks. *"Was it Linus who said, 'Get lost'?" asked Lucy.*

QUESTIONABLE MARKS

Sometimes a question comes wrapped inside another question. When you meet a sentence like this—*What do you mean, "What did I do to my hair"*—where does the question mark go? (No, you can't use two!) Does it go inside the closing quotation marks, or outside?

It's up to you. The answer depends on which question you want to emphasize.

If you want to emphasize the inner question, put the question mark inside the quotation marks. *How many of you have asked yourselves the question, "Who am I?"*

If you want to emphasize the overall question, put the question mark outside the quotation marks. *What do I say when the waiter asks, "Which wine, sir"?*

The same principle works with exclamations inside exclamations, and with sentences that have both exclamations and questions. Don't use two marks. Decide which part of the sentence you want to emphasize. The following examples combine questions and exclamations.

Here the questions are emphasized:

The kid drives me nuts by constantly asking, "Why?"
Did you hear someone cry, "Help"?

And here the exclamations are emphasized:

The kid drives me nuts by constantly asking, "Why"!
Did you hear someone cry, "Help!"

See also the note on page 197.

THE LESS SAID: WHEN NOT TO QUOTE

Sign painters seem to love quotation marks. They don't care how a word is spelled, as long as it's enclosed in quotes. I don't know much about the sign-painting business—maybe they get paid extra for punctuation. Here are a few signs of the times I've spotted:

Nail salon: *Our Instruments Are "Sterilized"*
Pizzeria: *"Free" Delivery*
Locksmith: *"Fast" and "Friendly" Service*

There's no reason for quotation marks in any of those signs. The intent may be to emphasize the quoted words, but a bright color or a different typeface would do a better job.

In fact, quotation marks used like that can mislead the reader. They're sometimes used in a skeptical or sarcastic way, to indicate that what's quoted isn't meant seriously: *Uncle Oscar's regular Friday-night "volunteer work" turned out to be a poker game.*

The moral is: Don't quote it if you don't have to. And the next time your pipes spring a leak and a truck marked *"Licensed" Plumber* pulls up to your door, don't say I didn't warn you.

THE SLANT ON TITLES

You may have wondered why some titles, like *Vogue* and *The Adventures of Huckleberry Finn*, most often appear in the slanting letters called italics, while others, like "How Do I Love

Thee?" and "My Funny Valentine," usually appear in ordinary type enclosed in quotation marks.

Customs vary on how titles should be written. In most newspaper writing, for example, all titles are in plain type, though not all go inside quotation marks.

My advice is to follow conventional practice. Put the names of longer works, like books, movies, and plays (and magazines and newspapers), in italics. Put the names of shorter works, like stories, songs, and poems that aren't book-length, in ordinary type with quotation marks.

USE ITALICS

ALBUMS: *Abbey Road*, *Soultrane*

BOOKS: *The Cat in the Hat*, the *Oxford English Dictionary*

MOVIES: *Million Dollar Legs*, *Mad Max: Fury Road*

NEWSPAPERS, MAGAZINES: *Miami Herald*, *The New Yorker*

TV SERIES: *Jeopardy!*

PAINTINGS, SCULPTURES: Duchamp's *Nude Descending a Staircase*, Rodin's *The Burghers of Calais*

PLAYS, MUSICALS, OPERAS, BALLETS: *Macbeth*, *Guys and Dolls*, *The Magic Flute*, *Swan Lake*

USE QUOTATION MARKS

ARTICLES: "The Cellulite Cure: Fact or Fiction?"

ESSAYS: "Civil Disobedience," by Henry David Thoreau

POEMS: "The Raven," by Edgar Allan Poe

SHORT STORIES: "The Secret Life of Walter Mitty," by James Thurber

SONGS: Cole Porter's "Begin the Beguine"

NOTE: Where titles are concerned, classical music has its own variations on the theme. Here, too, usage varies widely. I recommend writing the formal names of symphonies, concertos, sonatas, and similar compositions in ordinary type without quotation marks: Mozart's Symphony No. 41 in C, Beethoven's Piano Sonata No. 23 in F minor, Schubert's Piano Quintet in A. But if you use a nickname, put it in italics: Mozart's *Jupiter* Symphony, Beethoven's *Appassionata* Sonata, Schubert's *Trout* Quintet.

SCREEN SHOTS

As for the titles of websites, blogs, and electronic publications, the rules are still evolving. But here are some simple guidelines that I think are reasonable.

I recommend italics for the names of online publications, including periodicals, encyclopedias, dictionaries, and so on, as with print equivalents: *The New York Times*, *Vanity Fair*, *Slate*, *HuffPost*, *Wikipedia*, *Merriam-Webster Unabridged*, *OED Online*.

However, I recommend using regular type for the names of social media sites, blogs, and databases: Facebook, Twitter, Language Log, The Grammarphobia Blog, Project Gutenberg, Early English Books Online. I use regular type and quotation marks for the titles of individual blog posts, articles, and other items published online.

CHAPTER 9

THE COMPLEAT DANGLER

A FISH OUT OF WATER

Life would be pretty dull if everyone's English were perfect. Without slips of the tongue, we wouldn't have spoonerisms, named after the Reverend William A. Spooner, a dean at Oxford. He was known for his tongue-tanglers, though most of the ones attributed to him (like "It is kisstomary to cuss the bride") are apocryphal.

And we wouldn't have malapropisms, either. Mrs. Malaprop was a character in an eighteenth-century play whose bungled attempts at erudite speech led her to declare one gentleman "the very pineapple of politeness!" and to say of another, "Illiterate him . . . from your memory."

We're lucky that English, with its stretchy grammar and its giant grab bag of a vocabulary, gives us so much room for verbal play, if not anarchy. As Groucho Marx said, "Love flies out the door when money comes innuendo," and it's hard to imagine him saying it in Esperanto.

Naturally, if you have room to play, you have room to make mistakes. And English sentences are often constructed without regard for building codes. I've grown almost fond of one common error, the dangler. It's a word or phrase (a group of words) that's in the wrong place at the wrong time, so it ends up describing the wrong thing. Here comes one now: *Strolling along the trail, Mount Rushmore came into view.* Whoops! The opening phrase, *strolling along the trail*, is a dangler. Why? Because it's attached to the wrong thing, *Mount Rushmore.* The way the sentence stands, the mountain was out taking a stroll.

Danglers show up in newspapers and bestsellers, on the network news and highway billboards, and they can be endlessly entertaining—as long as they're perpetrated by someone else. When you're doing the talking or writing, the scrambled sentence isn't so amusing. See if you can tell what's wrong with these examples.

> **Born at the age of forty-three**, *the baby was a great comfort to Mrs. Wooster.* (Whoops!) As the sentence is arranged, the baby—not his mother—was forty-three. (The opening phrase, *born at the age of forty-three*, is attached to *the baby*, so that's what it describes.) Here's one way to rearrange things: *The baby,* **born when Mrs. Wooster was forty-three**, *was a great comfort to her.*

> **Tail wagging merrily**, *Bertie took the dog for a walk.* (Whoops!) See how *tail wagging merrily* is attached to *Bertie*? Put the tail on the dog. **Tail wagging merrily**, *the dog went for a walk with Bertie.*

As a den mother, *Ms. Basset's station wagon was always full of Cub Scouts.* (Whoops!) The phrase *as a den mother* is attached to *Ms. Basset's station wagon.* Attach it to the lady herself. *As a den mother*, *Ms. Basset always had her station wagon full of Cub Scouts.*

Danglers are like mushrooms in the woods—they're hard to see at first, but once you get the hang of it they're easy to find. Although the wild dangler may lurk almost anywhere in a sentence, the seasoned hunter will look in the most obvious place, right at the beginning. If the first phrase is hitched to the wrong wagon—or to no wagon at all—it's a dangler.

Some kinds of opening phrases are more likely than others to be out of place. I'll show you what to look for.

THE USUAL SUSPECT

Always suspect an *ing* word of dangling if it's near the front of a sentence; consider it guilty until proved innocent. To find the culprit, ask yourself whodunit. Who's doing the *walking, talking, singing*, or whatever? You may be surprised by the answer. In each of these examples, there's a "whoops." To find it, look at the phrase containing the *ing* word and look at whodunit.

After overeating, *the hammock looked pretty good to Archie.*
Who ate too much in this sentence? The hammock! If a person did the overeating, the opening *ing* phrase

should be attached to him. ***After overeating****, Archie thought the hammock looked pretty good.*

On returning home*, Maxine's phone rang.* Who came home? Maxine's phone! To show that the owner of the phone was doing the returning, put her right after the opening phrase. ***On returning home****, Maxine heard the phone ring.*

Walking briskly*, the belt of her raincoat was lost.* Who's the pedestrian? The belt! What's attached to the opening phrase is what's doing the walking. If you want to say *she* was walking briskly, put her right after the opening phrase. ***Walking briskly****, she lost the belt of her raincoat.*

PIN THE TAIL ON THE DONKEY

Have you ever seen children at parties pinning the tail on the wrong part of the donkey? Well, sometimes adjectives (words that characterize nouns) get pinned to the wrong part of a sentence and become danglers. Here's a sentence with its "tail" in the wrong place.

Dumpy and overweight*, the vet says our dog needs more exercise.* (Whoops.) The description *dumpy and overweight* should be pinned on the dog, not the vet. Here's one remedy. ***Dumpy and overweight****, our dog needs more exercise, the vet says.* But a more graceful solution would be to rewrite the sentence completely.

The vet says our dog needs more exercise because she's **dumpy and overweight**.

Adjectives (such as *dumpy* and *overweight*) like to be pinned as close as possible to what they describe.

HITCH YOUR WAGON

A dangling adverb at the front of a sentence is a lot like a horse that's hitched to the wrong wagon. Adverbs (words that characterize verbs) can be easy to spot because they often end in *ly*. When you see one, make sure it's "hitched" to the right verb. In this example, what went wrong at the hitching post?

> **Miraculously** *we watched as the surgeon operated with a plastic spoon.* (Whoops.) As the sentence stands, the opening word, *miraculously*, refers to the watching, not the operating. That's because the closest verb is *watched*. To fix things, put the *ly* word closer to the right verb. **Miraculously**, *the surgeon operated with a plastic spoon as we watched.* Here's another solution: *We watched as the surgeon* **miraculously** *operated with a plastic spoon.*

Adverbs (such as *miraculously*) like to be hitched to the nearest verb. For more about troublesome adverbs, see page 144.

ROADS TO NOWHERE

You can easily be led astray when a sentence has a road sign at the very beginning. The kind of sign I mean is a preposition, a word that shows position or direction (*at*, *by*, *on*, *with*, and so on). If the sign is in the wrong place, you end up on the road to nowhere. Try to avoid this kind of dangler.

> ***At the age of ten***, *my father gave me a puppy.* (Whoops.) As the sentence is written, Dad was only a boy! The opening phrase, *at the age of ten*, is attached to *my father*—an obvious mismatch. If the sign is to point in the right direction, the sentence has to be rearranged. ***At the age of ten***, *I was given a puppy by my father.* Or: *My father gave me a puppy when I was ten.*

EXCEPTIONS THAT MAKE THE RULE

Some expressions are so common that they're allowed to dangle at the beginning of a sentence, even though they're not connected to anything in particular. We treat them as casually as throat-clearing.

For example, we may say: **Generally speaking**, *pigeons mate for life.* The pigeons aren't the ones doing the speaking, naturally, and no one would make such a connection. These expressions apply to the statement as a whole, not to a single part of it. (Words like *hopefully* and *frankly* can act in a similar way; see pages 95–96.)

Other stock phrases that can dangle to their hearts'
content include *strictly speaking, barring unforeseen circumstances, considering the alternative, assuming the
worst, judging by appearances, after all, by and large, on
the whole, admittedly, put simply, given the conditions,
in the long run, in the final analysis, to tell the truth, contrary to popular belief, to be sure,* and *to be perfectly frank.*

Introductory phrases like these have become so familiar
that they have earned the right to be exceptions to the
rule. Are they necessary? That's another issue. For more
about throat-clearing, see pages 255–256.

TO'S A CROWD

Some of the hardest danglers to see begin with *to*. Beware of
the sentence that starts with an infinitive (a verb form usually
preceded by *to*, for instance *to run, to see, to build*). The opening phrase has to be attached to whoever or whatever is performing the action. Here's an opening phrase that leaves the
sentence scrambled.

> ***To crack an egg properly,*** *the yolk is left intact.* (Whoops.)
> As the sentence is written, the yolk is the one cracking
> the egg. The opening phrase, *to crack an egg properly,* is
> attached to *the yolk,* not to whoever is doing the crack-
> ing. Let's put a cook in the kitchen. ***To crack an egg
> properly,*** *you must leave the yolk intact.* Here's an even

simpler way to say it: **To crack an egg properly**, *leave
the yolk intact.* (The subject is understood to be *you.*
This is called an imperative sentence, since someone's
being told to do something.)

Owners' manuals, you'll notice, are chock-full of dangling
infinitives. Does this sound familiar?

> **To activate widget A**, *doohickey B is inserted into slot C.*
> If the one trying to activate the silly thing is *you*, make
> *you* the subject. **To activate widget A**, *you insert doo-
> hickey B into slot C.* Or you can delete the *you*, since
> it's understood to be the subject. **To activate widget
> A**, *insert doohickey B into slot C.*

A LIKELY STORY

Looking for a dangler? Then look for a sentence that starts
with *like* or *unlike*. More than likely, you'll find a boo-boo.
Here's a likely candidate.

> **Like Alice**, *Fran's face-lift cost plenty.* (Whoops.) The
> phrase *like Alice* is a dangler because it's attached to
> the wrong thing: *Fran's face-lift.* Presumably Fran's
> face-lift is like Alice's, not like Alice. Make sure the
> things being compared really are comparable. There are
> two ways to fix a sentence like that. **Like Alice, Fran
> paid plenty for her face-lift.** Or: **Like Alice's, Fran's
> face-lift cost plenty.**

CHAPTER 10

DEATH SENTENCE

DO CLICHÉS DESERVE TO DIE?

Tallulah Bankhead once described herself as "pure as the driven slush." And bankruptcy has been called "a fate worse than debt." We smile at expressions like these out of relief, because we're braced for the numbing cliché that fails to arrive.

Nothing is wrong with using a figure of speech, an expression that employs words in imaginative (or "figurative") ways to throw in a little vividness or surprise. But it's an irony of human communication that the more beautiful or lively or effective the figure of speech, the more likely it will be loved, remembered, repeated, worn out, and finally worked to death. That's why some people will tell you that the Bible and Shakespeare are full of clichés!

So crowded is our stock of figurative language that every profession—legal, corporate, fashion, artistic, literary, and so on—seems to have a collection all its own. A tired book critic, for example, will say a novel is "a richly woven tapestry," "a tour de force," or "a cautionary tale," one whose characters are either "coming of age" or experiencing "rites of passage." For corporate "high rollers," what matters is the "bottom line," or whether a company is "in play" or its stock has "gone south."

Trite writing sometimes has a fill-in-the-blank feeling, as if it were written according to a pattern. There's the *blank-as-a-blank* pattern: *bald as a billiard ball, white as a sheet*. And there's the *blanklike-blank* pattern: *viselike grip, childlike innocence*. And even a *blanking-blank* pattern: *deafening crash, sneaking suspicion*.

The problem here isn't the pattern; it's the words that fill in the blanks. If they're tired and predictable, you need some platitude adjustment.

Are all clichés and familiar turns of phrase to be summarily executed? No. Let your ear be your guide. If a phrase sounds expressive and lively and nothing else will do, fine. If it sounds flat, be merciless.

One more point.

It's far better to trot out a dependable cliché, and to use it as is, than to deck it out with lame variations (*the tip of the proverbial iceberg*) or to get it wrong ("unchartered seas" instead of *uncharted* ones; "high dungeon" instead of *dudgeon*). And two or more unrelated figures of speech shouldn't be used one after another, whether they're clichés or not (*He got off his high horse and went back to the drawing board*). That's called mixing your metaphors, and there's more about it at the end of this chapter.

There's no way to eliminate all clichés. It would take a

roomful of Shakespeares to replace them with fresh figures of speech, and before long those would become clichés too. Vivid language is recycled precisely because it's vivid. But think of clichés as condiments, the familiar ketchup, mustard, and relish of language. Use when appropriate, and don't use too much. When you're dressing up a hamburger, you don't use béarnaise sauce. You use ketchup, and that's as it should be. But you don't put it on everything. Some dishes, after all, call for something special. Here are some of today's more overworked condiments.

ACID TEST. Overuse and you flunk.

AFTER ALL IS SAID AND DONE. Enough said.

AGREE TO DISAGREE. People never really *agree to disagree*. They just get tired of arguing.

AN ALBATROSS AROUND HIS NECK. Bird-brained.

ALL WALKS OF LIFE. Get a walker.

APPLE OF HIS EYE. Myopic.

AT THE END OF THE DAY. Let's put it to bed.

AT FIRST BLUSH. Embarrassing.

BACK TO THE DRAWING BOARD. Back to *Roget's Thesaurus*.

THE BALL IS IN YOUR COURT. Double fault.

BEAT A DEAD HORSE. Inhumane.

BEHIND THE EIGHT BALL. Dirty pool.

BETTER LATE THAN NEVER. Better never.

BETWEEN A ROCK AND A HARD PLACE. Too confining.

BITE THE BULLET. Save your teeth.

BITTER END. This is right up there with *making ends meet*.

BLANKET OF SNOW. Nature is a *fertile field* (there's another one) for clichés. Besides *blankets of snow*, beware *sheets of rain* (which of course *rain cats and dogs*), *calms before the storm*, *devastating earthquakes*, *raging torrents*, *bolts from the blue*, *steaming jungles*, *uncharted seas* (which are likely to become *watery graves*), *wide-open spaces*, *places in the sun*, and anything *silhouetted against the sky*. See also GOLF-BALL-SIZED HAIL later in this chapter.

BLESSING IN DISGUISE. Not disguised well enough.

BOGGLES THE MIND. It's all right to be boggled once in a while, but don't make a habit of it.

BONE OF CONTENTION. This geriatric expression is getting osteoporosis.

BORED TO TEARS. There has to be a more exciting way to complain of boredom.

BOSOM BUDDY. Get it off your chest.

BOTTOM LINE. Get off your bottom and find a better way to say it.

BROAD DAYLIGHT. The sun has set on this one, and on *light of day*.

BRUTE FORCE. A 98-pound weakling.

A BUG GOING AROUND. Another way of saying you don't know what you've got.

BY HOOK OR BY CROOK. This one hangs out in the same crowd with *hook, line, and sinker* and *lock, stock, and barrel*.

CALM BEFORE THE STORM. Take a rain check.

CAN OF WORMS. Don't open this one too often. And don't unnecessarily disturb its beastly cousins *nest of vipers* and *hornets' nest*.

CAN'T SEE THE FOREST FOR THE TREES. See your ophthalmologist.

CAST A PALL. Bad casting.

CHAMPING AT THE BIT. Rein it in. And no, don't make it "chomping"!

CHECKERED CAREER. Forever plaid.

COME TO A HEAD. Sometimes seen as *bring to a head*, this phrase has its humble beginnings in dermatology. Need I say more?

COOL AS A CUCUMBER. Using this too much is simply uncool.

COUNT YOUR CHICKENS. Lays an egg.

CRYSTAL CLEAR. Of quartz not.

CUT TO THE CHASE. Doesn't cut it.

CUTTING EDGE. Dull.

DAYS ARE NUMBERED. A phrase that's not just overused, but depressing.

DEAD AS A DOORNAIL. Why a doornail, anyway? See also **PASSED AWAY** on page 231.

DIAMOND IN THE ROUGH. And watch those *pearls before swine*, too. When accessorizing your language, remember that a little jewelry goes a long way.

DISCREET SILENCE. Silence makes good clichés (*chilly silence, eloquent silence, pregnant silence*). And in the silence, of course, you can *hear a pin drop*.

DRAW A BLANK. This is what you do when you run out of clichés.

EACH AND EVERY. The resort of a weak writer, like *one and the same* and *any and all*.

EASIER SAID THAN DONE. What isn't? As for *no sooner said than done*, it's a promise that's seldom kept.

ERRAND OF MERCY. The truly merciful don't resort to clichés.

FAR BE IT FROM ME. When you say this, you're about to butt in where you don't belong. If you do want to be a buttinsky, though, use it correctly (not "far be it for me").

FATE WORSE THAN DEATH. Bury it.

FELL THROUGH THE CRACKS. An unconvincing way of saying something is not your fault. And don't make it worse by saying "fell between the cracks."

FEW AND FAR BETWEEN. This is what fresh expressions are becoming.

FOOD FOR THOUGHT. I'd say this expression is *from hunger*, but that's another cliché.

FOOLS RUSH IN. And when they get there, they announce their presence with clichés.

FOREGONE CONCLUSION. A pedestrian way of saying that something was no surprise.

FORESEEABLE FUTURE. The future is not foreseeable. Anyone who knows otherwise should be in the commodities market.

GARDEN VARIETY. Needs pruning.

GENERAL CONSENSUS. Disagreeable.

GENERATION GAP. It's degenerated.

GET NOWHERE FAST. It's a cliché, all right, but it's better than *spinning your wheels*.

GET THE SHOW ON THE ROAD. This expression closed in New Haven.

GLASS CEILING. This phrase, like *level playing field*, is getting overworked. Hasn't it become a little transparent?

GOLF-BALL-SIZED HAIL. Why golf balls? How about plums or Ping-Pong balls for a change?

GREEN WITH ENVY. It's not your color.

GRIM REAPER. One scythe fits all.

GRIND TO A HALT. Grease it.

HEAD OVER HEELS. I've never understood this one. Wouldn't *heels over head* make more sense?

HEATED ARGUMENT. It's getting tepid.

HIS OWN WORST ENEMY. Not unless he stabs himself in the back.

HIT THE GROUND RUNNING. It limps.

HOOK, LINE, AND SINKER. Throw it back.

HOPE SPRINGS ETERNAL. Hopeless.

I HEAR WHAT YOU'RE SAYING. People who say this have no ear for language.

IGNORANCE IS BLISS. I wouldn't know.

IMPENETRABLE FOG. Clear your head (maybe we should bring back *thick as pea soup*).

IN THE FINAL ANALYSIS. See a shrink.

IN THE NICK OF TIME. "Just in time" isn't good enough?

IN NO UNCERTAIN TERMS. Terminate it.

INNOCENT BYSTANDER. Why is a *bystander* always *innocent*? Has anybody given him a lie-detector test?

IT GOES WITHOUT SAYING. Then don't say it.

JUMP-START. Beware of claims that anything other than a car (the economy, for example) can be *jump-started*.

LAST BUT NOT LEAST. If it's not least, then don't put it last.

LEAPS AND BOUNDS. Gazelles and antelopes, maybe even lizards, move by *leaps and bounds*; few other things do.

LEAVE NO STONE UNTURNED. Stone cold.

LEGENDARY. This and *fabled* are much overused. What legend? What fable? Unless you're Aesop or the Brothers Grimm, give these words a vacation.

LET'S TOUCH BASE. Let's not. (The same goes for *Let's do lunch*.)

LEVEL PLAYING FIELD. Falls flat.

LIGHT AT THE END OF THE TUNNEL. Oncoming train?

LIKE A HOUSE ON FIRE. Call 911.

LOCK, STOCK, AND BARREL. Oh, shoot.

LOW ON THE TOTEM POLE. Taboo.

MAKE A KILLING. The best thing to be said about this cliché is that it's better than being *taken to the cleaners*. Don't use either of them to excess.

MASS EXODUS. Drop the *mass*, unless you mean a crowd leaving St. Patrick's Cathedral.

MEANINGFUL DIALOGUE. This was a dumb expression to begin with. Drop *meaningful*. In fact, *dialogue* is pretty dumb, too. Don't people have talks anymore?

MOMENT OF TRUTH. Ever notice that it's always bad news?

MORE THAN MEETS THE EYE. If you've got a good eye, there's not that much more.

MORE THE MERRIER. Not if you're doing the cooking.

NARROW ESCAPE. It's getting a bit thin.

NEEDLE IN A HAYSTACK. Lose it.

NIP IT IN THE BUD. This nipping of buds has to stop.

ON THE GROUND. Let's ground this one.

ON MY WATCH. Watch it.

ONE FELL SWOOP. One too many.

ONLY TIME WILL TELL. Time's up.

OUTSIDE THE BOX. Box its ears.

PANDORA'S BOX. Put a lid on it.

PASSED AWAY. You've probably noticed that death is a favorite playground of clichés. This is too bad. In situations where people most need sincerity, what do they get? Denial. There's no shame in saying somebody died, but the vocabulary of mortality avoids it. Think again before using moribund expressions like *passed away* or *passed on* (sometimes reduced to just *passed*), *untimely end, cut down in his prime, called to his Maker, called away, great beyond, this mortal coil, transitioned peacefully, joined the great majority, bought the farm, hopped the twig* (a variation on *fell off his perch*), *kicked the bucket, gone to a better place, handed in his dinner pail, checked out, grim reaper, in the midst of life, irreparable loss, broke the mold, vale of tears, time heals all, words can't express, tower of strength,* or *he looks like he's sleeping.*

PET PEEVE. Muzzle it.

PIECE OF CAKE. Stale.

PLAY HARDBALL. Three strikes.

PLAY IT BY EAR. Don't wear it out, except at the piano.

POLITICAL HOPEFULS. I vote no.

POWERS THAT BE. This is much overused by powers that wannabe.

PREEXISTING CONDITION. We're probably stuck with this, but it's a redundancy (that means it repeats itself, like *end result, final outcome, new initiative,* and *close proximity*).

PUSHING THE ENVELOPE. Only if you're sorting letters.

RAISE THE BAR. May it go belly-up.

REACH OUT TO. Reach for something less smarmy.

RELIABLE SOURCE. This implies that your other sources are lying scoundrels.

ROLLER COASTER. This phrase (usually preceded by some descriptive term like *emotional* or *fiscal*) comes up a lot in news stories about natural disasters, crippling illness, the federal budget, and the Olympic Games. Let's hope the ride will soon be over.

RUDE AWAKENING. A snooze.

SADDER BUT WISER. Some people are *sadder but wiser* after hearing *a word to the wise.* These are nice old expressions that could be with us for a long time if they're treated gently, but *only time will tell.*

SCREAM BLOODY MURDER. Keep your voice down.

SEA OF FACES. These are often *bright and shining faces.* Commencement speakers, please give these expressions a sabbatical.

SEAT OF THE PANTS. Don't wear them out.

SERIOUSLY CONSIDER. This isn't just hackneyed, it's insincere. If someone tells you he'll *seriously consider* your suggestion, he's already kissed it off. That goes double if he has promised to give it *active* or *due consideration.*

SHATTERED WITH GRIEF. Why does this phrase make us think of insincere widows?

SHOT IN THE ARM. Tetanus, anyone?

SICKENING THUD. This was a lively image in the first five thousand mystery novels where it appeared. The *sickening thud* usually came after *a shot rang out.*

SIGH OF RELIEF. An old bromide.

SILVER LINING. Tarnished.

SLIPPERY SLOPE. Don't fall for it.

SPINNING YOUR WHEELS. Shift gears.

STICKS OUT LIKE A SORE THUMB. So does this hackneyed expression.

STOCK IN TRADE. Trade it in.

STRAW THAT BROKE THE CAMEL'S BACK. One hump or two?

SWEET SPOT. It's gone sour.

TAKE THE BULL BY THE HORNS. You first.

TARNISHED IMAGE. The *tarnished image* (distantly related to the old *blot on the escutcheon*) could use some polishing. Put it back in the cupboard.

TEAM PLAYER. When your boss says you should be more of a *team player*, that means she wants you to take on more of her work.

THICK AS THIEVES. Thieves are not that thick, anyway. Otherwise, plea bargaining would never work.

TIGHT SHIP. Sinking fast.

TILL THE COWS COME HOME. Don't wait up.

TIP OF THE ICEBERG. A tip of the hat to anyone who can come up with something better.

TO THE MANNER BORN. If you're going to use a cliché, respect it. This Shakespearean phrase (it comes from *Hamlet*) means "accustomed to" or "familiar with" a manner of living. (Some dictionaries now accept the upstart "to the manor born" as meaning privileged since birth. Give it no respect.)

TONGUE IN CHEEK. The only expression more trite than *tongue in cheek* is *tongue firmly in cheek*. Let's retire them both.

TOUGH ACT TO FOLLOW. Get a new routine.

TRIALS AND TRIBULATIONS. Whine not.

TRUST IMPLICITLY. Never believe people who say you can trust them implicitly.

TUMULTUOUS APPLAUSE. This one went out with the Monkees.

24/7. Time out!

UP IN THE AIR. Let's come up with a more down-to-earth way of saying this.

VIABLE ALTERNATIVE. Well, it beats the alternative that doesn't work.

WAR-TORN. This cliché stays alive because, regrettably, there are always enough wars to go around. A place that's *war-torn*, by the way, is sure to be *embattled* or *besieged*.

WHAT MAKES HIM TICK. This image is winding down.

WIN-WIN SITUATION. A lose-lose expression.

WORLD-CLASS. No class.

METAPHORS BE WITH YOU

Is it any wonder we love figures of speech? Just think how dull language would be without them. The metaphor, the most common figure of speech, lets us use one image—any image we want!—to conjure up another. Imagination is the only limit. This gives us about a zillion ways (give or take a few) of saying the same thing.

The phrase *volley of abuse*, for example, uses the image of a fusillade of bullets to describe an outpouring of anger. This metaphor leaves behind a single vivid picture.

But if that image has to compete with another (as in *The* **volley of abuse** *was the* **straw that broke the camel's back**), we have what's called a mixed metaphor. No clear picture emerges, just two dueling ideas (bullets versus straws). If you've heard it's unwise to mix metaphors, this is why: The competing images drown each other out, as in *There's always a* **silver lining** *at the* **end of the tunnel**, or *Don't* **count your chickens** *till the* **cows come home**.

Some people are so wild about metaphors that they can't resist using them in pairs. This may work, if the images don't clash: *Frieda viewed her marriage as a* **tight ship**, *but Lorenzo was plotting a* **mutiny**. Since the images of *tight ship* and *mutiny* have an idea in common (sailing), they blend into one picture. But usually when two figures of speech appear together, they aren't so compatible. In that case, the less said, the better.

CHAPTER 11

THE LIVING DEAD

LET BYGONE RULES BE GONE

The house of grammar has many rooms, and some of them are haunted. Despite the best efforts of grammatical exorcists, the ghosts of dead rules and the spirits of imaginary taboos are still rattling and thumping about the old place.

Sometimes an ancient prohibition becomes outdated, or it may turn out that a musty convention was never really a rule at all. The trouble is that these phantoms are hard to displace, once they take hold in our minds. It's no longer considered a crime to split an infinitive or end a sentence with a preposition, for example, but the specters of bogus or worn-out rules have a way of coming back to haunt us. In the interest of laying a few to rest, I dedicate to each a tombstone, complete with burial service. May they rest in peace.

🪦 **TOMBSTONE:** Don't split an infinitive.

R.I.P. An infinitive is a verb in its simplest form, right out of the box. It can usually be recognized by the word *to* in front of it: *Blackbeard helped him* **to escape**. But the *to* isn't actually part of the infinitive and isn't always necessary: *Blackbeard helped him* **escape** *and no one saw him* **escape**. As a preposition, a word that helps position words in relation to one another, the *to* lets us know an infinitive is coming.

The truth is that the phrase "split infinitive" is misleading. Since *to* isn't part of the infinitive, there's nothing to split. A sentence often sounds better when the *to* is close to the infinitive: *Dilbert decided* **to mention** *dating in the workplace*. But there's no harm in separating them by putting a descriptive word or two in between: *Dilbert decided* **to discreetly mention** *dating in the workplace*.

A sentence like that sounds natural because in English, the best place for an adverb (like *discreetly*) is right in front of the word it describes (*mention*). Where else could *discreetly* go? Putting it anywhere else—say, before or after *decided* or *dating*—would change the meaning. So go ahead and split, but don't overdo it. Not: *Dilbert decided* **to discreetly and without referring to the boss's secretary mention** *dating in the workplace*.

Sometimes, rewriting a sentence to avoid a "split" makes it ridiculous. Try rearranging the words in this example: *Kiri's landlord wanted* **to flatly forbid** *singing*. Or this one: *He threatened* **to more than double** *her rent*. Or this: *The landlord* *is expected **to strongly oppose** weaker noise regulations.* See what I mean?

Writers of English have been merrily "splitting" infinitives since the 1300s. It was considered perfectly acceptable until the mid–nineteenth century, when Latin scholars—notably Henry Alford in his book *A Plea for the Queen's English*—misguidedly called it a crime. (Some linguists trace the taboo to the Victorians' slavish fondness for Latin, a language in which you can't divide an infinitive.) This "rule" was popular for half a century, until leading grammarians debunked it. But its ghost has proved more durable than Freddy Krueger.

TOMBSTONE: It's wrong to end a sentence with a preposition.

R.I.P. Here's another bugaboo that English teachers used to get worked up over.

We can blame an eighteenth-century English clergyman and Latin scholar named Robert Lowth for saddling us with this one. He wrote the first popular grammar book to say that a preposition (a positioning word, like *at, by, for, into, off, on, out, over, to, under, up, with*) shouldn't go at the end of a sentence. This idea caught on, even though great literature from Chaucer to Shakespeare to Milton is bristling with sentences ending in prepositions. Nobody knows why the notion stuck—possibly because it's closer to Latin grammar, or perhaps because the word *preposition* means "position before," which seems to suggest that a preposition shouldn't come last.

At any rate, this is a rule that modern grammarians have long tried to get us out from under.

TOMBSTONE: *Data* and *media* are strictly plural nouns and always take plural verbs.

R.I.P. It's time to admit that *data* has joined *agenda*, *erotica*, *insignia*, *opera*, *stamina*, and other technically plural Latin and Greek words that have become thoroughly Anglicized as singular nouns taking singular verbs. No plural form is necessary, and the old singular, *datum*, can be left to the Romans.

As for *media*, it's singular when you mean the world of mass communications, which is most of the time. *The **media** **was** in a frenzy.* But it's occasionally used as a plural to refer to the individual kinds of communication. *The **media** present **were** TV, radio, newspapers, and the blogosphere.* The singular in that sense is *medium*. *The liveliest **medium** of all **is** the blogosphere.*

TOMBSTONE: Always put the subject of a sentence before the verb.

R.I.P. Says who? Tell it to Tennyson (*"Into the valley of Death / Rode the six hundred"*). He didn't mind putting his subject (*the six hundred*) after the verb (*rode*).

True, most of the time a sentence with its subject (the one doing the action) before the verb (the action being done) sounds more forceful and direct than one written the other way around. *Edgar was more mysterious* is punchier than *More mysterious was Edgar.* But every now and then it's appropriate to put the verb first (*Says who?* for instance), and literature is full of poetic examples of verbs preceding their subjects. (Just ask Edgar: "*Quoth the Raven, 'Nevermore.'*")

> **NOTE:** If a sentence starts with *there*, its real subject follows the verb, as in ***There** was a young man from Darjeeling*. (The subject isn't *there*; it's *man*.) Sentences starting with *there* get a bad rap in many grammar guides. There's nothing wrong with them, either. See pages 60–61 and 250.

TOMBSTONE: It's wrong to start a sentence with *and* or *but*.

R.I.P. And why is it wrong? There's no law against using *and* or *but* to begin a sentence.

Over the years, some English teachers have enforced the notion that conjunctions like *and* and *but* should be used only to join elements within a sentence, not to join one sentence with another. Not so. It's been common practice to begin sentences with conjunctions since at least as far back as the tenth century. But don't overdo it, or your writing will sound monotonous.

TOMBSTONE: Use *than I* in comparisons, not *than me*.

R.I.P. The eighteenth-century schoolmasters strike again! They were the first to condemn sentences like *Percy is older **than me***, insisting on *older **than I***. Why? Because they decided that *than* shouldn't be used as a preposition.

However, for over five hundred years great writers and

ordinary people alike have treated *than* as a preposition. And prepositions are usually followed by *me, him, her, them, us,* and other object pronouns.

Today, authorities recognize that *than* can be used as either a preposition or a conjunction.

As a preposition, it's followed by an object pronoun (*Percy is older **than me***). As a conjunction, it's followed by a subject pronoun (*Percy is older **than I***), or you can add the understood verb if you like (*Percy is older **than I am***).

Both uses of *than*—preposition and conjunction—are correct. The only difference is that ending a sentence with a subject pronoun (like *I*) sounds stiffer and more formal than ending it with an object pronoun (like *me*).

In more complicated comparisons, though, a solitary pronoun after *than*—as in *Percy trusts Eustace more than **me***—can be misleading (see pages 12–13). If so, just stretch the sentence out to make your meaning clear:

> *Percy trusts Eustace more **than he trusts me***.
> *Percy trusts Eustace more **than I do***.

TOMBSTONE: Don't split the parts of a verb phrase (like *has been*).

R.I.P. This has never been a legitimate rule. It's a by-product of the famous superstition about splitting an infinitive. See pages 78–79 and 238–239.

▌ TOMBSTONE: *None* is always singular.

R.I.P. Not always. In fact, *none* is more likely to be plural.

Many people seem to have been taught (mistakenly) that *none* always means "not one" (as in **None** *of the chickens* **is** *hatched*). But most authorities have always believed that *none* is usually closer in meaning to "not any (of them)" than to "not one (of them)." So it's considered plural in most cases and takes a plural verb: **None** *of the chickens* **are** *hatched*.

None is singular only when it means "none of it"—that is to say, "no amount": **None** *of the milk* **was** *spilled*.

If you really do mean "not one," say "not one." There's more about *none* in the chapter on plurals, pages 28–29.

▌ TOMBSTONE: Don't use *whose* to refer to inanimate objects.

R.I.P. Here's a musty old custom whose time is up. There's nothing wrong with using the possessive *whose* for inanimate objects. *Never buy a* **car** **whose** *odometer doesn't work.*

A related misconception is that you shouldn't use *'s* with inanimate things (as in *This* **car's** *odometer is broken*). Apparently, the thinking goes, inanimate things aren't as possessive as living ones. Silly, right? Well, this book's position is that yesterday's custom can be safely ignored.

🪦 **TOMBSTONE:** Use *It is I*, not *It is me.*

R.I.P. This is another ordinance that's out of date. You can use *It is* (or *It's*) *me, That's him, It's her,* and similar constructions instead of the also correct but much stuffier *It is I, That's he,* and *It's she.*

Similarly, it's fine to say *Me too.* The alternative, *I too,* is still grammatically correct, but unless you're addressing the Supreme Court or the Philological Society, you can drop the formality.

There's more about *I* and *me* on pages 10–14.

🪦 **TOMBSTONE:** Never use *who* when the rules call for *whom.*

R.I.P. We can't dump *whom* entirely, at least not just yet. But modern grammarians believe that in conversation or informal writing, *who* is acceptable in place of *whom* at the beginning of a sentence or clause (a clause is a group of words with its own subject and verb): ***Who's** the package for? You'll never guess **who** I ran into the other day.*

Where *whom* should be used after a preposition (*to, from, behind, on,* etc.), you can substitute *who* in casual situations by reversing the order and putting *who* in front. *"From **whom**?"* becomes *"**Who** from?"*

There's a more detailed discussion of *who* versus *whom* on pages 7–10.

TOMBSTONE: Never use *that* instead of *who* to refer to people.

R.I.P. Despite what you may have heard, a person can be either a *that* or a *who*. In fact, *that* has been used for people as well as animals and inanimate things for some eight hundred years, and it's standard English. *The **girl that** married dear old Dad was Mom.*

A thing, however, is always a *that*. *He took her on a Paris **honeymoon that** broke the bank. Fortunately, it was a **bank that** allowed overdrafts.*

There's more on *that* versus *who*, including how to refer to animals, on page 7.

TOMBSTONE: Always use an active verb and avoid a passive one.

R.I.P. It's true that a passive verb (*The getaway car **was driven by** Bonnie*) makes for a wimpier, more roundabout sentence than an active one (*Bonnie **drove** the getaway car*). The more straightforward sentence puts the one performing the action (*Bonnie*) ahead of the one being acted upon (*the getaway car*), with the verb in between: subject . . . verb . . . object.

But the direct route isn't always the best route. The passive might be more appropriate in cases like these.

- When there's a punch line. You might want to place the one performing the action at the end of the sentence for emphasis or surprise: *The gold medal in the five-hundred-meter one-man bobsled competition* **has been won** *by a six-year-old child!*

- When nobody cares whodunit. Sometimes the one performing the action isn't even mentioned: *Witherspoon* **is being treated** *for a gunshot wound, and Hermione* **has been arrested***.* We don't need to know who's stitching up Witherspoon or who put the cuffs on Hermione.

TOMBSTONE: Never use a double negative.

R.I.P. My advice on double negatives: Never say never.

The double negative wasn't always a no-no. For centuries, it was fine to pile one negative on top of another in the same sentence. Chaucer and Shakespeare did this all the time to accentuate the negative. It wasn't until the eighteenth century that the double negative was declared a sin against the King's English, on the ground that one negative canceled the other. (Blame Robert Lowth, the same guy who decided we shouldn't put a preposition at the end of a sentence. He could have saved us all a lot of trouble by going into a different line of work.)

As for now, stay away from the most flagrant examples (*I didn't do nothing*; *You never take me nowhere*), but don't write off the double negative completely. It's handy when you want to avoid coming right out and saying something: *Your blind date is not unattractive. I wouldn't say I don't like your new haircut.* For more on double negatives, see page 273.

TOMBSTONE: Don't use *I will* in place of *I shall*.

R.I.P. Once upon a time, refined folk used *I shall* or *we shall* to refer to the simple future, not *I will* or *we will*. But *will* has edged out *shall* as the people's choice. *Shall* is still used with *I* and *we*, however, in a polite offer or proposal: **Shall I** **freshen your drink, or shall we** *go?*

There's more about the demise of *shall* in the chapter on verbs, page 80.

TOMBSTONE: Use *more than* instead of *over*.

R.I.P. You may have been told by some pedant that *over* doesn't apply to numbers, only to quantities. Not so. It's fine to use *over* in place of *more than* or *in excess of.* The belief that this is wrong is a widespread misconception concocted by nineteenth-century newspaper editors. *Dad's new car gets **over** ten miles to the gallon.*

TOMBSTONE: Don't use *since* to mean "because."

R.I.P. Now and then, an extremely conservative grammarian will suggest that *since* should be used only to indicate a time period (*since Thursday*, for example). Forget that, if you ever heard it. *Since* doesn't always mean "between now and" or "from the time that." It can also mean "because" or "for the reason that." **Since** *you asked me, I'll tell you.* People have been using *since* in this way for over five hundred years.

Just be sure the meaning can't be confused, as in **Since** *we* *spoke, I've had second thoughts.* In that case, *since* could mean either "from the time that" or "because," so it's better to be more precise.

▌ **TOMBSTONE:** Don't use *while* to mean "although."

R.I.P. In the past, some grammarians believed that *while*, which comes from an Anglo-Saxon word meaning "time," should be used only to mean "during the time that."

But there's a long tradition, going back at least to the sixteenth century, of using *while* at the head of a sentence or a clause to mean "although" or "whereas": **While** *he may be short, he's wiry.*

Just be sure the meaning can't be confused, as in **While** *he reads the* Times, *he watches the news on CNN.* In this case, *while* could mean either "during the time that" or "although." Pick one of those and avoid the confusion.

One more thing about *while.* Some people overuse it as a way to vary their sentences and avoid using *and.* Let's not wear out a useful word for no good reason. If *while* isn't meant, don't use it. Not: *Wally wears suspenders,* **while** *his favorite shoes are wingtips.*

▌ **TOMBSTONE:** Use *lighted*, not *lit*.

R.I.P. There's nothing wrong with using *lit* for the past tense of *light: Paul* **lit** *two cigarettes, then gave one to Bette.*

NOTE: Many people also turn up their noses at *dove* instead of *dived*, and at *snuck* instead of *sneaked*. But times change and so does English. Dictionaries now accept both *dove* and *snuck*, but I wouldn't recommend *snuck* in formal writing. It's a free country, though. If you like 'em, use 'em. See pages 112 and 126–127.

TOMBSTONE: Use *have got*, not *have gotten*.

R.I.P. People who take this prohibition seriously have gotten their grammar wrong.

At one time, everyone agreed that the verb *get* had two past participles: *got* and *gotten*. (The past participle is the form of a verb that's used with *have*, *had*, or *has*.) It's true that the British stopped using *have gotten* about three hundred years ago, while we in the Colonies kept using both *have got* and *have gotten*. But the result is not that Americans speak improper English. The result is that we have retained a nuance of meaning that the unfortunate Britons have lost.

When we say, *Fabio **has got** three Armani suits*, we mean he has them in his possession. It's another way of saying that he *has* or *owns* them.

When we say, *Fabio **has gotten** three Armani suits*, we mean that he *has acquired* or *has obtained* them.

It's a useful distinction, and one that the British would do well to reacquire.

▌ TOMBSTONE: Drop the *of* in *all of* and *both of*.

R.I.P. Some members of the Redundancy Police think *of* is undesirable in the phrases *all of* and *both of*, except in front of a pronoun (*all of me, both of them*, etc.). They frown on sentences like **Both** *of the thieves spent* **all** *of the money*, and would prefer **Both** *the thieves spent* **all** *the money*.

Either way is correct. There's no law against keeping *of*, but by all means drop it if you want to. You can't please all of the people all the time. For more on dropping *of*, see pages 132 and 147.

▌ TOMBSTONE: Don't start a sentence with *there*.

R.I.P. There is no doubt that a statement starting with *there* begins on a weak note. It's weak because *there* is a phantom subject, standing in for the real one. *There is a party going on* is a different way of saying, *A party is going on*. The real subject in both cases is *party*.

Some English teachers frown on starting a sentence with *there*, possibly because they prefer keeping the real subject before the verb. Never mind. There's nothing wrong with it. In fact, literature is full of splendid examples: *"***There** *is a tide in the affairs of men, which, taken at the flood, leads on to fortune."* There's more about this on pages 60–61 and 241.

▌ TOMBSTONE: Don't say "Go *slow*" instead of "Go *slowly*."

R.I.P. Both *slow* and *slowly* are legitimate adverbs. In fact, *slow* has been a perfectly acceptable adverb since the days of Shakespeare and Milton.

Adverbs can come with or without *ly*, and many, like *slow* and *slowly*, exist in both forms. Those without the tails are called "flat adverbs," and we use them all the time in phrases where they follow a verb: "sit *tight*," "go *straight*," "turn *right*," "work *hard*," "arrive *late*," "rest *easy*," "sing *sharp* (or *flat*)" "aim *high*," "play *fair*," "come *close*," and "think *fast*." Yes, *straight*, *right*, *hard*, and the rest are bona fide adverbs and have been for many centuries.

TOMBSTONE: Don't use *they* to refer to *everybody* or *someone*.

R.I.P. In today's English, there's nothing wrong with a sentence like *Everybody can eat what **they** want* or *Someone left **their** carry-on in the overhead bin*.

English speakers quite normally use *they* and its other forms (*them, their, themselves*) to refer to an indefinite subject—an unknown person or persons of unknown gender. Today the best authorities agree that this usage is not only natural but grammatically correct. So good English does not require awkward *he or she* substitutes (*Everybody can eat what **he or she** wants; Someone left **his or her** carry-on in the overhead bin*).

For a couple of centuries, this use of *they* was regarded as bad English. The objection was that *they* is plural while the indefinite pronouns—*everybody, anyone, somebody, nobody*, and so on—are grammatically singular. (After all, we use such pronouns with singular verbs: *Everyone **goes**,* not *Everyone **go**.*) This explains why generations of schoolchildren were taught to use *he* instead of *they* for an unknown somebody-or-other.

Recently, the clunky but more inclusive *he or she* has become common.

But there was never a need to avoid *they*. Since the 1300s, long before anybody objected, people consistently used *they* for an indefinite person. And they never stopped, despite the naysayers. Why?

Because words like *everyone* and *nobody* and *somebody* don't mean just one. They're technically singular but they're psychologically plural, since their meaning is "all people," "no people," "some people," and so on. Modern grammarians now recognize what ordinary speakers have known all along— there's no conflict in using *they*, *them*, *their*, and *themselves* to refer to an indefinite word that has a plural feeling.

In fact, this isn't the only case of a pronoun changing its spots. *You* was originally plural, and used only as an object, not a subject. There were once four forms of the word: *thou*, *ye*, *thee*, and *you*. Over time, the four forms were combined into one all-purpose *you*. (For more about the evolution of *they* and company, see pages 16–19 and 43–44.)

CHAPTER 12

SAYING IS BELIEVING

HOW TO WRITE WHAT YOU MEAN

A good writer is one you can read without breaking a sweat. If you want a workout, you don't lift a book—you lift weights. Yet we're brainwashed to believe that the more brilliant the writer, the tougher the going.

The truth is that the reader is always right. Chances are, if something you're reading doesn't make sense, it's not your fault—it's the writer's. And if something you write doesn't get your point across, it's probably not the reader's fault—it's yours. Too many readers are intimidated and humbled by what they can't understand, and in some cases that's precisely the effect the writer is after. But confusion is not complexity; it's just confusion. A venerable tradition, dating back to the ancient Greek orators, teaches that if you don't know what you're talking about, just ratchet up the level of difficulty and no one will ever know.

Don't confuse simplicity, though, with simplemindedness. A good writer can express an extremely complicated idea clearly and make the job look effortless. But such simplicity is a difficult thing to achieve, because to be clear in your writing you have to be clear in your thinking. This is why the simplest and clearest writing has the greatest power to delight, surprise, inform, and move the reader. You can't have this kind of shared understanding if writer and reader are in an adversary relationship.

Now, let's assume you know what you want to say, and the idea in your head is as clear as a mountain stream. (I'm allowed a cliché once in a while.) How can you avoid muddying it up when you put it into words?

There are no rules for graceful writing, at least not in the sense that there are rules for grammar and punctuation. Some writing manuals will tell you to write short sentences, or to cut out adjectives and adverbs. I disagree. The object isn't to simulate an android. When a sentence sounds nice, reads well, and is easy to follow, its length is just right. But when a sentence is lousy, you can take steps to make it more presentable.

This goes for all writing, online as well as off. Good English is clear English: it's efficient, precise, sensible, economical, sometimes even beautiful. In fact, good English is especially important in cyberspace because the speed and brevity conspire to muddle your message. And the reader's short attention span only makes things worse.

Here are eighteen general principles that are good for all

kinds of writing. You may not want to follow all of them all of the time, though it's not a bad idea.

1. SAY WHAT YOU HAVE TO SAY.

Unless you're standing at a lectern addressing an audience, there's no need to clear your throat. Your listeners aren't finding their seats, putting down their forks, wrapping up a conversation, or whatever. Your audience—the reader—is ready. So get to it.

These are the kinds of throat-clearing phrases you can usually ditch:

> **At this juncture** *I thought you might be interested in knowing . . .*
> **Before we begin,** *perhaps it would be valuable to recall . . .*
> **I can assure you** *that I'm sincere when I say . . .*
> **In light of recent developments** *the possibility exists that . . .*

And once you've started, resist the temptation to pad your sentences with meaningless stuffing. Be merciless with phrases like these:

AT THIS POINT IN TIME. Why not just *now*?

IF AND WHEN. Use either *if* or *when*; you seldom need both.

IF I DO SAY SO MYSELF. You just did.

IF I MAY. You need permission?

IF YOU WILL. This is only slightly better than *ahem*.

THAT SAID. Yes, we heard you.

UNLESS OR UNTIL. One or the other will usually do, unless
or until you're getting paid by the word.

(Of course, some messages could do with a bit of cushion-
ing: *We at the bank feel that under the circumstances you would*
want us to bring to your attention as soon as possible the fact
that . . . your account is overdrawn.)

2. STOP WHEN YOU'VE SAID IT.

Sometimes, especially when you're on a roll and coming up
with your best stuff, it's hard to let go of a sentence (this one,
for example), so when you get to the logical end you just keep
going, and even though you know the reader's eyes are glazing
over, you stretch one sentence thinner and thinner—with a
semicolon here, a *however* or *nevertheless* there—and you end
up stringing together a whole paragraph's worth of ideas before you finally realize it's all over and you're getting writer's
cramp and you have to break down and use a period.

When it's time to start another sentence, start another
sentence.

How do you know when it's time? Well, try breathing along
with your sentences. Allow yourself one nice inhalation and
exhalation per sentence as you silently read along. If you start
to turn blue before getting to the end, either you're reading too
slowly (don't move your lips) or the sentence is too long.

3. USE PLAIN WORDS.

Big words are seductive, I know. But they don't impress people
nearly as much as you think. Some writers think that simple,

clear, straightforward language isn't flashy enough, so they toss in complexities. Why merely *say* something, when they can *declare, assert, expostulate, announce,* or *asseverate* it? Instead, avoid the hot air, and choose the simple word over the complicated one.

Get out your red pencil and look for stuff like this:

CALCULUS. This word is often used in a fuzzy, pseudo-scientific way to mean "reasoning" or "thinking" or "method." Save it for when you're writing about higher mathematics.

DIALOGUE. Windy writers like to *dialogue,* or to *have a dialogue.* Don't talk to them. (The only thing worse than a *dialogue* is a *meaningful dialogue.* See page 230.)

IMPACT. When used as a verb, this word *impacts* me the wrong way. If you don't want to give the rest of the world a headache, use *impact* only as a noun.

INTERFACE. People who like to *dialogue* also like to *interface.* Don't interface with them.

MONIES. This is how a bureaucrat says *money.* I guess *money* sounds too much like . . . money.

PARADIGM. It masquerades as a two-dollar word, but it's really worth only about twenty cents. A *paradigm* (the *g* is silent: PAIR-a-dime) is simply a pattern or example. What it *isn't* is a standard of perfection (that's a *paragon*).

PARAMETER. Weak writers like to use scientific-sounding words to lend authority to limp sentences. So they use *parameter* to mean a boundary, a characteristic, a component, an element, a feature, an ingredient, a part, a

perimeter, a quality, or a requirement. When a word is
used for too many things, it ends up meaning nothing.

TRANSPIRE. This is how a stuffed shirt says "happen" or
"occur" or "take place." It's just stuffing.

UNPRECEDENTED. Very few things are unprecedented.
Don't use this word to refer to something unusual,
uncommon, odd, unexpected, rare, exceptional, curious,
irregular, offbeat, or surprising. No matter how extraordinary something sounds to you, there's probably a
precedent for it.

4. BE DIRECT.

Too many writers back into what they have to say. A
straightforward statement like *He didn't intend to mow down
your perennial border* comes out *His intention was not to mow
down your perennial border.*

Don't mince words. If what you mean is *Mom reorganized
my closet brilliantly*, don't water it down by saying, *Mom's re-
organization of my closet was brilliant.*

Here are a couple of other examples:

Their house was destroyed in 1993. Not: *The destruction of
   their house occurred in 1993.*
We concluded that Roger's an idiot. Not: *Our conclusion
   was that Roger's an idiot.*

If you have something to say, be direct about it. As in geom-
etry, the shortest distance between two points is a straight line.

5. PUT THE SUBJECT CLOSE TO THE VERB.

Nobody's saying that sentences can't be complex and interesting; they can, as long as they're easy to follow. But we shouldn't have to read a sentence twice to get it. Here's an example that takes us from Omaha to Kansas City by way of Pittsburgh:

*The **twins**, after stubbornly going to the same high school despite the advice of their parents and teachers, **chose** different colleges.*

Find a way to say it that puts the doer (the subject, *twins*) closer to what's being done (the verb, *chose*): *The **twins chose** different colleges, after stubbornly going to the same high school despite the advice of their parents and teachers.*

The closer the subject is to the verb, the less likely the reader will get lost. If you need a compass to navigate a sentence, take another whack at the writing.

6. PUT DESCRIPTIONS CLOSE TO WHAT THEY DESCRIBE.

A television journalist in the Farm Belt once said this about a suspected outbreak of hoof-and-mouth disease: *The pasture contained several cows seen by news reporters that were dead, diseased, or dying.*

Do you see what's wrong? The words *dead, diseased, or dying* are supposed to describe the cows, but they're so far from home that they seem to describe the reporters. What the journalist should have said was: *Reporters saw a pasture containing several cows that were dead, diseased, or dying.*

When a description strays too far, the sentence becomes awkward and hard to read. Here's an adjective (*bare*) that has strayed too far from the noun (*cupboard*) it describes: *Ms. Hubbard found her **cupboard**, although she'd gone shopping only a few hours before, **bare***. Here's one way to rewrite it: *Although she'd gone shopping only a few hours before, Ms. Hubbard found her **cupboard bare***.

And here's an adverb (*definitely*) that's strayed too far from its verb (*is suing*): *She **definitely**, if you can believe what all the papers are reporting and what everyone is saying, **is suing***. Put them closer together: *She **definitely is suing**, if you can believe what all the papers are reporting and what everyone is saying*.

The reader shouldn't need a map to follow a sentence.

7. AVOID PRONOUN PILEUPS.

A sentence with too many pronouns (*he, him, she, her, it, they, them,* and other words that substitute for nouns) can give your reader hives: *Fleur says Judy told **her** boyfriend **she** got a nose job and already regrets **it***.

Whose boyfriend? Who got the nose job? Who regrets what?

When you write things like this, you know the cast of characters. It won't be so clear to somebody else. Don't make the reader guess. Here's a possibility: *Judy already regrets telling **her** boyfriend about **her** nose job, or so Fleur says*. Or maybe this: *Fleur says **her** boyfriend heard about **her** nose job from Judy, who already regrets telling him*.

8. DON'T BELABOR THE OBVIOUS.

Some writers can't make a point without poking you in the ribs with it. A voice isn't just pleasing; it's pleasing *to the ear*.

You don't just give something away; you give it away *for free*. The reader will get the point without the unnecessary prepositional phrases (phrases starting with words like *by*, *for*, *in*, *of*, and *to*): pretty *in appearance*, tall *of stature*, few *in number*, blue *in color*, small *in size*, stocky *in build*, plan *in advance*, drive *by car*, assemble *in a group*. You get the picture.

Speaking of redundancies, think twice before using expressions like *advance reservations*, *final conclusion*, *foreign import*, *free gift*, *prerecorded*, *follow behind*, or *safe haven*. Do I hear an echo? See also PREEXISTING CONDITION, page 232.

9. DON'T BE AFRAID TO REPEAT A WORD.

It's better to repeat a word that fits than to stick in a clumsy substitute that doesn't. Just because you've called something a spider once doesn't mean that the next time you have to call it an arachnid or a predaceous eight-legged creepy-crawly.

Editors sometimes call this attempt at elegant variation the Slender Yellow Fruit Syndrome. It is best explained by example: *Freddie was offered an apple and a banana, and he chose the slender yellow fruit.*

10. BE CLEAR ABOUT WHEN AND WHERE.

The butler found a candid photo of Bertie in a compromising position with one of the maids in the conservatory.

What happened in the conservatory? Is that where the photo was found, or where it was taken? And where was the maid?

This may be the meaning: *In the conservatory, the butler and one of the maids found a candid photo of Bertie in a compromising position.* Or this: *The butler found a candid photo, taken in the conservatory, of Bertie and one of the maids in a compromising position.*

Now consider this one: *Aunt Agatha threatened to disinherit Bertie when she caught him gambling on Sunday.*

Goodness, look at the time! Where does Sunday fit in? Is that when the threat was made, or when Bertie was caught, or when gambling was forbidden?

Maybe this is the meaning: *Aunt Agatha threatened to disinherit Bertie on Sunday when she caught him gambling.* Or perhaps the *when* should be an *if*: *Aunt Agatha threatened to disinherit Bertie if she caught him gambling on a Sunday.*

Where are we? When is it? These are questions the reader shouldn't have to ask.

11. PUT YOUR IDEAS IN ORDER.

Don't make the reader rearrange your sentences to figure out what's going on. The parts should follow logically. This doesn't mean they should be rattled off in chronological order, but the sequence of ideas should make sense. Here's a notice that a hurried librarian might have written:

Books can't circulate when they're on your shelves instead of ours. So please return any overdue books you have at home. Overdue books are a serious problem for our library. If you don't bring them back, we'll post your name on the bulletin board.

What's wrong with this picture? Look at the order of the sentences. One of them—*Overdue books are a serious problem for our library*—interrupts two others that are clearly a couple and shouldn't be separated. So where does the stray belong?

I'd put it up front, where the train of thought begins, since it tells us why the notice is being written in the first place:

Overdue books are a serious problem for our library. Books can't circulate when they're on your shelves instead of ours. So please return any overdue books you have at home. If you don't bring them back, we'll post your name on the bulletin board.

12. IMAGINE WHAT YOU'RE WRITING.

Picture in your mind any images you've created.

Are they unintentionally funny, like this one? *Uma bent over backward to impress her yoga teacher.* Or how about this one: *The bereaved family covered the mirrors as a reflection of its grief.* If you don't see what's wrong, reflect on it for a moment.

Are there too many images, as in this sentence? *The remaining bone of contention is a thorn in his side and an albatross around his neck.* Give the poor guy a break. One image at a time, please.

CALL ME EMAIL

This may come as a shock to some of you, but email (or other digital writing) is no excuse for lousy English. Sure, it's often informal, but informal shouldn't mean incoherent.

The things we like about email—the speed and breezy style—can lead to misunderstandings. So email unto others as you would have them email unto you. Here's how.

- *Be specific in the subject line.* And be sure it doesn't sound like spam.
- *Get to the point.* The guy at the other end doesn't have all day.
- *Watch your English.* If you write to Aunt Mildred and she cares about grammar and spelling and profanity and such, then you should too.
- *Go easy on the cybertalk.* Use acronyms, emoticons, and emojis only if Professor Higgins will get them—and welcome them.
- *Don't forget to use the shift key.* It's difficult to read writing that's ALL CAPITALS (please, no shouting!) or all lowercase.
- *Say what you're replying to.* The Little League coach might have a short memory.
- *Can this be true?* The Internet is full of misinformation, so don't spread it around. When you come across an astounding "fact," don't just copy, paste, and send. Check it out (see the next page). If you can't verify it, don't believe it.
- *Adjust your attitude.* Are you being a little . . . abrupt? impatient? nasty? Kindness is never out of place, and you'll never regret it later.
- *Read your message again before sending.* You'll be surprised at what you find.

13. CHECK YOUR FACTS.

A young friend of mine once wrote an article about the Underground Railroad and referred to the great abolitionist "James Brown." The man's name was *John* Brown. And he never sang "I Feel Good."

Look up anything that could conceivably be wrong—names, events, numbers, dates, places, and so on. Start with the "who" and proceed through the "what," "when," "where," and "why." If you can't verify it, don't treat it as fact.

14. CHECK YOUR MATH.

If a number seems too astonishing to be true, it probably isn't.

- Verify any addition, subtraction, multiplication, or division. Don't just run your eyes over the figures. Get out the calculator.
- When comparing numbers, avoid the phrases "times more than" and "times less than." Fifty, for example, is not five times more than ten. It's four times more (four times ten, or forty, more) than ten. And ten is not five times less than fifty. It's four times less (four times ten, or forty, less) than fifty. See what I mean? Even when used correctly, "times more than" and "times less than" are misleading. Instead, try "as much as" and "as many as." *Ten is a fifth as much as fifty, and fifty is five times as many as ten.*
- Watch increases and decreases. Any number that falls 100 percent hits zero. Nothing decreases by more than 100 percent without going into a negative number. For

example, a decrease to ten, from an original fifty, is not a drop of 500 percent—it's a drop of eighty percent (the drop, forty, is eighty percent of fifty). And an increase to fifty, from an original ten, is not a rise of 500 percent—it's a rise of 400 percent (the increase, forty, is four times, or 400 percent of, ten).

• Don't confuse *percent*, *percentage*, and *percentage point* (see also page 58). A *percent* is one-hundredth of something, so it's generally used with a number. *Sixty* **percent** *of the customers* [or sixty out of every hundred] *are children*. A *percentage* can be any part of a whole, so it's never used with a number, only an ordinary description. *That's an enormous* **percentage**. A *percentage point* is the difference between one percentage and another. *The percentage rose from fifty percent last year to sixty percent this year, an increase of ten* **percentage points**. (No, this is NOT an increase of ten percent! It's an increase of twenty percent—ten parts of fifty. Do the math.)

• Be careful adding one percentage to another. If 8 percent of American men and 12 percent of American women are overweight, that doesn't mean 20 percent of all American adults are overweight. The overall number lies in between, because you don't add the numbers, you average them. Assuming there are equal numbers of men and women, the average would be 10 percent. This bring us to my final point.

• Take care when using words like *average*, *mean*, *median*, and *norm*. Let's say a play group has seven children, aged

1, 2, 2, 2, 3, 5, and 6. The *average* (same as *mean*) age is 3, the sum of the ages (21) divided by the number of children (7). The *median* age is 2, the number that falls in the center of the lineup. The *norm* (an imprecise term) is under 3, since that's where most of the ages fall. (Let's hope there's more than one adult supervising *that* play group!)

15. DON'T MAKE YOURSELF THE CENTER OF THE UNIVERSE.

Of course we want to know what happened to you. Of course we care what you think and feel and do and say. But you can tell us without making every other word *I* or *me* or *my*. Next time you write a text, an email, or a letter (remember letters?), look it over and see how many sentences start with *I*.

You can prune phrases like **I** *think that* or *in* **my** *opinion* or *let* **me** *emphasize* from your writing (and your talking, for that matter) without losing anything. Anecdotes can be told, advice given, opinions opined, all with a lot fewer first-person pronouns than you think.

This doesn't mean we don't love you.

16. GET THE BIG PICTURE.

Forget the details for a minute. Step back and take a look at what you've written. Have you said what you wanted to say? After all, leaving the wrong impression is much worse than making a couple of grammatical boo-boos. Get some perspective.

17. REVISE AND CONQUER.

Assuming you've made your point, ask yourself whether you could make it more smoothly. Somebody once said that in good writing, the sentences hold hands. See if you can give yours a helping hand. It may be that by adding or subtracting a word here or there, you could be even clearer. Or you could switch two sentences around (see tip No. 11), or begin one of them differently.

18. READ WITH A FELONIOUS MIND.

There's no easy way to raise your writing from competence to artistry. It helps, though, to read with a felonious mind. If you admire a passage in a book or article or letter or memo, read it again. Why do you like it, and what makes it so effective? When you find a technique that works, steal it. (I said the technique, not the words! Stealing words is a serious offense.)

GLOSSARY

ABBREVIATION. A shortened form of a word or phrase, like *Rd.* for "Road" or *MD* for "Medical Doctor" or *USA* for you know what. See also **PERIOD**.

ACTIVE. See **SUBJECT** and **VERB**.

ADJECTIVE. A word describing or characterizing a noun. It can come before the noun (***pink*** *sweater*) or after (*The sweater is* ***pink***). Adjectives also come as comparatives (*pinker*) and superlatives (*pinkest*). Because an adjective adds something to a noun, it's called a modifier or a qualifier; we say it "modifies" or "qualifies" the noun.

ADVERB. A word that describes or characterizes a verb (*He grunted* ***lugubriously***). It can also characterize an adjective (*He is* ***very***

lugubrious) or another adverb (*He grunted **very** lugubriously*). An adverb is called a modifier or a qualifier; we say it "modifies" or "qualifies" another word.

APOSTROPHE. A mark of punctuation that's used to make nouns possessive (*Albert's coat*) or to show where letters have been omitted, as in contractions (*wouldn't*). Only in rare cases—let me emphasize *rare!*—is an apostrophe used to form a plural (*dot all the i's*).

ARTICLE. The three articles (*a*, *an*, *the*) are actually tiny adjectives that tell us whether a noun refers to a particular thing (***the** chair, **the** ottoman*) or just one of those things (*a chair, **an** ottoman*). *The* is called the definite article; *a* and *an* are indefinite articles.

BRACKETS. Marks of punctuation used in quoted material or excerpts to enclose something that's not part of the original, like an explanatory aside. *"The weight of the Empress of Blandings [1.2 tons] is a well-kept secret,"* said Lord Emsworth's pigman.

CLAUSE. A group of words with its own subject and verb. A simple sentence might consist of only one clause: *Ernest had left for Paris.* More complex sentences have several clauses, as shown in this example: *I learned | that Ernest had left for Paris | when I got his hotel bill.* Independent clauses make sense alone (*I put on a sock . . .*), but dependent, or subordinate, clauses don't (*. . . that had no mate*).

CLICHÉ. A figure of speech that's lost its sparkle. When you find yourself using one, nip it in the bud—or maybe I should put that another way.

COLLECTIVE NOUN. A noun that stands for a group of people or things, like *total* or *number*. It can be considered singular (*The* **number** *is staggering*) or plural (*A* **number** *of them have gone their separate ways*).

COLON. A punctuation mark that can be used to introduce a statement, a series of things, a quotation, or instructions. It's like a traffic cop that stops you and alerts you about road conditions up ahead.

COMMA. A punctuation mark that indicates a pause. If it were a traffic signal, it would be a yield sign, separating ideas and preventing pileups. Commas can be used between the clauses in a sentence or the items in a series.

COMPARATIVE. See **ADJECTIVE**.

CONDITIONAL CLAUSE. A clause that starts with *if, as if, as though*, or some other expression of supposition. The verb in a conditional clause has an attitude: that is, it takes on different forms, or "moods," depending on the speaker's attitude or intention toward what's being said. When the clause states a condition that's contrary to fact, the verb is in the subjunctive mood (*If I* **were** *you* . . .). When the clause states a condition that may be true, the verb is in the indicative mood (*If I* **was** *late* . . .). For more on the conditional, see **VERB**.

CONJUNCTION. A connecting word. The telltale part of this term is "junction," because that's where a conjunction is found—at the junction where words or phrases or clauses or sentences are joined. The most familiar conjunctions are *and, but,* and *or.* And it's fine to start a sentence with one. But not too often. Or you'll overdo it.

CONSONANT. Generally, a letter with a "hard" sound: *b, c, d, f, g, h, j, k, l, m, n, p, q, r, s, t, v, w, x, y, z.* Sometimes the consonants *w* and *y* act like vowels, which are letters with a "soft," open-mouthed sound. And occasionally consonants (such as *g, h,* and others) are seen but not heard.

CONTRACTION. It's usually two words combined into one, with an apostrophe showing where letters are omitted. The most common contractions consist of a verb plus *not* (*do + not = don't*); a pronoun plus a verb (*they + are = they're*); or a noun plus a verb (*Bob + is = Bob's*). Don't confuse the last example with the possessive (*Bob's dog*).

DANGLER. A word or phrase in the wrong place that ends up describing the wrong thing: ***After napping****, the card table was set up.* Who was napping? Unless it's the table, change the sentence: ***After napping****, Oscar set up the card table.*

DASH. A punctuation mark that interrupts a sentence to insert another thought. One can act like a colon: *It was every mother's nightmare—ringworm.* Or a pair of dashes can be used like parentheses: *The remedy was easy enough—a simple oral medication—but what would she tell the neighbors?*

DICTIONARY. A reference that lists words in alphabetical order and gives their spellings and pronunciations, their meanings, and sometimes their origins—including words that aren't quite up to standard, like *alright*. The fact that a word can be found in the dictionary doesn't mean it's all right. Once more: Read the fine print!

DOUBLE NEGATIVE. This is what you get when you combine a negative verb (like *have not* or *is not*) with another negative term: a pronoun (like *nothing* or *nobody*), an adverb (like *hardly* or *never*), a conjunction (like *neither* or *nor*), or a word with a negative beginning (like *in* or *un* or *non*). Not all double negatives are no-nos. Here are some flagrant examples of don'ts: *I have not seen nobody. It wasn't hardly worth it. He is not there neither.* On the other hand, here are some allowables: *It's not inconceivable. She's not unappealing.*

ELLIPSIS POINTS. Punctuation that indicates an omission, or ellipsis, in a quotation. The three dots can show the omission of a word—in this case a naughty one: *"Get off my lawn, and take your . . . dog with you!" he shouted.* Or they can show where a sentence trails off: *"Now let me think. . . ."* (Notice that when the ellipsis points come at the end of a complete sentence, a period precedes them, so you end up with four dots instead of three.) If you want to emphasize the incompleteness of the trailing off, however, you may end with a space, then just three dots: *"But I could have sworn . . ."*

EXCLAMATION POINT. A punctuation mark that comes after something that's exclaimed: *"I passed!" said Pippa.* Go easy on exclamation points and save them for the really startling stuff.

FIGURATIVE. Language is figurative when it uses words in imaginative or out-of-the-ordinary ways. In the process, the truth is often stretched to make a point. If you were being literal, you might say: *Bob's dog is big and stocky.* But to be more vivid, you could say: *Bob's dog is built like a refrigerator.* See **LITERAL**.

FIGURE OF SPEECH. A word or phrase that's **FIGURATIVE** (see above) or imaginative: *She knows how to push his buttons.* When it gets stale, it becomes a **CLICHE** (which see).

GERUND. A word that's made of a verb plus *ing* (*bowling*, for example) and that acts as a noun. ***Bowling** is his first love.* A gerund is sometimes called a verbal noun. But the same *ing* word is a participle if it acts as an adjective (*He's a **bowling** fool*) or part of a verb (*He was **bowling***).

GRAMMAR. A system of rules for arranging words into sentences. We adopt rules when we need them and discard them when we don't, so the rules change over time.

HYPHEN. A mark of punctuation that looks like a stubby dash. It is used to join words together to make new terms (*self-conscious*), as well as to link syllables when an oversized word, like *humongous* here, breaks off at the end of a line and continues on the next.

IDIOM. A phrase whose overall meaning can't be explained by the meanings of the individual words. Idioms don't necessarily make sense (*that dress isn't you; the elephant in the room; under the weather*).

IMPERATIVE. A verb is imperative when the speaker is expressing a command or request: ***Lose*** *twenty pounds, Jack.* See **MOOD**.

INDICATIVE. A verb is indicative when the speaker is expressing a straightforward statement or question: *Jack **lost** twenty pounds.* See **MOOD**.

INFINITIVE. A verb in its simplest form (*sneeze*, for example). While the preposition *to* is usually a signal that the infinitive is being used (*to sneeze*), it's not part of the infinitive itself. Putting an adverb in the middle (*to loudly sneeze*) is fine—you're not really "splitting" anything.

INTERJECTION. A word (or words) expressing a sudden rush of feeling: *My word! Help! Wow! Oh, damn!*

INTERROGATIVE. An expression is interrogative if it asks a question: *Got that?*

INTRANSITIVE. See **VERB**.

ITALIC. The slanting print (*like this*) that's often used for emphasis (*Holy cow!*) or for the titles of long works like books, movies, and plays (*The Wizard of Oz*). Italic letters may also be used to set something apart, like the examples in this book: *Jerry Lee's performance was a homage to Moon Mullican.*

JARGON. Language used by windbags and full of largely meaningless, pseudotechnical terms that are supposed to lend the speaker an aura of expertise. The advantage of jargon is that you can use it to discuss things you know little about, and without really saying anything. But even when you know what you're talking about, technical language can be confusing to someone who isn't another expert. *Jargon* comes from an old word for "chattering" or "twittering."

LITERAL. True or "to the letter"—the opposite of figurative. The adverb *literally* is sometimes used to emphasize or exaggerate a figure of speech: *My hair **literally** stood on end.* But don't go too far: *The boss **literally** had kittens after we let the cat out of the bag.* See **FIGURATIVE**.

METAPHOR. This is the most common **FIGURE OF SPEECH** (which see). A metaphor takes the language normally used for one thing and applies it to something else: *His stomach began to growl. The moon was a silver coin upon the water.*

MOOD. Verbs have attitude. They take on different forms, called "moods," that reflect the speaker's attitude toward what's being said. There are three principal moods in traditional English grammar. In an ordinary statement or question about facts, the verb is in the **INDICATIVE** mood. (*He **is** on my foot.*) In a wish or an *if* statement that's contrary to fact, the verb is said to be in the **SUBJUNCTIVE** mood. (*I wish he **were** not on my foot. If he **were** not on my foot, I could go.*) If what's being said is a command or a request, the verb is in the **IMPERATIVE** mood and the subject is understood to be *you*. (***Get** off my foot!*)

NOUN. A word that stands for a person, place, thing, or idea. A common noun starts with a small letter (*city* or *girl* or *religion*, for example); a proper noun starts with a capital letter (*Memphis* or *Molly* or *Methodist*).

OBJECT. A noun or pronoun that's acted on by a verb. It can be something you give, for instance, or somebody you give it to. An indirect object is the person or thing on the receiving end of the action, and a direct object is who or what ends up there: *Harry gave **me*** [indirect object] *the **flu*** [direct object]. Think of it as a game of catch—you throw a direct object to an indirect object. Additionally, a noun or pronoun at the receiving end of a preposition (*to* and *from* in these examples) is an object: *Harry gave the flu to **me**. He is from **Chicago**.*

PARENTHESES. Marks of punctuation used to enclose an aside (either a whole sentence or words within a sentence).

PARTS OF SPEECH. The eight categories of words in traditional grammar: noun, pronoun, adjective, verb, adverb, preposition, conjunction, interjection. This sentence uses all of them: *But* [conjunction] *gosh* [interjection], *you* [pronoun] *are* [verb] *really* [adverb] *in* [preposition] *terrible* [adjective] *trouble* [noun]*!*

PASSIVE. See **SUBJECT** and **VERB.**

PERIOD. This is the stop sign of punctuation. It shows where a declarative sentence, one that states something, ends. The period is also used in some abbreviations (*St.* for "Street," *Dr.* for "Doctor," *p.m.* for "post meridiem"), but many abbreviations have dropped the dots (*MD, US*), so check the dictionary.

PHRASE. A group of related words without its own subject and verb, like *glorious sunset* or *in the meantime* or *to spill the beans* or *gently swinging in the breeze.* A group of words with both a subject and its verb is a clause.

PLURAL. More than one; just one is **SINGULAR** (which see). Plural nouns generally have endings different from singular ones (*berries* versus *berry,* for instance), though there are exceptions (*sheep, deer,* and others).

POSSESSIVE. Showing ownership. With most nouns, you get the possessive form (or "case") by adding 's (*Alice's* cousin) or the preposition *of* (*a cousin **of Alice***). A "double possessive" uses both methods (*a cousin **of Alice's***).

PREPOSITION. A word that "positions" or situates words in relation to one another. The roots of the term *preposition* mean "put before," which is appropriate, because a preposition usually comes before a noun or pronoun: *Her cousin is **from** Philly.* (Contrary to what you may have heard, however, it can indeed go at the end of a sentence.) The prepositions we use most are *about, above, across, after, against, ahead of, along, among, around, as, at, away from, before, behind, below, beneath, beside, between, but* (in the sense of "except"), *by, down, except, for, from, in, in back of, in front of, inside, into, like, of, off, on, onto, out, out of, outside, over, past, since, through, throughout, to, toward, under, until, up, upon, with, within, without.* Some of these words can serve as other parts of speech as well (adverbs, conjunctions, etc.).

PRONOUN. A word that can be used in place of a **NOUN** (which see). Pronouns fall into these categories:

- A personal pronoun can be a subject (*I, you, he, she, it, we, they*); an object (*me, you, him, her, it, us, them*); or a possessive (*my, mine, your, yours, his, her, hers, its, our, ours, their, theirs*). Some of these (*my, your, his, her, its, our, their*) are also called possessive adjectives, since they describe (or modify) nouns.

- A reflexive pronoun calls attention to itself (it ends with *self* or *selves*): *myself, yourself, himself, herself, itself, ourselves, yourselves, themselves.* Reflexive pronouns are principally used to emphasize (*She **herself** is Hungarian*) or to refer to a subject already named (*He blames **himself***).

- A demonstrative pronoun points out something: *this, that, these, those.* It can be used by itself (*Hold **this***) or with a noun, as an adjective (*Who is **this** guy?*).

- An indefinite pronoun refers to a vague or unnamed person or thing: *all, another, any, anybody, anyone, anything, both, each, either, every, everybody, everyone, everything, few, many, much, neither, no one, nobody, none, one, other, several, some, somebody, someone, something, such* (**All** *is lost*; **Such** *was the state of the Union*). Some of these, too, can serve as adjectives.
- An interrogative pronoun is used to ask a question: *what, which, who, whom, whose* (**Who's** *on first?*).
- A relative pronoun introduces a dependent (or subordinate) clause: *that, what, whatever, which, whichever, who, whoever, whom, whomever, whose* (*He's the guy* **who** *stole my heart*).

PUNCTUATION. The signs and signals in writing that aid the flow of language. They call for stops, starts, slowdowns, and detours. The familiar marks of punctuation include the period, the comma, the semicolon, the colon, the question mark, the exclamation point, parentheses, the dash, the hyphen, the apostrophe, quotation marks, and ellipsis points.

QUESTION MARK. A punctuation mark that comes at the end of a question.

QUOTATION MARKS. Punctuation marks that surround spoken or quoted words.

SEMICOLON. A punctuation mark for a stop that's less final than a period. It's like a flashing red light; it lets you drive on after a brief pause. You'll often find it between clauses in a sentence and between items in a series.

SENTENCE. A word or group of words that expresses a complete thought; in writing, it begins with a capital letter and has a concluding mark like a period, a question mark, or an exclamation point. Most sentences have a subject and a verb, but not all. An imperative sentence, which demands an action, may have only a verb (*Run!*). An interrogative sentence, which asks a question, may also have only one word (*How?*). An exclamatory sentence, which expresses emotion, may have only a word or a phrase (*Good heavens!*). The declarative sentence, the most common kind, conveys information and is likely to have a subject, a verb, and an object—usually in that order: *He ate my fries.* See also **MOOD**.

SIBILANT. A consonant sound that hisses, like *s, z, sh, zh, ch,* and *j.* Nouns that end in sibilants sometimes have special ways of forming plurals and possessives.

SINGULAR. Only one; more than one is **PLURAL** (which see). A noun or a verb is singular if it applies to a single person, place, or thing.

STUFFED SHIRT. A person likely to use jargon; similar to a windbag. See **JARGON**.

SUBJECT. The star of a sentence. In an active sentence, the subject is who or what performs the action (***Barkley*** *walks on a leash*). In a passive sentence, the subject is acted upon (***Barkley*** *is walked on a leash*). Subjects can be nouns (***Bert*** *plays*), pronouns (***He*** *plays*), phrases (***Bert and Ernie*** *play*), and even certain forms of verbs (***Playing*** *keeps them busy*). A complete subject can have lots of accessories (***Sensible Bert and harebrained Ernie*** *play*), while a simple or basic subject consists of the bare essentials (***Bert and Ernie*** *play*). See also **VERB**.

SUBJUNCTIVE. A verb is in the subjunctive (see **MOOD**) when the intention is to express:

- A wish (*I wish Jack **were** here*).
- A conditional (*if*) statement that's contrary to fact (*If Jack **were** here . . .*).
- A suggestion or demand (*We insist that Jack **be** here*).

SUPERLATIVE. See **ADJECTIVE**.

SYLLABLE. Part of a word that is pronounced as a single unit. The word *syllable* has three syllables, pronounced like this: SIL-la-bul. *Word* is a one-syllable word.

TENSE. What a verb uses to tell time. The basic tenses—present, past, future—and the variations on them tell us when an action takes place, took place, will take place, would have taken place, and so on. We're always telling time with verbs, since whenever we use one, there's a "when" built in. See **VERB** for examples of some common verb tenses at work.

TRANSITIVE. See **VERB**.

VERB. An action word. In a sentence, it tells you what's going on: *She **sells** seashells*. Verbs are called transitive when they need an object to make sense (*Henry **raises** dahlias*) and intransitive when they make sense without one (*Flowers **die***). Some verbs are both transitive (*She **eats** peas*) and intransitive (*Let's **eat***). See also MOOD and TENSE.

A verb is active when the action is performed by the subject (*Henry **raises** vegetables as well as dahlias*). A verb is passive when the action is performed upon the subject (*Vegetables **are raised** too*).

The four principal parts of a verb are the infinitive (*eat*), the past tense (*ate*), the past participle (*eaten*), and the present participle (*eating*). These are the building blocks of the various tenses. Here's what some common verb tenses look like, for the first person singular (*I*) and the verb *eat*. As you can see, tenses beyond the simple ones require an auxiliary, or "helping," verb (some form of *have* or *be*).

	PRESENT	PAST	FUTURE	CONDITIONAL
SIMPLE	I eat	I ate	I will eat	I would eat
PERFECT	I have eaten	I had eaten	I will have eaten	I would have eaten
PROGRESSIVE	I am eating	I was eating	I will be eating	I would be eating

VOWEL. A letter with a "soft," openmouthed sound: *a, e, i, o, u,* and sometimes *y*. However, *u* and *eu* can act like consonants, letters with "hard" sounds (as in *universe* and *Europe*).

BIBLIOGRAPHY

Here are some books you may find helpful, including many that I turn to again and again. (A dictionary isn't optional, though. It's required.)

STANDARD AND ETYMOLOGICAL DICTIONARIES

The American Heritage Dictionary of the English Language, 5th ed. Boston and New York: Houghton Mifflin Harcourt, 2016. Online at https://ahdictionary.com.

The American Heritage Dictionary of Indo-European Roots, 3rd ed. Revised and edited by Calvert Watkins. Boston and New York: Houghton Mifflin Harcourt, 2011. Available online at https://ahdictionary.com/word/indoeurop.html.

Chambers Dictionary of Etymology. Edited by Robert K. Barnhart. New York: Chambers, 2006.

Dictionary of Word Origins: The Histories of More Than 8,000 English-Language Words. John Ayto. New York: Arcade, 2011.

Merriam-Webster Online Dictionary. Springfield, Mass.: Merriam-Webster, 2018. Originally based on *Merriam-Webster's Collegiate Dictionary,* 11th ed., this version is regularly revised and updated. Available at https://www.merriam-webster.com.

Merriam-Webster Unabridged Dictionary. Springfield, Mass.: Merriam-Webster, 2018. Originally based on *Webster's Third New International Dictionary of the English Language, Unabridged,* this online version is regularly revised and updated. Available by subscription at http://unabridged.merriam-webster.com.

Oxford Dictionaries Online. Oxford and New York: Oxford University Press, 2018. This online dictionary is regularly revised and updated. Available at https://en.oxforddictionaries.com.

Oxford English Dictionary Online. Oxford and New York: Oxford University Press, 2018. By subscription at http://www.oed.com.

Webster's New World College Dictionary, 5th ed. Boston and New York: Houghton Mifflin Harcourt, 2016.

GRAMMAR, USAGE, AND WRITING

The Cambridge Grammar of the English Language. Rodney Huddleston and Geoffrey K. Pullum. Cambridge, England: Cambridge University Press, 2005.

The Chicago Manual of Style, 17th ed. Chicago and London: University of Chicago Press, 2017.

The Columbia Guide to Standard American English. Kenneth G. Wilson. New York: Columbia University Press, 1996.

A Comprehensive Grammar of the English Language. Randolph Quirk et al. London: Longman, 1985.

Essentials of English Grammar. Otto Jespersen. Tuscaloosa and London: University of Alabama Press, 1994. This edition reproduces the original, which appeared in 1933.

Fowler's Dictionary of Modern English Usage, 4th ed. Edited by Jeremy Butterfield. Oxford and New York: Oxford University Press, 2015. This is the most recent incarnation of *A Dictionary of Modern English Usage*, by H. W. Fowler, originally published in 1926. Subsequent editions were edited by Sir Ernest Gowers (1965) and by R. W. Burchfield (1996, 1998, and 2004).

A Grammar of the English Language, Vol. I, *Parts of Speech*; Vol. II, *Syntax*. George O. Curme. Essex, Conn.: Verbatim, 1993.

Merriam-Webster's Dictionary of English Usage. Springfield, Mass.: Merriam-Webster, 1994. Abridged as *Merriam-Webster's Concise Dictionary of English Usage*. Springfield, Mass.: Merriam-Webster, 2002.

The Origins and Development of the English Language, 7th ed. John Algeo and Carmen Acevedo Butcher. Boston: Wadsworth, 2014.

Oxford English Grammar. Sidney Greenbaum. Oxford and New York: Oxford University Press, 1996.

The Reader Over Your Shoulder: A Handbook for Writers of English Prose. Robert Graves and Alan Hodge. Introduction by Patricia T. O'Conner. New York: Seven Stories Press, 2018.

Simple & Direct: A Rhetoric for Writers, 4th ed. Jacques Barzun. New York: Harper Perennial, 2001.

Style: Toward Clarity and Grace. Joseph M. Williams. Chicago: University of Chicago Press, 1995.

Words Fail Me: What Everyone Who Writes Should Know About Writing. Patricia T. O'Conner. San Diego and New York: Harvest/Harcourt, 2000.

Words into Type, rev. 3rd ed. Marjorie E. Skillin, Robert M. Gay, et al. Englewood Cliffs, N.J.: Prentice Hall, 1974.

INDEX